Special Issue
From Cuba
Edited by John Beverley

boundary 2

an international journal

of literature and culture

Volume 29, Number 3

Fall 2002

Duke University Press

boundary 2

boundary 2

an international journal of literature and culture

Founding Editor   William V. Spanos

Editor   Paul A. Bové

Review Editor   Daniel O'Hara

Managing Editor   Margaret A. Havran

Editorial Collective

Jonathan Arac, Columbia University
Paul A. Bové, University of Pittsburgh
Joseph A. Buttigieg, University of Notre Dame
Margaret Ferguson, University of California, Davis
Michael Hays, Soka University of America
Ronald A. T. Judy, University of Pittsburgh
Marcia Landy, University of Pittsburgh
Daniel O'Hara, Temple University
Donald E. Pease, Dartmouth College
William V. Spanos, SUNY at Binghamton

Editorial Board

Charles Bernstein, SUNY at Buffalo
Rey Chow, Brown University
Arif Dirlik, University of Oregon and Duke University
Wlad Godzich, University of California, Santa Cruz
Stuart Hall, Open University, U.K.
Fredric Jameson, Duke University
Karl Kroeber, Columbia University
Masao Miyoshi, University of California, San Diego
Edward W. Said, Columbia University
Hortense Spillers, Cornell University
Gayatri Spivak, Columbia University
Cornel West, Harvard University

Advisory Editors

John Beverley, University of Pittsburgh
Eric Clarke, University of Pittsburgh
Terry Cochran, University of Montreal
Christopher L. Connery, University of California, Santa Cruz
Kathryne V. Lindberg, Wayne State University
Jim Merod, BluePort Sound Archive, La Costa, Calif.
Aamir R. Mufti, University of California, Los Angeles
R. Radhakrishnan, University of Massachusetts, Amherst
Bruce Robbins, Columbia University
Rob Wilson, University of California, Santa Cruz

Corresponding Editors

Jenaro Talens, University of Geneva, Switzerland; University of Valencia, Spain
Q. S. Tong, University of Hong Kong

Contents

Introduction

John Beverley

The intention of this collection is to run the U.S. economic blockade of Cuba, which is also a kind of cultural and intellectual blockade. Anyone in this country who has had anything to do with Cuba—journalists, schol-ars, professionals, students, artists, film producers, executives, sports fig-ures, politicians, ordinary tourists—is aware of the major and minor incon-veniences the embargo, now over forty years old, imposes. To put this issue together, even the simplest thing, such as calling up a contributor to check on a passage, meant finding inventive and often devious ways of getting around obstacles. To obtain copyright releases, for example (not something the Cuban contributors cared much about, since intellectual work in Cuba has traditionally been in the public domain, but a sine qua non for *bound-ary 2*'s publisher, Duke University Press), required asking friends (and in one case, even strangers) who were visiting Cuba for one reason or other to try to locate the parties whose signatures were needed and bring the signed permission forms back with them, since mail service between the island and the United States is at best erratic. Without e-mail, in fact, the collection would have been impossible. But even e-mail to and from Cuba suffered

boundary 2 29:3, 2002. Copyright © 2002 by Duke University Press.

inexplicable crashes and blockages. E-mail messages to someone in Cuba or from someone in Cuba to me not getting through? Well, then, one could triangulate via so-and-so in New York, whose e-mail—for some reason—to so-and-so in Havana, who was in contact with that someone you wanted to reach in the first place, was getting through. And so, months behind schedule, little by little, one way or another—*de cierta manera*—the material for this collection began to accumulate.

But it goes without saying, of course, that one of the unstated aims of the embargo is precisely to make it difficult for U.S. citizens to have access to what Cubans are thinking, writing, creating, and arguing in Cuba today. Successive U.S. administrations have justified the embargo in part on the grounds that genuine freedom of speech is not possible in Cuba. But it is the relative silence imposed on Cuba by the embargo that makes it seem that there is only one voice in Cuba—the voice of the party, or of Fidel Castro— that "civil society" exists only in opposition to the regime and the goals of Cuban socialism, that the only ethically and intellectually honest positions in Cuba are those of "dissidents," that ideological pluralism and independence of thought exist only among those who have left Cuba. In this way, the defense of intellectual freedom can and has been mobilized against the Revolution, at the same time that the effects of the embargo include a coercive restriction of our own intellectual freedom and access to information in this country.

No one denies that Cuba has one of the most educated populations in the Americas, a population, moreover, that, whatever the controls on news and information it has to put up with (and they are extensive), has because of Cuba's own modern history and global role a broad and sophisticated grasp of what is going on in the rest of Latin America, the United States, Africa, the Middle East, China, Vietnam, Japan, the former Soviet Union, and both Western and Eastern Europe. This is, in other words, not a population that lacks the wherewithal to think for itself. Yet the dominant assumption is that because of repression, Cubans in Cuba cannot think for themselves (this is not to say that it is always easy or possible to speak freely in Cuba).

During the pre-1989 golden age of Cuban-Soviet relations, Cubans, perhaps to mark a distance from their erstwhile ally, were fond of so-called Popov jokes. Popov is the stereotypical earnest but dim-witted Soviet Party hack. Thus, for example (question in a course on Marxism-Leninism course for party cadre that Popov has been obliged to attend): "Popov, what do you call the period of transition between feudalism and capitalism?" Popov, hesitating, and then uncertainly, responds: "Socialism?" There was a prop-

erly Cuban variant of this, involving Popov's Cuban counterpart, "Norberto,"
let's say. Thus (question in a Cuban party cadre school): "Norberto, what
is socialism?" Norberto, hesitating, and then uncertainly, responds: "The
period of transition between capitalism and capitalism?"

What is paradoxical about the bitter humor of these jokes is that they
register the crisis of communism, but in a peculiarly communist or Marxist
way, as if they were affirming Marxism in the very act of marking its demise.
Antonio José Ponte, represented here by "The Supervised Party," is one
of Cuba's most talented younger writers and an explicit proponent of both
political and economic liberalization. Nevertheless, the key image he uses
to illustrate what he considers the immobilism of the Revolution—the image
of the clocks of Paris stopped by Jacobin sharpshooters at the moment of
triumph of the French Revolution—is drawn from Walter Benjamin's *Arcades
Project*, and Ponte's own piece ends with a profane "illumination," also in the
style of Benjamin, that seems to suggest a utopian dimension amidst the
despair and misery of the "Special Period" in contemporary Havana.

These cases—the Popov jokes and Ponte's explicit and implicit debt
to Benjamin—indicate one of the main themes of this collection: the existence of something like a specifically "socialist" form of civil society in Cuba.
Where in general the idea of civil society has been used in contemporary
political theory as an anticommunist device (in the most common argument, political struggle in communist societies is seen as the struggle of civil
society as such against a monolithic party-state), any observer of the current scene in Cuba will confirm the existence of a set of sensibilities, expectations, values, forms of leisure, and life possibilities that are specific to the
Cuban form and experience of socialism even as they constitute a ground
from which criticisms of this or that aspect of Cuban socialism or the regime
can be made.

In that sense, the real problem for a capitalist restoration in Cuba
will be not so much the authority of Fidel Castro and his associates or the
political monopoly of the Communist Party—indeed, as in the case of China,
both the *nomenklatura* and the party have proven in some ways amenable
to working with capital—as the often quite egalitarian values and expectations sedimented in Cuban culture and everyday life during the forty-year
longue durée of the Revolution. A *longue durée* that is now reaching its end,
however? That remains to be seen. Whatever happens, it is clear that Cuba
will not simply return to being what it was in 1959.

Like Palestine in some ways, and for some of the same reasons,
Cuba represents a point of irresolution within the world system: On the one

hand, with the collapse of the Soviet Union, the Revolution faces an impasse (what the official concept of "special period in times of emergency" is meant to signify is that while elements of socialism remain in place in Cuba, the possibility of building a fully socialist society has to be put on hold, for the time being or perhaps permanently[1]); on the other hand, the regime insists on maintaining at least symbolically Cuba's character as a socialist society, and while it has shown itself ready to wheel and deal with everyone from Spanish hotel chains to Francis Ford Coppola and his Hollywood buddies, it resists simply returning to the capitalist fold like the prodigal son. Predictions of the imminent fall of Castro have been a staple of political journalism in the United States, Latin America, and Europe since 1989, when the Cuban economy entered a period of near meltdown. Perhaps the most egregious of these was Andres Oppenheimer's 1992 opus, *Castro's Final Hour: The Secret Story behind the Coming Downfall of Communist Cuba.* A decade later, of course, Castro remains in power, and there are slight but significant signs of economic recovery in Cuba, at the expense, however, of opening up the country to global capital and sharpening internal class divisions.[2]

Despite the visibility of the doom-and-gloom school represented by such journalists as Oppenheimer, who echo in a pseudosophisticated, "soft" form the more hard-core revanchist positions of the Miami exile community, there has been a noticeable shift in U.S. thinking about and attitudes toward Cuba, particularly in the aftermath of the Elián González affair (the popularity of Wim Wender's film *The Buena Vista Social Club*, and the accompanying CDs, is perhaps one index of that shift). Behind the facade of the overtly hard-line, anti-Castro position of the Bush administration (and certainly Bush owes the contested Florida election largely to the political clout and perhaps also to the electoral dirty tricks of the Miami Cuban community), there is a split between "business" Republicans, who favor normalizing relations with Cuba, and "ideological" Republicans, who want to maintain and even intensify the embargo (I write this in the midst of Jimmy Carter's visit to Havana in May 2002). At the same time, the very difficult conditions of the "Special Period" have led to an ongoing discussion about the project

1. In which case, the features of the Special Period anatomized in many of the contributions here would become simply the new form of Cuban society, politics, and culture.
2. Oppenheimer's spectacular miscalculation, it is worth noting parenthetically, did not prevent him from becoming an authority on Latin America in the U.S. media, where he could be heard most recently as part of the chorus of champions of democracy prematurely celebrating the failed military coup against the elected government of Hugo Chávez in Venezuela.

of the Revolution and its expectations for the future that are shaping policy and thought in Cuba itself in significant ways.

From Cuba seeks to represent this discussion, a discussion which, of necessity, has had to engage all of the practical and theoretical problems posed by the collapse of the Soviet Union and the crisis of the "great narrative" of Marxism itself; the possibilities and limits of the nation-state and nationalism in the context of globalization; the question of what it means to think from a situation of historical catastrophe; the role of civil society and formal democracy in post-Communist societies; the question of women's liberation and gay rights, and of continuing—some will say even increasing—racism and discrimination directed against black Cubans; the impact of multiculturalism and postmodernism on recent Cuban art and culture; and so on. The main criterion for inclusion in the collection is that the authors represented here are still either resident in Cuba or have their main residence in Cuba and write from that situation. Without wanting to privilege "staying"—the regime has sometimes made "staying" in itself a badge of honor in order to discredit or relativize the authority of intellectuals and artists who have left for one reason or another (and there are often good reasons to leave)—the collection seeks nevertheless to represent the problematic of "those who stay," via rigorous and contemporary (on the whole, though some important pieces are from the early and mid-nineties) statements in a variety of genres (essay, poetry, short story, interview, chronicle, performance) that assume fully the dimensions of the crisis of the Cuban model of socialism and the extreme difficulties and contradictions—both external and internal—it faces.

One thing I hope the collection will show is that there is considerable realism and ideological diversity in current Cuban discourse. But, given the continuing polarization between Cuba and the United States, widespread dissatisfaction in Cuba, and competing policy lines within the regime and the party, there is also anxiety and tension around open discussions of the current situation. In an intellectual version of *jineterismo* (the practice of young men and women in Cuba selling sexual companionship to tourists for dollars), some of what is produced in Cuban culture today is "for export," so to speak: that is, on the one hand, an apologetic, rhetorical revolutionary "officialese" produced by the regime; on the other, "dissident" discourses calculated to win the approval of U.S. and European audiences and the exile community in Miami, but not necessarily representative of core positions in Cuba itself. The material I chose for this special issue seeks a balance between these alternatives. Whatever the strength or limitations of the writing included here, I think it is fair to say that it is writing by Cubans for Cubans, but also writing that, in translation, allows us to listen in.

The contributors include figures from an older, pre-revolutionary generation, such as Cintio Vitier and Fina García Marruz, who have resurrected a kind of Catholic-utopian nationalism in the place of an increasingly bankrupt orthodox Marxism, or the respected literary critic Ambrosio Fornet—something like Cuba's Lukács, if he will forgive me the comparison; others whose coming of age coincides with the triumph and consolidation of the Revolution in the sixties, such as the late Tomás Gutíerrez Alea, perhaps Cuba's most important modern film director, or the poets Miguel Barnet and Nancy Morejón; younger figures, some identified with the Revolution, such as Rafael Hernández, one of the intellectuals who opened up the influential discussion of the concept of civil society in Cuba, or Fernando Martínez Heredia, whose essay "In the Furnace of the Nineties" is considered by many a definitive statement of the crisis, or the literary critics Margarita Mateo and Desiderio Navarro; others with more critical or dissident positions, such as the art critic Gerardo Mosquera, the poet and independent journalist Raúl Rivero, the writer José Prats Sariol, or Antonio José Ponte, mentioned earlier; others who are in some ways politically unclassifiable but who maintain lives and careers in Cuba and an identification—sometimes tragic—with the country's fate, such as the poet/critic Víctor Fowler, the poet Reina María Rodríguez, or the performance artist Tania Bruguera.

My selection is, of course, to some extent arbitrary and accidental, as in all such anthologies. Although I have visited Cuba often in the last twenty-five years and have good friends and contacts there, I am not a Cuba specialist. My choices for this collection depend, then, to a large extent on the suggestions and good services of those friends and contacts. Any connoisseur of the artistic and intellectual scene in Cuba today will have his or her own list of half a dozen or so names that should have been included. Some I simply didn't know about; some were, for one reason or another, unavailable. I do think the voices and positions included here, however, are representative of a range of positions in dialogue or debate among intellectuals and artists in Cuba today. And while not everyone who should have been included is in this collection, many of those who are would be in any comprehensive anthology of contemporary Cuban writing.

The core idea of "from Cuba" as a principle of selection also began to unravel somewhat in the process of putting together the collection. One of the characteristics of the current situation is that the once familiar dialectics of "those who go"/"those who stay," exile/loyalty to the Revolution, the island/the diaspora, "inside" and "outside," are themselves shifting dramatically, a fact several of the contributions here attest to (I am thinking in particular of Antonio Eligio's piece on recent Cuban art and Fowler's impressions of his visit to the United States, "A Traveler's Album"). There are several figures I intended to include when I first conceived the idea of this collection two years ago but who have left Cuba in the interim (for example, the self-described postmodernist Emilio Ichikawa Morín). There are others who, by the time this volume appears, may well also have left Cuba for good. And there are others who, as noted, have begun to "circulate" between Cuba and the diaspora. One of the key contributors here is Haroldo Dilla, whose work is, to my mind, the most incisive portrait of Cuba in the Special Period from a position sympathetic to the goals of Cuban socialism if not its reality. Dilla used to be affiliated with the CEA, the Center of the Study of the Americas, one of the prestigious think tanks set up in an expansive moment by the regime precisely to think out of the box of socialist orthodoxy. But the CEA was closed down in 1996, it is said on the initiative of Raúl Castro, for exceeding its mandate, and Dilla now works as a researcher at FLACSO (Latin American Faculty for Social Sciences) in the Dominican Republic. Yet his essay here, on the political dynamics of the Special Period, begun in Havana and completed in Santo Domingo, is "from Cuba" in some sense.

Clearly writing "from there," on the other hand (specifically from Madrid, which has become a new center, rivaling Miami in some ways, for Cuban émigré culture), was the late writer and filmmaker Jesús Díaz. I met Jesús several times in the eighties and felt an immediate affinity with him. We shared some of the same political experiences and inclinations (for example, both of us were closely involved with the Nicaraguan Revolution). Jesús, who began his career as one of the young Turks of the Cuban Communist Party, became, in his influential films and novels, one of the sharpest portraitists of the inner contradictions and dangers of the revolutionary process. If he had remained in Cuba, he would certainly have been included here. Indeed, he would have had pride of place. Fed up with the frustrations and difficulties of Cuban life and seeing little chance of major change, Jesús never returned to Cuba from a research fellowship in Germany in the early nineties. Migrating eventually to Madrid, he founded there what is probably the most important Cuban émigré journal, *Encuentro de la cultura cubana*. As the title (which unintentionally but nevertheless unfortunately recalls the CIA-financed *Encounter* of the Cold War years) suggests, the idea of *Encuentro* was to provide a forum in which Cuban intellectuals in Cuba could dialogue with those who, for one reason or other, and at one time or other, chose to leave, like Jesús himself. And to some degree the journal has been able to accomplish that (several writers represented in this collection have published in *Encuentro*, and Antonio José Ponte in particular is on the current editorial board).

But, by the fatal logic that tends to turn every conversation about Cuba into a shouting match at some point, whatever its initial good intentions, *Encuentro* has become in effect an exile publication, which rarely has anything good to say about Cuba and which publishes primarily those intellectuals in Cuba who are explicitly identified with a dissident or "liberal" position, like its own. As such, it cannot represent the full array of intellectual and artistic voices "from Cuba": Intellectuals in Cuba who are pro-Castro or who, despite criticisms and reservations, remain committed to the project of the Revolution are less and less likely, I believe, to publish anything more than a rebuttal in its pages.

It was my sense of the failure of *Encuentro* to engage fully with the work of intellectuals and artists who have remained in Cuba that was one of the inspirations for this collection. But the fatal logic of extreme ideological polarization happens from the other side, too. I very much wanted to include something by Abel Prieto, the open-minded and charismatic Cuban minister of culture—himself a talented writer of short fiction—who was one of the main forces behind greater tolerance and pluralism in the cultural field in the nineties. I met Abel at—of all places—the University of Minnesota around 1980, when we were both up and coming nobodies, and I kept in touch with him off and on over the years. He was one of the first names that occurred to me for this collection. I sent him at least a dozen e-mail messages over several months asking him to give me something of his to include. His response was silence, as if my messages weren't getting through (so I made sure to follow up with personal entreaties from mutual acquaintances in Cuba, again to no avail). Abel is no doubt a very busy man, with more important claims on his time than a special issue of *boundary 2*; but I have learned to understand from previous experiences in Cuba that this kind of "polite" silence, if you will, is a way of saying no without saying no directly, particularly to foreigners like me, whose good opinion might be important in some small measure in the future.

There was a moment, early on in this project, when I wanted to include in the collection a piece by Fidel Castro himself. Through a mutual friend, I was offered the text of a speech on globalization Fidel gave at the South Summit two years ago. To have been able to list *el comandante* himself in the table of contents in simple alphabetical order was part of the image of Cuban intellectual life I was hoping to present: that there was not a single, monolithic voice, that Fidel's voice was certainly a commanding one, but not the only one. But that hope turned out to be illusory, like so many others connected to Cuba. My intermediary got wind of the fact that I intended to include a piece by a noted dissident (his characterization was stronger: a "counterrevolutionary"), and he let me know in no uncertain terms that it would be inappropriate for Fidel to appear in such company. He also withdrew his own contribution. For a brief moment, I thought the project was about to unravel, that everyone who felt more or less the same way was going to follow that lead, leaving me essentially with the "dissidents" already represented by what I saw as the failed project of *Encuentro*. But the others "stayed," and that in itself is already a sign of a change.[3]

I need finally to indicate my personal stake in all this. For intellectuals and activists of my generation, the generation of the sixties (I am months away from my sixtieth birthday), the Cuban Revolution represented the possibility of a break with both the claustrophobic culture of Cold War capitalism and the authoritarian version of socialism—famously dubbed by Che Guevara "goulash communism"—represented by the Soviet Union and the "People's Democracies" of Eastern Europe, a break that coincided fortuitously with our own coming of age. Jean-Paul Sartre was one of the first major European intellectuals to declare his solidarity with the Revolution, seeing it as a concrete embodiment of his own existentialist ethics of engagement. I was a great fan of Sartre at the time (before structuralism, as it were). But the book that really galvanized those of us who were in college in this country in the early sixties was C. Wright Mills's *Listen, Yankee*, which began with an injunction that is worth repeating today:

> No matter what you may think of it, no matter what I think of it—Cuba's voice is a voice that must be heard in the United States of America. Yet it has not been heard. It must now be heard because the United States is too powerful, its responsibilities to the world and to itself are too great, for its people not to listen to every voice of the hungry world. . . . If we do not listen to them, if we do not hear them well, we face all the perils of ignorance—and with these, the perils of dangerous mistakes.[4]

3. I would like to think that Fidel might have actually enjoyed the rough egalitarianism of being lumped together in alphabetical order with both loyalists and dissidents—the mantle of power, after all, weighs heavily—but I am not sure that would be the case.

4. C. Wright Mills, *Listen, Yankee: The Revolution in Cuba* (New York: Ballantine Books, 1960), 7.

This was four years before the escalation that would lead the United States, and my generation, into the Vietnam War. *Listen, Yankee* was a brilliant act of ventriloquism, in which Mills created from a mosaic of his interviews with the young revolutionaries in Cuba a synthetic voice speaking to a North American reader in a series of what he called "letters," explaining different aspects of the social, historical, and ideological forces behind the Revolution. Mills was no fool, and much of what he had to say holds up well; but some of his predictions or hopes—for example, that Castro's revolutionary dictatorship would give way in time to new forms of mass democracy, or that Cuba would not necessarily become communist or be drawn into the Soviet orbit—were clearly too optimistic. There has been a lot of water under the bridge since *Listen, Yankee* appeared in 1960, and we have all modified our initial enthusiasm for the Cuban Revolution in one way or another (for some, like Ronald Radosh or David Horowitz, the lesson of what they now take to be a youthful indiscretion has led them to the neoconservative right). Like the Revolution itself, Mills was expressing essentially a modernist conception of intellectual agency, development, and national liberation struggle. Where he created from many voices one voice—the voice of someone like himself—to speak for the Revolution, my ventriloquist gesture here—a consciously postmodernist one—is to allow many voices to speak for me. Yet, there is still something of that initial identification and enthusiasm in what I do here, expressed not so much as a defense of the status quo of Cuba as a desire to keep open a horizon of possibility that the defeat of Cuban socialism would surely eclipse. My hope is that the dialogue this collection sets up, between different voices in Cuba itself, and between those voices and ourselves and Cubans in this country, could be the framework of a new kind of territoriality in which the huge promise of the Revolution can somehow remain alive, and perhaps emerge anew. I do not think it diminishes it to call that territoriality, which can exist at present only perhaps as a textual space, utopian.

• • • •

It remains for me to thank those who helped put this project together. The idea of doing this collection in the first place came from Paul Bové, whose example, friendship, and support are implicated in it. Meg Havran performed the difficult task of closely editing sometimes murky manuscripts and attending to the myriad details that are involved in an enterprise such as this. Roberto Fernández Retamar, Desiderio Navarro, and, especially, Luisa Campuzano of Casa de las Américas in Havana were fundamental in securing much of the material included here, even as they sometimes disagreed with some of my own choices. On the other side of the political aisle, so to speak, José Prats Sariol played a similar role. Ernesto Grossman, Esther Gottleib, and George Yudice were also helpful as "couriers" and in other ways. In a way, I owe the initial inspiration and many of the contacts for this special issue to my former student Goffredo Diana. A word finally about the translations. Unless otherwise indicated, they are by Dawn Duke, a graduate student in the Department of Hispanic Languages and Literatures at the University of Pittsburgh. Working way beyond the call of duty, Dawn provided rough drafts in English of the material that I subsequently reworked. The superb translations of the poetry of Reina María Rodríguez and Omar Pérez are by Kris Dyskstra and Nancy Gates Madsen. The Cuban American novelist Achy Obejas provided the fine translation of Tania Bruguera's performance piece. Marta Hernández at Duke translated Carlos Aguilera's "Trip to China." Sujatha Fernandes at the University of Chicago was one of my "couriers" between Havana and Pittsburgh; she also obtained and translated a group of Cuban rap songs that I hoped to include (unfortunately, we could get copyright permission for only one of them). My Cuban American neighbor down the road at Carnegie Mellon University, Kenya Dworkin, contributed in a number of important ways to the translations. The new Duke University Press journal *Nepantla* provided us with a translation of Desiderio Navarro's "In Medias Res Publica," and the University Press of Florida provided us with a translation of Rafael Hernández's important essay "Looking at Cuba," which is part of a forthcoming collection of his work. I personally revised and sometimes reworked slightly all the translations, so the ultimate responsibility for their accuracy is mine. I do want to say, in this respect, that I am not always sure we—the translators and I—solved correctly all of the linguistic puzzles these texts presented. In the interest of readability, I also introduced some changes or cuts in the texts that their authors may not approve of. I hope these betrayals—inevitable in any translation—are minor, however, and that the end result captures at least partially their personal voice and views.

Trip to China

Carlos A. Aguilera

Translated by Marta Hernández

Roads

Roads in China are made of mud. The mud is red, and when it hardens, it looks like a flat clay sculpture. There is an area on the outskirts of Beijing where the mud is gray. They call it "round enamel vase."

The roads are long and, one may add, steep and narrow.

They have two lanes: one on the left, for pedestrians, with an invisible separation that everyone seems to respect; another on the right, for long trucks made in the Republic. Anyone with a car (for example, a '75 Oldsmobile) wanting to travel these roads has to get an official permit from the federal authorities at least a week in advance. Failure to do so will result in a fine, and the driver will be taken to the nearest police station, where his license will be suspended for several months.

Chinese roads are very complex. There are valley roads and mountain roads. The first three days after leaving Beijing, we drove on mountain roads.

boundary 2 29:3, 2002. Copyright © 2002 by Duke University Press.

They make one's life very difficult, not only because of their constant verticality but also because of the drizzle and fog, and because they seem endless.

For a Chinese person everything is much easier, of course. According to Michaux, there's a proverb in the West that says, "Only a Chinese can draw a line in the horizon." After climbing for three days on the Beijing–Outskirts of Beijing Road, I couldn't stop telling myself this proverb.

The trip is shorter on mountain roads. One needs three days of driving through the mountains to get out of Beijing and five days on valley roads (which are often much bumpier and have many more curves). The difference is that valley roads are paved.

A mountain road connects with two or three valley roads. One, in general, goes straight ahead and leads to some town or museum; another runs backward, to plain or a piece of ruined wall; and one branches off the first and gets lost in x direction.

According to Great Mongol, the driver assigned to us by the Ministry of Culture, the roads that seem to end as they pass through some little town branch out and merge again with the main artery of the valley, forming, with big and small rings, a serpent that spreads across the country.

Mud is the big problem on the mountain roads. When it rains, the mud makes it almost impossible to drive. When it doesn't, the thin quality of the dirt, much finer than any type of soil we have in the West, makes it very slippery, and it becomes difficult for cars and even for people to move forward.

On a very sunny day we saw a line of ten trucks skidding into one another constantly. All they could do was bump up against each other.

On mountain roads there are rocks. Not small or overhanging rocks. Huge rocks. Rocks the size of a Westerner's house.

On these rocks, the traveler may come across, for his entertainment, the so-called Chinese-Monkey. This is a man who climbs the rocks only with his hands, without using his feet. When he reaches the top, he jumps up and down triumphantly, as if his "heroic feat" could never be repeated.

These rocks make the landscape more beautiful. They make it harsh, and when you look at them closely, they smell like lead, cow shit and lead. From a distance, they look like cardboard rocks.

In the West, landscape means green: grasslands with rivers, lakes, mountains, etc. Not in China. In China, landscapes are mental. Stones turn into gazing little brains whose eyes cannot rest for more than a minute; they watch you.

Once, on our way from Shexuon to Huangcheihuan, we saw several people hitting and trying to strangle each other. Suddenly, one of them ran to the edge of the mountain (cliff), opened his arms, and threw himself off. This kind of suicide appears to be quite common in the Republic. It is called a *dislocated movement into sleep.*

There are many food stands along the mountain roads. They are run by people dressed up in regional folkloric costumes who sing in a low voice while their customers stick their fingers in the sweet and sour sauce, and lick them off.

The food stands are small. They can accommodate at most two people and a medium grill with small rectangular pieces of coal. While the owner serves someone, his wife crouches next to a wooden stool and looks on. Later she rushes to offer some *xixím* and nacre-colored sticks. As they withdrew after serving us, the couple mentioned that the sticks mean good luck and that each visitor gets a pair of them.

These food stands are renown all over the Republic.

At night, they are illuminated with lanterns of different colors.

Great Mongol

Great Mongol is small (1.62 meters, approximately), yellow, with almond-shaped, fatty eyes. His beige coat and his way of walking make him seem like a little man in an Ozu film. He is around fifty-two years old.

He knows how to avoid big trucks on mountain roads and passes cars with special care. He refers to them as the enemy (closing and opening his hand). He drives very fast on the valley roads, speeding up or slowing down, depending on our "picture-taking" needs.

Some nights, when we stop at a hotel, Great Mongol sings. He goes to karaoke bars (*repetition boxes*, in Cantonese), where he performs pop songs: "New York, New York" à la Frank Sinatra, or Chinese ballads. Neither

Maki nor I understand anything, so we prefer to observe the scene or go out to town and "chat."[1]

When Great Mongol goes to a repetition box, he can stay there for two or three hours. Everyone sits around a table and speaks in a low voice. If someone makes a joke, they smile and let out a single laugh, with a sudden explosion that ends abruptly. Not as in the West, where the laughter is prolonged.

When someone decides to sing, everyone falls silent. They look at the set with wide-open eyes and applaud. Afterwards, they invite the singer over to their table and make him drink Dragon Tail and chew Little Sky Worms. They ask about the singer's family and introduce him to other guests after bowing their heads. Later they all bid each other farewell.

Because he knows songs in English, people applaud twice as loudly when Great Mongol performs. He is then "obliged" to sing over and over again.

If the applause he gets is insufficient, the next day Great Mongol drives as if the mud roads were actually paved. He accelerates like a madman and brakes suddenly, bangs the steering wheel, kicks the floor . . .

If the applause is sufficient, he drives in a good mood, adjusting his speed to allow us to take Polaroid pictures and asking permission to turn on the radio.

On such days, he is of great help. He talks little and chooses places that, according to him, are pure photo opportunities. When I ask why, he says, "Westerners don't know the single brush stroke . . ."

He has a slow manner.

Repetition Boxes

The repetition boxes (*huanxhipó*) are small, unlike those in the West, with only four or five tables and a big TV screen. The singer stands in the middle,

1. Because of "inadequate development of the material," my traveling companion, Maki, speaks little or not at all in this text. I didn't know how to "write her in," so to speak. The reader should not think, however, that things always went this well with us. In addition to the little smiles and the photo opportunities we shared during our travels, there were arguments, fights, even the occasional outburst of male violence. Thus, it should be understood that if Maki plays a small role here, it is due to a "lack of synthesis" (or "inadequate development of the material") and not a desire for revenge or an oversight on the part of the author. A trip, however anchored in facts it may be, is also a fiction.

and people applaud when he or she finishes. Only Westerners laugh during the performance.

The waitresses in the repetition boxes are young girls or women, fifteen to twenty-five years old, dressed in miniskirts with a red checkered design and white blouses. They don't wear jewelry, only a tattoo on their upper right arm. To call them, the customers snap their fingers and say, "Miss." Everyone thinks, for some reason, that we all speak English, and they are always eager to practice it. When they realize that someone is not American, they smile.

They don't sell alcoholic beverages in repetition boxes. They sell *xixím*, as in the food stands along the road, and tea from different parts of the country.

There is a tea called Dragon Tail, another called Waters of the Yangtze, and yet another called Spring Walk.

Dragon Tail is served with oil. They brew it with *buanxhi* (beet sugar) to taste. The label says that it is good for rheumatism. It is made from flowers native to Huangcheihuan.

Waters of the Yangtze is served cold. It is bright red and served in small porcelain bowls with a design of transparent eyelets. When people hold up their bowls, they can see the eyelets change color according to the kind of light they get. This tea comes from Jiayúm in Central China.

Spring Walk is white. It is made by grinding stems of the guin bush, which grows in Xonjhia. These are then fermented with cinnamon, ginger, and flower petals. It is consumed throughout the Republic, sometimes mixed with peanut powder, which blends in the different flavors. They call it the tea of dialogue because of its thickness (and because it needs to be sipped slowly).

Repetition boxes are not ornamented.

The walls are lined with a dark taffeta, which looks like the fabric plumbers use to carry their tools. Lights hang from handcrafted lanterns of different colors for every season: red in winter, green in fall, white in spring, blue in summer.

At the end of the year, repetition boxes become Little Rice Halls. Women dress in traditional costumes that vary from one ethnic group to another and serve dishes with half-cooked ingredients. Then they form a line to perform a New Year's celebration ritual.

It is "prohibited" to go to bed early that night.

Lanterns

In the Republic, lanterns are made out of paper.

In the West, lights are hidden behind different sorts of objects, but in China there are no variations. Craftsmen make the lanterns out of paper (rice, onion, or bark paper), and it is only the ideogram, or picture, on them that varies.

For the Chinese, perfection is not about inventing new things constantly. It is about reaching the last degree of subtlety in the repetition of the same. Hence the millenary practice of this art.

Lanterns can be square, spherical, or rectangular, pleated when they are intended for the hall of a house or unpleated if they are to hang in a hotel lobby.

Some have landscapes painted on them: a bird on a branch, a stone, a bridge, a hunting scene . . . Others have ideograms with hopeful messages.

The inside of these lanterns is very simple: a wooden framework made of thin, square sticks that are bonded together by a special glue. The structure is left in the open air for two days, then wrapped and sold.

Due to its success, nowadays this craft has become somewhat vulgarized. For example, in a *go-go* in Jiayúm, we saw big paper lanterns (almost a meter long) with masochistic erotic representations: a Chinese man whips another one, while a woman licks his scars with her tongue and another woman sodomizes him with a handheld phallus.

However, the lanterns are usually small and have traditional messages, such as "Good luck for the future" or "Those who do not trust their own family cannot trust themselves."

These lanterns have been exported since the early sixties.

Valley Roads

Valley roads are broad. They cross the country from province to province and make it easier to travel and transport merchandise. There is not a single village or city that does not depend on them. When people have to buy something, they go to one of the establishments on the roads. The same applies when someone wants to relax. The roads are pipelines of impulses. People drive very fast on them and stop only when they get bored or hungry. One problem: This makes trips longer.

If a mountain road reduces the distance from one place to another, an *asphalt* road goes around the obstacle until it reaches another exit and then continues.

In the Republic, there are no valley roads that run straight for more than eighty kilometers. There is always a rise or a ditch, a detour, or a slope.

This has turned China into a chaos, where the constant flow of cars and persons resembles worms burrowing through the rotten eye of a dead animal.

Time stands still on valley roads. Trips are so long that little green cabins to relax in are now multiplying alongside hotels, coffee shops, garages, roadside movie theaters, Buddhist temples.

The traveler goes into one of these cabins (which are usually found in groups of five, more or less) and, with a hard ball, breaks objects that crack and make a glasslike noise: vases, cups, mirrors, picture frames, etc.

It is said that this sound is more relaxing than one or two hours of sleep, and so it seems. After having driven valley roads for five days and mountain roads for three more days, we laugh again and talk about the possibilities that a photographer interested in "the *political* ritual of objects" and the problem of "areas of devastation around cities" can find in a society of contrasts.

Valley roads have very dangerous curves.

On one of the valley roads (Zhuixin-Luanpong), we witness one of the most widely reported car crashes in the Republic: Two Fiat trucks collide head-on; eight are dead, and the road is closed for six hours.

According to the authorities, the passengers' bodies were guillotined several times, and only a leg and some body parts of the two children who were in the vehicles were found. In this area (Luanpong South Curve), the landscape is barren. In every direction, one sees great expanses of land, burned trees, pestilence.

In other places, one can see a village in the far distance, peasants in rice paddies, mountains, or the remains of Chu's Great Wall. But not in this area: only blood stains and constant crashes, bones.

The most exquisite landscape that we see in valley roads is a coffee shop (half American-style, half traditional) surrounded by cows and a large meadow with feeding troughs for water.

We are told that the coffee shop's owner is also the owner of the cows, and that every morning, he takes them to graze behind his business until it gets dark, and then he herds them back into a hut for the night.

This is so because in the Republic animals are strictly controlled.

The owner of the cows, who is also a businessman, hires the regional police force (*huanzzú*) to control illegal traffic and indiscriminate animal slaughter. This has turned the *huanzzú* into a very efficient machine of repression that has the power to search the entire area and inspect every village. In the short stretch between Huangcheihuan and Juyonggtai we were stopped and checked ten times.

When a foreigner arrives in a town, the villagers usually try to sell him small Buddha carvings or ivorylike representations of the goddess Zhao Tú raising her arms and sprinkling the countryside with rain.

The sellers set up tables and ocher canopies with English inscriptions in their doorways, light sandalwood incense, move about, and invite the prospective customer to observe "the harmony coming from the faces of Buddha, Zhao Tú, or Mo Lao Zhu." If the customer wants something, he has only to stretch his arm and say, with a half-open mouth, "that one." The sellers immediately put the representation in a small box, bow, and give it to him.

A carving of Buddha costs about seventy cents in U.S. currency.

Opium Dens

Opium dens are forbidden in the Republic.

The dens were legally closed in the seventies, and opium and the culture that had emerged around it were considered to be "depravities." For twenty years, all the "emperors" from East to West were jailed, and it was not permitted to utter their names in public.

If a Westerner wants to visit an opium den, he has to make a *descent into hell*, first, because of the scarcity of opium and the fear created by governmental repression; second, because of the current control of the *wangxhi* and the remoteness of their locations.

There are no more than twelve opium dens in China, hidden in old country houses or in deserted provincial towns. They are full all the time, however, and they empty out only when they run out of opium or when, for one reason or another, people cannot get to them.

A pipe is the first thing one gets in an opium den. They are long and have a bronze inscription with their name and year of manufacture (for example, *Sun over Jiayúm*, 1912).

Opium is the second thing one is given.

In spite of what we usually think in the West, there are several kinds of opium, although the dens of western China have only three: grey opium (or Bird's Smile), green-bladder opium (or Dragon's Breath), and red-mud opium (or Stars Behind the Mountains).

Grey opium arouses feelings and soothes physical pain. It makes one sleep, gives comfort, relief . . . In a nonrefined state, it is soluble in water.

Green-bladder opium produces hallucinations and sexual arousal. People take it to improve their sexual performance; it can be smoked or chewed.

Red-mud opium intensifies feelings. People become more lucid. It is popular with students. They smoke it or mix it with tobacco before exams.

According to Wei, who works at *Sun over Jiayúm*, people get an opium high only after they have smoked three pipes and then seen "the bull making waves in the lake."

The faces of those who frequent the opium dens are amazing. Thin as a rail, toothless, dark gums, sunken chins, pale. They talk and walk alone, holding a pipe in their mouths, and looking for all the world as if they had just accessed a complex and difficult engram.

They are called *gutún*, which means "those who revolve around their heads."

Women also go to the opium dens, although something odd happens in their case: They are given free opium in exchange for the narration, delivered from a podium, of what they "observed" during their smoke. For example, while we were smoking the opium of arousal, a woman claimed that she was "seeing" a horse turning around a tree that produced rats instead of fruit.

I began brooding about the image of a mouse (or a rat) hanging from a branch, and suddenly I started smelling rats everywhere: crane rats and hammer rats, ax rats and mouth rats, which bit me and hurled themselves at me showing their teeth. One of them said, "I am above the concept of rat," and tried to cut off my arm.

One of the features found in the opium dens is a rectangular white screen. When the women finish talking, they show porn videos or *amateur* videos of young girls talking about their sexual experiences. It seems that the latter are the most popular. They don't depict scenes of violence or of people having sex in different positions. They show only close-up head shots of girls describing how they had sex with such and such a person. However, these stories are full of little details.

When there are no videos on the screen, it is quiet in the opium dens, and one becomes aware of soft music, which helps metabolize the opium in a nebulous atmosphere, where things—including heads and pipes—seem to be floating.

Months later, after we had returned to the West, we received a letter from Great Mongol, in which he wrote that some of the dens had been shut down. He included pictures of some of the locales and of the people being arrested. One of the pictures shows a person whose hands are being tied by a policeman, while another one kicks him in the head.

This operation was called in the newspapers "moving furniture without disturbing the dust."

Contortionism

In China, contortionism is a tradition. People learn it from family to family, and they practice it in improvised circuses or on the edge of the road. Sometimes the contortionist is a woman; other times there are two contortionists, a woman and a man or two men.

A female contortionist we later nicknamed Zhinku Woman was, in our opinion, the most astonishing. She dislocated herself very slowly, and her movements had more to them than the simple technical pleasure resulting from her feet rotations. She performed her act so calmly that we almost did not notice it, like a spring strongly twisted over itself. One of her poses was performed on top of a cow. When she finally attained the most bizarre position, the cow would start to walk through the audience, showing off the pose from different angles and under different light conditions. While she was still entering the pose, the cow stayed still, whipping its tail and making a cracking sound. The woman's rigidity and the sonorous swing of the tail were a show in themselves.

What was incredible about this contortionist was that when she performed, she didn't move her eyes. She had such concentration that she could stay for hours without looking at anything. When she was done, she would undo her knot, begin rising slowly while moving her arms, flexing her shoulders and elbows, and bending her legs, until she could finally stand up.

Once we picked her up (on the stretch of road between Zhinku and Befendong), and she told us, "Contortionism is the art of speaking without being heard."

Cotton Ticks

The cotton tick is small, ochre-colored, and lives in colonies. Tick colonies are organized into states; it is one of the most feared populations of Western-Southern-Central China.

It is well known that a plague of ticks can devour entire fields of cotton in a few hours.

The interesting thing about this insect is that it not only destroys the plant but also hollows out and impoverishes the earth, something that doesn't happen with locusts or tapeworms. Due to the poisons and insecticides used for their destruction, when tick colonies settle somewhere, the ground begins to crack and turn to sand (*funxawhi*), causing extremely productive fields to become wastelands.

Because the cotton tick is very small (no longer than two centimeters), its population is very large and voracious. During the daytime, the males usually devour cotton, nibble at leaves and grind stems, whereas the females build tick colonies.

When they exterminate a colony of ticks, the peasants shovel them into four or five mounds the size of a *suizhú* (tool hut). Afterwards, they cover the surrounding ground and the mounds with oil and set them on fire. There is no movement more beautiful than that of a female tick racing to escape immolation, and that of the spreading fire frying them to a crisp.

A few of the ticks manage to save themselves from the fire. These the children catch, cut into halves, grill, and later eat as snacks.

Cotton ticks can live up to four months in favorable conditions.

War Museums

War museums are little puppet theaters. They feature huge black and white photographs with captions that identify the hero, his home city, his dates of birth and death. The eyeless, tortured, or dead men in these pictures are known in the region as "sons of the people."

Behind the war museums are small cemeteries that consist of a stone vault with glass windows and little boxes with dust inside. In front of the vault, some stone benches for family and friends to sit on.

Because the war museums are tense places, the musicians of the Republic, "induced" by the State, compose solemn pieces to create an atmosphere of sorts and lend these places the pathos they would not have otherwise.

Thus, when we were walking through Fonxhuá museum with a group of Lithuanians, we saw several women frightened by the "power" of the pictures and the music, which cracked over their heads like a hammer.

The comic gesture came from Lola, a white crane,[2] who was both the symbol of the museum and the pet of comrade Chung—the secretary of finance of the Republic. Lola spent her time running after the Lithuanian women and pecking at the panels where the pictures of the sons of the people were venerated by visitors day after day. When we left, we saw how those faces, with cavities in their eyes and blood stains on their mouths, more than heroes, seemed like puppets pierced by horror.

Since the logic of a museum is to impose a feeling of naturalness, one of its strategies is the showcase: boots with mud/saliva, pieces of watches with remains of skulls, shingles with bullet holes, stained chamber pots.

This has turned Fonxhuá into one of the most popular museums in the Republic. There, people can find the hands of Colonel Wong—the military

2. So called because of the color its feathers and feet take on when it flies.

genius of guerrilla war—in a glass case. According to the leaflet ("Treasures of Fonxhuá Museum"), Wong was captured by the regular army, and one of the ways in which he was tortured involved cutting his hands off little by little, until he bled to death. Later, his hands were given to the Maoist Popular Front and exhibited as an ideological fetish *for the instruction of future generations.* (When you look at them closely, each hand has an inventory number and an identifying ideogram.)

In spite of their relation to death, these war museums are excellent places to take a rest. They help one escape the tedium caused by the days spent on the road, and they have small shops where little flags with slogans from the Republic and pleated parasols are sold. One unpleasant fact though: It is forbidden to take pictures.

Highways

The highways of western China are famous. They wind like worms around the periphery and connect towns by forming passages of movement in all directions.

The best thing about these highways is that they don't make you feel tired. They have been designed with big ramps along the sides and shaded overlooks from which to observe the nearby cities.

Huangcheihuan can thus be viewed in relation to Yantzú lake or in relation to the bridges that cross the different bends in the rivers which subdivide the city into two islands: the South (old city), with small antique shops and a bohemian atmosphere that has no parallel anywhere else in the Republic; and the Northeast (new city), with its concentration of heavy industry and the most technocratic prisons in the entire country.

What is most amazing about these highways is that they cross the city very harmoniously, arching over the highest buildings or the trailer houses that can be found almost everywhere in the Republic. And they accomplish this without breaking up the architecture or the landscape, turning the city into an iron cage or a kind of flying hardware store.

One morning, as we were walking across Huangcheihuan, we had the impression that we were the characters in some North American documentary about the Midwest.

Temples are one of the highways' many attractions. They are painted green and have a narrow room, in which a one-meter-high cardboard Buddha sits.

Since trips from one province to the other take so long, the monks of the Republic carry these prefabricated temples along the roads (hanging them on the back of trucks that they drive themselves) and "open" them on certain stretches of highway. It is not unusual to see a small line in front of the temple, with one or two people praying or an entire family in silence.

They call the trucks carrying these temples and a small Buddha painted in white "highway Buddhism."

The difference between this kind of Buddhism and the one practiced in traditional temples is in the way the small ritual drum (ko'on) is played: much more lightly and without interruptions, with several beats repeating without variation while people are in "repose." This music continues until the user "wakes up" or gets up, and it doesn't stop suddenly but rather gets slower and then ends after a few seconds.

The price of entrance into these places is twenty yuan.

If one of these trucks breaks down or has a flat tire, the monks will repair it by themselves. According to Great Mongol, the monks are bad drivers and good mechanics, and they have caused hundreds of crashes and provoked many extremely dangerous situations on the highways. People still remember the day when one of these monks fell asleep, drove into a school in the Shi region, killed fourteen children, and ran away, while a smiling Buddha statue fell off the truck and remained standing upright amid the blood and the wailing. Since then, thousands of believers end their pilgrimage at that place, which they call "Buddha's dwelling in Shi."[3]

The truth is that every time we see a monk repairing a truck or rinsing the grease off his hands, we wonder how this is at all possible and smile. More than monks, they look like little devils out of a Buñuel film.

---

3. To be precise, of the different kinds of Buddha figures (smiling, of harmony, melancholy, drenched with muddy water . . .), the Buddha of fertility is the most popular. He is represented with a severe face in which there are no signs of sadness, and it is the only version of the Buddha in which he appears without crossed or hanging arms; here they extend forward with open fingers. Couples pray for fertility to this figure, and it is a custom for women to kiss the index finger (of the right hand) three times, saying as they do, "Buddha of fertility, show me the way" (xicho padme kung no fa). As they leave, they should bow their heads and not turn their backs on the figure until they are outside the temple. In order for their wish to be granted, they should drink the tea called Spring Walk for three days in succession.

The week before leaving, we stopped along one of the valley roads and tried to take a picture of the monks. They didn't allow it. At first they were very reticent, and after hiding their faces, walking in different directions, and screaming at each other, they approached us with closed fists and threw stones at us. When we were far enough away from them, we stopped and made faces at them. One of them laughed, took out his penis, and urinated. That attitude threw into crisis everything we had been thinking about Buddhism up until then.

The *Huangcheihuan Sun* has reported that there are more than a thousand trucks devoted to Buddha in the Republic.

B.

Beijing is an empire. It is the political city par excellence and, according to what we were told, nothing happens there without the State knowing about it. To assure this, the State applies extreme measures: It makes all citizens spy on each other and accuse each other in front of courts that are set up to pass judgment on individuals and construct a chain of guilt/redemption.

People still talk about the case of some carpenters who, charged with the illegal sale of polished wood, accused—over time—more than fifty-two people, including managers and skilled workers who were in charge of controlling the market and regulating prices. This caused wood to become unavailable and made people involved in sculpture, carpentry, etc., look for different jobs, until the authorities forgot about the case and the wood business recovered again.

One should not be horrified by this, however. The people of Beijing are very phlegmatic, and they like to take life as a comedy of errors. Trials awaken a "desire for continuity" rather than anguish.

If one had to define B. with a word, it would be *maquette*. The city rises over a grid of straight avenues (with wide streets), and its architecture is "modern-traditional." From a high vantage point, Beijing looks like a Northern European city. But this impression is illusory. Beijing is like a caricature, and, more than a city, it seems like a fun house. Buildings have been finished off with neon signs and fake windows; houses, nominally neoclassical, have pagoda roofs or some other element emphasizing the fusion of styles.

The same happens with the churches: Thirty percent are Catholic. They are built with some kind of material derived from plastic (reinforced with rubber and gravel) and are painted red or magenta, and decorated with bits of glass all around and a cross above. With a grin on his face, Great Mongol says that *those* are God's coffee shops.

The machines that multiply money are another of the other attractions of B. (*gonsuwhoxig*). Young people gather around them and, by inserting only a few pennies, they make the equivalent of five dollars. The problem comes when these machines jam. Chinese good humor collapses, and people kick the machines until they work again or vomit up the coins. Then they leave, smiling, and try another one.

One afternoon, as we were walking to the house of Lu Zhimou (the writer), we saw how some teenagers removed the shell from one of these machines, punched the custodian—the district security officer—and then ran away.

Beijing is nonetheless a quiet city. There are very few thieves, and violent deaths are due mostly to the curfew after ten at night and not to assaults or burglaries. After ten, it is impossible to get any kind of transportation, and sick or injured people have to wait until six the next morning to get to hospitals.

That is why many writers excused themselves for leaving early from Zhimou's home, explaining that anyone who is found in the street after curfew is sent to jail for contravening the official decrees of the Republic. Zhimou told us that the writers watch each other, and that, in order to meet Westerners, they have to ask the central authority for "advice." Anyone breaking the rule is likely to be exiled to a small provincial town.

When I tried to take a picture of the writers, they covered the lens of my camera and said no. The writers of the nation must not let the Western world look at them. They then got up, tucked in their shirts, and left. After a while, Zhimou's wife—in traditional dress and bracelets—appeared with some long pipes, boxes of opium, and tea.

(She didn't have to insist. We accepted.)

Airport

The Beijing Airport is like a fish bowl. It was built with thick glass, which amplifies its transparency, and has escalators that connect waiting rooms in the different buildings. When a plane lands or takes off, the escalators, with clear plastic sides and brown carpets, turn the airport into an anthill.

On top of the walls of the airport there are stained-glass windows. Not small or medium, but large windows. Four meters long, more or less. They represent the Chinese *Via Crucis* through history, and one of them has a giant Mao figure cutting the head off a dragon that has blood coming out of his mouth. This stained-glass window, which is right in front of the main runway, compels arriving passengers to stop and look at it.

When we stood close to the window, we read: "Only a great leader together with his people can behead a dragon."

In some other windows, Mao is reaping wheat with a sickle and teaching children how to read in school.

These stained-glass windows of striking colors separated by thin joints are the most photographed windows in the three buildings of the airport.

To get to the airport one has to travel several highways. First, there is the freeway heading to Shuking; then the one bordering Thermonuclear-2; then the one to the airport itself.

As is well known, these highways have "de-stressing" ramps, and when we stop on one of these, the distant panorama of workers unloading boxes of fish on the docks and peasants plowing the land for miles around seemed a coupling of a *single* unique space rather than two separate spaces.

The same happened with the cemetery. From far away, it was a rectangle, with signs and arrows; closer at hand, it was a place of meditation and "gathering."

It is interesting that in China, instead of taking flowers or food to cemeteries (as is common in other cultures), mourners bring stones adorned with some inscription or painted image. For example: "Your son who still loves you," or a picture of the family sitting around the table. There were some tombs with piles of stones on top of them, and others with two or three stones on the sides.

These cemeteries are very plain. There is only a cement cross made to imitate wood stuck in the ground and a small bronze plaque with the dates and names of the deceased.

Around the cemeteries, trees.

After kneeling for several minutes, Great Mongol told us how his father buried a butcher's hook in his mother's throat and then dragged her along

Shuking "to make her understand once and forever not to raise her voice in front of her husband." Afterwards he hung her in the town grocery store and ran away.

Later, it was learned, he was shot trying to cross the border into Siberia.

Beijing's airport is silent. People don't talk to each other or they talk quietly, at the same time bowing and bringing their mouths too close to each other. This movement makes them look like tumblers falling down and getting up.

When we presented our passports at the checkpoint, the officials began looking at each other and then at us, trying to superimpose our faces on the passport pictures. This took several minutes, which gave us time to say good-bye to Great Mongol and give him a farewell hug.

Once we were inside, a customs officer approached us and, using a sign language of sorts, made us understand that there were problems with our luggage. In the office, our Polaroid pictures (750 in total) were scattered over the table, and two officers were examining them carefully. When they became aware of our presence, the male officer (with bulging eyes and wearing a suit with red epaulets) came up to me and, tapping me on the chest with his finger, said, "You not know anything about China." I made no response and instead tried to register the details of the situation: iron table, three mid-size pictures of the Republic's leaders, gray walls, a male officer, a female officer, papers . . .

After placing the Polaroids in irregular piles, the male officer (who was stepping outside constantly and checking with someone who sounded like Great Mongol) said, "These are the pictures that you to take," and pushed toward me a little bundle of approximately two hundred pictures.

I took them and put them into a yellow envelope. When I asked about the other ones, he looked at us and said through a half-shut mouth, "Distort image of Republic" (and made a gesture meaning *end of discussion*).

We went out onto the runway and lined up to get on the plane. I looked at Mao once more. The veins of his face were swelling up, and no more blood was coming out of the dragon's mouth; instead, the dragon spun around frantically while laughing . . . I squeezed the little bundle with our pictures again. We climbed on board.

Three Poems

Miguel Barnet

•

A laborer's son,
he worked occasionally as a kitchen hand
in luxury hotels.
He wore ordinary clothes at work,
his young and coarse hands
showed some suspicious signs,
and his eyes seemed to stare at nothing.
Saturday nights
awakened in him strangely licentious desires,
mixed with a sentiment he knew was avarice.
Everything he had seen during the week
in the foreign exchange stores
became an obsession: blue jeans with a Texas label,
tiny round glasses, a silk shirt
that had never been put out on display.
To get these things he would sell his body to the first bidder

boundary 2 29:3, 2002. Copyright © 2002 by Duke University Press.

of any sex, since
what was important was the item, the wild fantasy dreamed of,
the blue jeans.
Like Cavafy, I wonder if in ancient times
Alexandria possessed a young man more beautiful,
more perfect than he.
There remains no statue of him, no painting, not even
an ordinary photograph,
hurled into oblivion, he was painfully devoured by a disease
that was the scourge of the century.
I remember him on a street in Havana asking the time
of a murderous clock.

•

Women burnt by the sun,
hot shoulders, broad hips,
selling guayaba sweets,
homemade pizzas, frutabomba drinks

Street dogs, abandoned,
sniffing the scraps,
drinking from puddles of water

Retirees
polishing windshields,
as before,
renting dreams for anxious tourists
in front of the bars.
As before,
the bright and silky manes
of the varnished Mitsubishis,
floating like a magic carpet over the city

Pimps, prostitutes,
young Communists, babalus,
schoolchildren still wearing red handkerchiefs around their necks
and the earth, the earth, fleshy and moist,
as before,
the earth that rejects profit,
that is not for sale.

The Sixties

Beautiful as a lie
were those years
that made the stones talk
that gave us wings
that gave us memory

How, then, am I not going to feel sad
that no one takes off his clothes
in the rain anymore
that no one wants to raise a flag
that no one hangs himself from a spiral staircase
that no one rips out his heart and hurls it
against the rocks
that no one gets lost
because the compass is connected to the SYSTEM

Beautiful as a lie
were those years
that now dribble away
like the ink
on the page of my notebook

Tania Bruguera. *El peso de la culpa* (The burden of guilt). 1997–99. Performance. Private collection. Courtesy of LiebmanMagnan, New York.

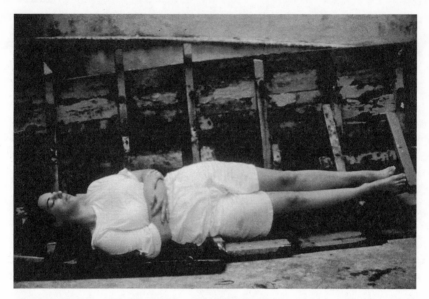

Tania Bruguera. *Miedo* (Fear). 1994. Performance. Courtesy of Liebman-Magnan, New York.

Tania Bruguera. *Tabla de Salvacion* (Table of salvation). 1994. Marble, wood, cotton. Installation. Courtesy of LiebmanMagnan, New York.

Tania Bruguera. *Destierro* (Displacement). 1998–99. Performance. Courtesy of LiebmanMagnan, New York.

Tania Bruguera. *Cabeza Abajo* (Head down). 1997. Performance. Courtesy of LiebmanMagnan, New York.

Tania Bruguera. *Cuerpo del silencio* (Body of silence). 1998. Performance. Courtesy of LiebmanMagnan, New York.

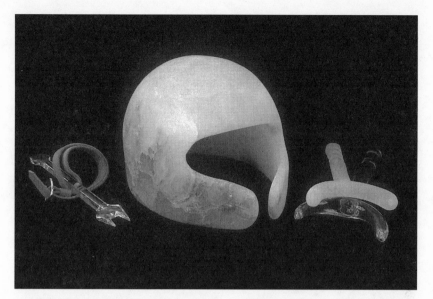

Tania Bruguera. *Engineer of Souls* series. 2000. Alabaster, glass, leather. Dimensions variable. Courtesy of LiebmanMagnan, New York.

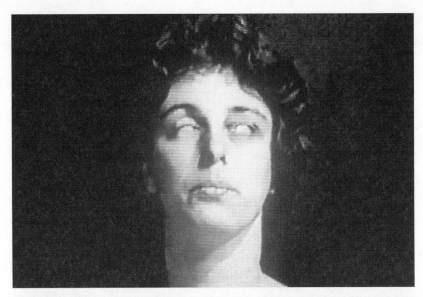

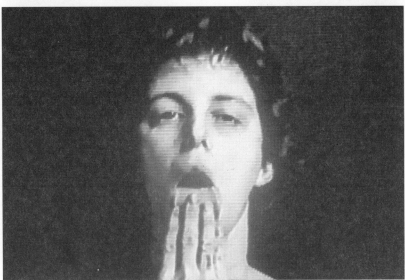

Tania Bruguera. *La Isla En Peso* (detail). 2001. DVD, edition of 3. Dimensions variable. Courtesy of LiebmanMagnan, New York.

Untitled (Havana 2000)

Tania Bruguera

Translated by Achy Obejas

You are standing in the inky black, a black that rises at the entrance, threatening to engulf you. This could be a place to die.

You don't know this place. It is a fortress. The ground is all cobblestones, rounded by time and water even before they arrived in Havana as weights in the belly of empty ships coming from far away, soon to be bursting with sugar and other treasures taken from the colonies. Like so many things that were supposed to be transitory, the stones remained, paved the thoroughfares, gave direction.

You are here out of curiosity, or guilt, or habit, or simply because something has called you to this dark and fetid place.

You remember every story you've ever heard about this place, about the time the Spaniards conquered Cuba, about the need to defend against

Because I don't write per se for performance, I hope this experimental text will serve as way to explore the ideas and intentions at play in this particular piece of mine, along with some of the comments and feedback that I was so grateful to receive from the audience.

boundary 2 29:3, 2002. Copyright © 2002 by Duke University Press.

Tania Bruguera. *Untitled.* VII Bienal de la Habana, 2000. Performance. Sugarcane, video, Cubans.

unseen enemies. As happens so many times, what was supposed to protect you from others has been turned against you.

This place, this settlement now turned into a tourist haven, has been the site where government after government, generation after generation, has shut off its detractors.

There's a smell, a rising fume, that you can't quite place.

In the darkness, you distinguish a sentry dressed in black at the entrance-way. The gates are open as if in invitation. Inside, to either side, there's a blur of iron bars, tiny rooms, cells. The sentry is serious but kind and, after a cursory check of your person, lets you inside.

The smell is unrecognizable, insistent.

Everything's black, as if the space inside had swallowed the light and with it all that you know, all that's recognizable. You step uneasily into the blackness. The floor is spongelike. Walking is tentative. You must do so slowly. Your feet are like a blind man's fingers. Your senses sharpen.

You are alone here, or not. You are implicated.

The more you proceed, the more you lose your sense of time. It's like a life sentence, in which time doesn't exist anymore, memories repeated over and over.

The smell intensifies, and the floor sinks under your foot; it is milled sugarcane, still fresh, still wet. Its vapors—sweet and vile—surround you. Your skin absorbs it, sucks it in.

You hear how the walls absorbed the cries of those waiting to die. The echo trapped here with you is like the ricochet of shots from a firing squad. The walls are rocks, consolidated pain, suppressed pain, all of it pain.

You are tempted to turn around, you are tempted to run out of here.

How far have you gone? How long have you been here?

The black seems infinite, then, just as you're about to give up, it dilutes, it begins to part, to make some sort of sense. You are no longer moving based solely on sound. Now you feel other presences, you sense heat.

You begin to discern a light in the distance, it's blue, it's a pinpoint. You can't tell if it's in front of you, below, or above. That light becomes your guide and your goal. As you near it, the light rises, hovers above you.

You crane your neck to look at the light. It is almost painful.

There are sounds, something brushes by, almost touching.

The light becomes images, becomes scenes: This is a man in the prime of his life; he swims, he waves, he marries, he hugs his son while wearing pajamas. This is a man as familiar to you as your own reflection: This is the view through the keyhole or lens—it doesn't matter, it's the same. (There's nothing intimate here, nothing you didn't know after all.)

This is a young and jolly Fidel unbuttoning his shirt, over and over, showing his human skin, boasting of being free from bulletproof vests.

Your neck hurts from straining to look up.

You are not alone.

You've been standing there for some forty years, or maybe five minutes.

Your pupils are wide open.

You turn to leave and you're abruptly struck by a long, whirling tunnel of light.

From its golden dust emerge shadows, black figures that beckon. They are naked Atlases in slow motion, moving almost imperceptibly, repeating their gestures ad infinitum: One rubs his body, as if trying to rid himself of the stench of the sugarcane, the sound of skin on skin like a murmur; another pries his mouth with his fingers to free the words stuck behind his clenched teeth; a third wipes his face with his forearm; the last bows.

Your feet sink in the milled, useless and infertile sugarcane as you head back toward the greater light. (Have you always walked this way?)

As you step out of the darkness, out of the dungeon, you are faced with the splendor and reality of light just beyond your grasp.

And, at least for a moment, you are blind.

We Are Losing All Our Values:
An Interview with Tomás Gutiérrez Alea

Michael Chanan

Michael Chanan: Titón, when I saw your film, *Fresa y Chocolate* (Straw-berry and chocolate), I left the theater thinking, among other things, that in a way, this film is a response to Néstor Almendros's documentary *Conducta impropia* (Improper conduct), which deals with the repression of homo-sexuals in Cuba. I think so, because, first, when you started in cinema at the end of the forties, you produced several shorts in 8-mm format with him, and, second, because it seems to me that in many of your films, underlying the explicit theme is a certain type of dialogue as much with some key ideas as with other filmmakers.

Tomás Gutiérrez Alea: Actually, it wasn't a preconceived dialogue, but, per-haps there is something to what you say. While I was preparing the film, I learned of Néstor's death, and it affected me a great deal; I was in quite a dramatic situation myself at the time, because I had been diagnosed with lung cancer and was given a very poor prognosis. Then, with the film having as its theme a homosexual in Cuba, well, inevitably, I had to link it to what Néstor had done. So, yes, in a certain way, *Fresa y chocolate* is an answer to *Conducta impropia*.

boundary 2 29:3, 2002. Copyright © 2002 by Duke University Press.

MC: How do you judge *Conducta impropia* as a representation of the problem of homosexual repression?

TGA: It's a documentary I would never have expected from Néstor, not because of its theme but rather because of the way in which it's presented. I think it's too overdrawn, too schematic, too simplified a version of reality, too manipulative. I mean, *Conducta impropia*, for me, is everything negative you could associate with socialist realism, but inverted. In my opinion, it was not interesting as a documentary; some of the testimonies it presented that are true were interesting; others, on the other hand, seemed absolutely exaggerated to me. Of course, I was conscious of the fact that homosexuals faced repression in Cuba, as when they were imprisoned in work camps.

MC: Wasn't that at the end of the sixties and the beginning of the seventies?

TGA: I don't remember the exact time, but I believe it was then, yes. In any case, it was a scandalous situation, so much so that the policy was ended abruptly when voices were raised in protest. But it's no less true that the repression and discrimination homosexuals have been subjected to in Cuba continued for many years. Even today, it's still there at the social level—I won't say the official level, but at the social and individual levels. The macho tradition of our country, as in many other, especially Latin American, countries, is very strong, and the rejection of homosexuals is visible in all of them. Therefore, I don't want to say that the testimonies Néstor collected were lies. The events related in *Conducta impropia* are almost all true, but only a part of the story is told, and it is not told in context. The real measure of these events is not given; instead, Néstor simply stated that there was repression. What he did seemed too simplistic to me, something that was not at the level of his talent. After all, it's with half-truths that you can make big lies, and, in my opinion, this is what he did.

MC: Did you two have a difference of opinion?

TGA: Yes, and as a result, we stopped talking to each other. Up to that point, even with him being in exile, I had seen him on two or three occasions. I had seen him in Cannes, I had been in his house in New York, we had spoken on the phone in Paris . . . But when he made that documentary, it really seemed to me that he didn't have the right to do something like that; I couldn't understand why he, who had already achieved success, who had already made his way in the United States, thanks to his talent and ability as a director of photography, and who, in any case, had broken ties with Cuba since the beginning of the seventies, was so bitter. I couldn't understand it. And then, well, I thought that my film could have been an answer to Néstor. I would have been very pleased if he had lived to see it, and maybe then we could have resumed a dialogue. I say this with a certain nostalgia, and I'm not very sure it would have been so.

MC: In order to produce those tacit or internal dialogues found in your films, you have to enter into other dialogues—for example, a dialogue with the context. If we think of the reasons you chose to make a film about a character who is portrayed in a double way as an artist-homosexual, with which other components of the context of Cuban reality are you dialoguing?

TGA: As you know, the film does not deal directly with the theme of intolerance in relation to homosexuals. In reality, what it's about is a much wider intolerance. It's centered on the homosexual, but it can be understood as a problem that goes much beyond, that transcends, the problem of the homosexual and becomes a much more general problem. Who, then, am I dialoguing with? Well, with people who, in one way or another, have to do with this situation, who are responsible for this situation, the intolerance, the ostracization of the person who is different, the nonacceptance of the person who thinks with his or her head.

MC: But perhaps it would be too simplistic to say that those responsible are "the Party," because the film shows different possibilities within the Party.

TGA: Well, with the most extremist, the most . . . I was going to say, the most orthodox section of the Party, but, it's not necessarily the most orthodox section, rather, with a part of the Party that likes to think of itself as orthodox, because persons who think they are orthodox believe that they act in accord with a belief, a doctrine, a very straitlaced manner of thinking. There, the difference between tolerance and understanding comes into play. In fact, the orthodox person is not tolerant, but he is not tolerant in the face of something that, in some way, disturbs his manner of perceiving the world, his way of confronting things. But he is capable of understanding other positions. To have an orthodox attitude is not necessarily to have a repressive attitude. That is what I believe, anyway.

MC: Tómas, we know that in Hollywood, the director of a film does not have the right to make the final cut, while in Europe, directors tend to have this right. How is it in Cuba? Who has the right to make the final cut?

TGA: In principle, the director. But, of course, since films are produced by the Cuban Institute of Film Art and Industry, the ICAIC, the head of the Institute reserves that right, above all at the political and ideological level, meaning that it is there that censorship is exercised. In reality, he has exercised this right in a peremptory way on very few occasions. Generally, things are discussed previously, and agreements are reached. I can tell you that in my case, I have had conflicts of this type only once. This was with my film *Hasta Cierto Punto* (Up to a certain point), and I believe the conflict was justifiable in this case. I wanted to discuss the paternalism of the State in this film and create a stimulus to provoke discussion of this problem. But the truth is that I hadn't done it in a sufficiently solid and consistent manner so that the discussion could develop in what I thought was the best way. So I realized that I couldn't insist on my approach, in spite of the fact that, theoretically, my position was right, because in the film itself I had not expressed it in a convincing and correct manner. So I preferred not to say it at all, if you understand?

MC: Yes, but your use of the word *correct* at this juncture inevitably makes one think of the phrase *political correctness*.

TGA: I'm very pleased that you've sounded the alarm, because that is not the issue here. I believe that instead of saying *correct*, I should say *effective* manner. In *Hasta Cierto Punto*, I didn't say what I wanted to say in an effective way, in a convincing way. Some things didn't come out well; they were not effective dramatically, and, at the same time, they were politically polemical. This made the film more vulnerable, and so I preferred to take these things out. And keep in mind that in our case, given the situation or mentality of being under siege, of a fortress under fire, surrounded by the enemy, there is a certain level of paranoia and suspicion. When a criticism is made under these circumstances, many people think this weakens our position in the face of the enemy. I think the opposite occurs. I think that if the criticism is good, if it's efficient, if it's profound, it makes us stronger and less open to manipulation. That's my position. But I also realize that, in practice, the suspicion and paranoia felt by many people could stop a film from coming out. So what happens? Some people believe that if some films are not sufficiently convincing, it's better that they don't come out at all. I don't agree—I think those films, too, should come out. But what is clear is that if a particular film is vulnerable, the polemic can be destructive for it. That makes me aware that our situation in this regard is somewhat difficult, since it forces us to do things very well. Criticism has to be made in a very effective way in order to be indisputable.

MC: Tell me about *Cartas del parque* (Letters from the park).

TGA: *Cartas del parque* is a film about love. It has nothing to do with the political circumstances we live in. It's a film about feelings, about love. I think it's a story told in such a way as to produce aesthetic pleasure, or at least that was my intention. In this sense, it's different from all the films I've made. It doesn't touch on any polemical aspect of our reality. When it came out, there were those who said that I was running away from problems, that I was taking refuge in these films because I didn't have the courage to confront our reality critically. When I made *La última cena* (The Last Supper), which is a historical film, they said I was avoiding the present by going into the past. Well, now I've made *Fresa y chocolate*, in which there is a strong criticism of our current reality, and they say I've put on a mask in order to make it seem as if it is possible to criticize in Cuba.

MC: It's as if they are looking for a film director who is a kind of philosopher for everyone. Why is this so?

TGA: This is so especially in the case of Cuban directors. North American directors aren't rebuked for making a film about love. And if they happen to make a film with some type of social criticism, well, okay. Although for the most part they make action films, and no one criticizes them for this.

MC: So why in Cuba should film directors assume the role of social critics?

TGA: Because there are no other voices. Journalism, for example, does not perform its mission of social criticism. In spite of this, people talk in corridors, in cafés, on the street, on sidewalks, in lines, but the problems of society are not discussed in the press. This is a great frustration, and one feels the need to speak out.

MC: How do you see the dynamic in Cuba now?

TGA: I believe that there has always been, on the part of the leadership of the Revolution, an ambitious idea of maintaining ideological purity, of avoiding contamination from abroad, and of transforming people based on their consciousness and not on material incentives. All this has as a consequence paternalism, formalism, idealism, and all that we have had to put up with all these years. This situation is what provokes a crisis of involution. We are losing all our values; all the values the Revolution had recuperated in human beings are deteriorating today to the point where it's becoming impossible to know when we will hit rock bottom, but we're near.

MC: To what extent has this situation been produced not by the internal dynamics of the Revolution but by the collapse of communism in the world, by the effects in Cuba of the collapse of the Soviet Union?

TGA: Come on, now! No! The Cuban crisis was not the result of the Soviet collapse. What happened is that the Soviet collapse unveiled or revealed a situation that was already not sustainable. It revealed that Cuba was living on the *subvention* or support of the socialist world, and especially of the Soviet Union, which is not a sane policy for any country. Cuba was not producing material goods; rather, it was producing politics and exchanging politics for oil. And this is a situation that, with the fall of the socialist bloc, left us naked. It is a situation in which no one knows how to function. At the same time, people continue to insist that consciousness is what moves us. If the Soviet Union had continued to exist, I don't know where we would have ended up. I believe that we were heading toward an irreversible crisis.

MC: How is it possible to overcome this crisis?

TGA: Well, sometimes a crisis generates a reaction, an answer. I think the only way of overcoming it would be—and perhaps I'm expressing a very idealistic Christian sentiment here—by means of understanding and love among people. We have to help one another, because if we don't, we're all going to perish. Of course, there have to be new economic mechanisms, intelligent mechanisms, so that people feel motivated to react in the most coherent way to these goals of human coexistence. You can't act solely on the basis of exhortations and sermons and calls for love, because love flourishes where people can love each other, not in sewers.

MC: Titón, after your 1968 film *Memorias del subdesarrollo* (Memories of underdevelopment), outside of Cuba there was some critical commentary that tried to place you in the position of a dissident. You rejected it. However, something of this has remained in your reputation. Where do you place yourself, then?

TGA: Well, some say I'm a dissident because I criticize Cuban reality; others say I'm a propagandist for the government because with this criticism I try to show that in Cuba there exists freedom when in fact there is none. What a dilemma, eh? It's absurd. I don't know where they will put me. In reality, I'm neither one nor the other. If a dissident is understood as someone who attacks the government to try to destroy it and erase all that the Revolution has been able to bring of benefit to the people, then I'm not a dissident. But, of course, I criticize within the Revolution everything that I think is a distortion of those objectives and those paths of hope—in other words, everything that has set us off the path, to the point of placing us where we are today, in a very dangerous and agonizing crisis. In this sense, I'm a critic, but I'm not a dissident. With regard to the idea others put forward—that I'm a propagandist—a kind of mask the government puts on for foreign consumption in order to make it seem like there is freedom . . . well, I believe that you would need to refer back to the content of my films. Of course they are complex films, critical films, but for that very reason, they are also an answer to the image certain people abroad have of Cuba, which is also a distorted image, a superficial image, in which there is no real analysis of our situation. I don't know what else I can tell you. I believe that throughout these years, I have followed a clear line in this sense: I have always had contradictions and have tried to express as fully as I could, as fully as my lucidity would allow me. I have said all I can say. And though I have been in a position to live much better outside of Cuba, well, I haven't done it, and in truth it has been a very great temptation, this possibility of being able to live off my work, in relative comfort, honestly, in a place where I don't have to work so hard just to be able to work. But I haven't done it, and I haven't done it because . . . I don't know how to explain it. Because it's not a rational decision, that's for sure. I could live better in other places, and in Cuba I have to put up with a lifestyle that is quite uncomfortable. But I believe that in Cuba, values exist that do not exist in other places, and I greatly regret that they are being perverted, and I try to fight to recuperate them. It's a very personal and intimate need.

Cuba: The Changing Scenarios of Governability

Haroldo Dilla Alfonso

Governability has become a useful label for a variety of often contradictory situations. This tends to happen in the social sciences when a term is appropriated by politics for less sophisticated uses than the search for new knowledge, or, inversely, when the social sciences borrow a term from politics with the intent of actualizing a conceptual problematic without the necessary prior internal critique. In the case of governability, the appropriations have been mutual.

It is not my intention to address this problem in this article, although its consequences are implicated in my argument. I will use *governability* operatively here to mean a relation of power between ruled and rulers, which in the most optimal conditions guarantees that the ruled act according to formally established norms and procedures. What we have here is a situation of relative and unstable equilibrium between diverse types of social demands and the institutional processing capacity of a given political system, which is not limited to positive administrative action or policy initiatives but also includes negative responses (the obliteration or repression of demands) and ideological and informational production that can act as a means of creation of new values. This last, ideological component of gov-

boundary 2 29:3, 2002. Copyright © 2002 by Duke University Press.

ernability has been a highly effective element in regimes with foundational aims, such as the Cuban one.

No political regime in Latin America has enjoyed greater stability than the one installed in Cuba after the triumph of the Revolution in 1959. In the course of four decades, there have been only three moments in which the discontent of sectors of the population has been translated into collective actions and outcomes that have been disruptive of the established order. The first of these occurred during the initial stages of the revolutionary process, when, over a period of five years, several centers of counterrevolutionary insurgency appeared in the mountain regions of the country, along with an upsurge in urban terrorism. The second happened in the spring of 1980, when discontented sectors occupied the Peruvian Embassy in Havana, precipitating the massive exodus to the United States from the port of Mariel. The third—another migratory explosion, known as the crisis of the *balseros*, or rafters—happened in 1994 and had as an additional ingredient widespread street protests, the most important of which took place in one of the most central neighborhoods of the capital city. In none of these three critical conjunctures did antisystemic forces represent a significant social base, however, and, in any case, the political class was able to mobilize sufficient countersupport. Similarly, each of the three situations mentioned was linked to U.S. policies hostile to Cuba, and each led to a massive exodus of discontents as part of the solution (although, as one might expect, the class basis of discontent and exile in the first conjuncture—the Cuban bourgeoisie and middle class—changes significantly in the second two).

One of the most notable characteristics of the Cuban process has been the specific role that violent repression has played as a mechanism of governability, especially in the early sixties, when the newly installed revolutionary state applied extremely repressive measures not only to the counterrevolutionary outbreaks but also to political dissidence within the Revolution itself or to forms of quotidian behavior the new leaders considered incompatible with a supposed revolutionary morality. Once this initial phase of consolidation was over, however, violent repression became more selective and punctual, and when its use was deemed necessary, the revolutionary political class could deploy it with the support of considerable sectors of the population. In the place of violent repression, the system began to deploy, primarily on ideological-cultural bases, diverse mechanisms of exclusion or anathematization of demands, sustained by a strict machinery of social-political control and regulation lubricated by the strong consensus in support of the Revolution.

Without recourse to this element of consensus, it is impossible to explain Cuban governability in the last forty years, or, for that matter, today. Of course, neither the type of consensus nor the way governability is articulated now are the same as in those distant times when Cubans of both sexes cheered the victorious bearded guerrillas, marched off to fight the invaders at the Bay of Pigs, or believed sincerely the idea that achieving a sugar harvest of 10 million tons would radically change their quality of life. A decade of crisis in the nineties, the impoverishment of a majority of the population, and an economic revival undertaken within the framework of the global capitalist market have changed many national political parameters. Cubans of the nineties are more politically conscious and sophisticated than their parents or grandparents were. The aim of this article is to analyze, then, the emergence of a new scheme of governability in the nineties and beyond, and its most relevant characteristics.

Economic Crisis or Systemic Decomposition?

From the very early stages of the Revolution onward, the Cuban state has enjoyed a quasi-monopolistic status in the assignment of resources and values, due to the virtual eradication of the market and alternative forms of property. This authority became virtually hyperbolic in the seventies, when the connection with the Soviet market and the subsidies it provided permitted the Cuban economy astonishing autonomy from its own social conditions, given that its reproduction ceased to depend on primary internal factors such as productivity and efficiency. The most salient form of this authority was the promulgation of severely centralized and bureaucratized development plans in which there was little space to debate alternatives. On this basis, it was possible to create a broad program of social benefits and expanded civic participation, and to produce upward social mobility around three key areas: full employment, education, and public health. This was, unquestionably, a historic achievement without precedent in Latin America, but it was also one of the forms of ideological capital of the state in relation to society.

At the same time, the state was able to produce a highly credible ideology without even moderately effective competitors. The revolutionary forces had been tremendously successful in putting down oppositional sectors and their organic intellectuals. An institution linked to counterrevolutionary politics as powerful as the Catholic Church, for example, was virtually silenced for more than two decades. The only active competing ideological producers—the United States and the exile groups, whatever their respective ideological orientations might have been—remained in a diametrically opposed corner and were easily anathematized by a revolutionary discourse that highlighted patriotic values. In such a situation, the ideological production of the state could also easily manage the challenge of what Goran Therborn has called the interpellations of the "good," the "existent," and the "possible,"[1] and present the new regime as the agent of a teleological march forward whose discursive dimension was congruent with a material base of economic development, equitable distribution, and national security. The core nuclei of this discourse reinforced a fusion of legitimacy and authority on the part of the regime and tended to present the actual course of things as the necessary outcome of the universal laws of history. The policies of the regime appeared to ordinary citizens as products of the social community itself, and therefore as unassailable, making it difficult, at the same time, to perceive "the moral fragility of positive law," as Juan Ramon Capella puts it.[2] Here the political obligation that any regime presupposes of its citizens was actualized as a self-assumed rather than imposed obligation.

And, of course, all this was possible because Cuban society was a social body in the process of decomposition and thus marked by a low level of universalization and social reflexivity, to borrow Anthony Giddens's terms. The dynamic of the Revolution generated the emigration not only of the bourgeoisie but also of a large part of the middle classes and the intellectuals, and in political terms it liquidated not only the Right but also the moderate Left. Faced with a false but apparently credible choice between a just and equitable social system and a political regime that would guarantee civil and political rights and democracy, the popular masses opted for the former.[3] The new political class in power expressed its limits not only in its incapacity to run the economy efficiently—Che Guevara's main anxiety in his Cuban years—but also in its inability to produce a superior democratic

1. Goran Therborn, *The Ideology of Power and the Power of Ideology* (London: Verso, 1980).

2. Juan Ramon Capella, *Fruta prohibida* (Madrid: Editorial Trotta, 1997).

3. The aversion—or, at the very least, indifference—of the Cuban population to a liberal democratic restoration was a constant found in the major sociological and anthropological studies carried out in Cuba in the sixties by Maurice Zeitlin, Paul Sweezy, and Oscar Lewis, among others. As late as 1974, a Chilean journalist who was studying closely the process of institutionalization of the Revolution got from an interviewee a confession that deserves to be transcribed here: "The Yankees also talk about democracy. . . . I prefer to hear the word socialism. . . . When I hear 'democracy' I feel a little shiver" (Marta Harnecker, *Cuba: dictadura o democracia* [Mexico: Siglo XXI, 1975]).

political order. The result could not be other than a very high concentration of political authority and a political voluntarism that was only further intensified by U.S. hostility to the Revolution and regional isolation.

In this sense, institutionalization was a transcendental moment in the evolution of the Cuban Revolution. Leaving aside its organizational and normative benefits, including a somewhat limited process of decentralization and supervision of arenas for direct participation, institutionalization was above all a moment when the socialist tendencies of the system were definitively frozen and the revolutionary process limited to modernizing and nationalist goals.[4] The socialist features survived in a distribution scheme that, as noted, guaranteed high levels of social equity and served as a key element of popular support.

This scheme of regulation began to show cracks in the eighties, largely because the upward social mobility unleashed by the Revolution itself generated an educated, complex social subject, whose level of qualification collided with the rigid norm of subordination the system imposed on it. But the real crisis came when the external economic subsidy provided by the Soviets disappeared, and it became clear that the national economy was incapable of guaranteeing its simple reproduction. The facts are well known. After exhibiting virtually stagnant growth between 1986 and 1989, the economy declined by 35 percent in the next four years. The import sector was seriously affected, and personal consumption declined drastically. Free social services, the Revolution's badge of honor, continued, but their quality was inevitably affected by the lack of resources.

The most important thing, for our purposes here, is to note that at the beginning of the nineties, Cuban society was facing a systemic crisis that affected not only the prevailing model of economic production and accumulation but also the system of social regulation and ideological-cultural production. Consequently, it also affected the reformulation of the prevailing scheme of governability. For the Cuban political class, and especially for the so-called historical leadership associated with Fidel Castro himself and the 1959 triumph of the Revolution, this signified a perplexing dilemma. In truth, it was not the first time that the revolutionary political class saw itself obliged to make substantial political reformulations. Between 1959 and 1961, it did this in masterful fashion, counting in its favor the enthusiastic support of the majority and the political sterility of the minority opposition. In the seven-

4. I analyze this process in my essay "Cuba: Cual es la democracia deseable?" in *La democracia en Cuba y el diferendo con los Estados Unidos*, ed. H. Dilla (Havana: Editorial de Ciencias Sociales, 1996).

ties, the political class undertook yet another reformulation of the project of the Revolution, with hardly any opposition to speak of, with less enthusiasm than a decade earlier, but also with the inestimable support of a superpower.

What has characterized the reformulations of governability at the end of the century, on the other hand, is that they have been launched in conditions that are new for a political class not used to having to allow competitors in the assignment of values and resources, and in which, moreover, any potential decision with long-term consequences not only leads inevitably to the appearance of new competitors but also accentuates the weakness or incapacity of the political class itself. The stress that this has produced has expressed itself in the last fifteen years in a series of forced marches and countermarches as much in the political as in the economic sphere, and, in particular, in an exceptionally contradictory relation between the exigencies of governability and the aspirations for a greater democratic opening.

The Three Moments of the Reformulation of the Nineties

The first of these moments corresponds to what was called officially the Process of Rectification of 1986–89, with its excessively optimistic goal of putting the Revolution on the "correct path" again. In point of fact, that path was characterized by a strong antimarket rhetoric, the recovery of national autonomy (in contraposition to both the United States and Soviet perestroika), and a strong reliance on ethical and nationalist arguments that had as their emblematic figures José Martí and Che Guevara. The second moment corresponds to an interregnum that began in 1990 and culminated in 1995. This was the most difficult stage in economic terms, the most intense phase of what has been called the Special Period, but paradoxically, it was the most open period in political terms.

While there are substantial differences between these two stages, there is a structural continuity that expresses itself in at least three aspects: the lack of an even moderately coherent model of economic accumulation, a climate of relative political tolerance, and the first signs since the consolidation of revolutionary power in the sixties of visible division among the political class.

During the eight or so years that these two stages cover, a reticence to adopt market mechanisms to reactivate the economy predominated. This reticence shifted from constituting the ideological backbone of the so-called Rectification (which aimed to curb the market reforms that had been introduced earlier in the eighties) to a somewhat half-hearted principle after 1989, when it became clear that there was no other path and the market began to enter the national scene through all available openings. Eventually, this gave rise to an implicit situation that some have called the model of a dual economy, an attempt to segment the economy into two spaces, a dynamic one linked to the world market and called upon to finance the second, which remained in crisis, ruled by central planning and generally concentrated on the internal market and traditional export activities. Behind this model, however, there was lacking a design that could bring together the possibility of reactivating the economy with the conservation of the social bases of the alliance or consensus sustaining the revolutionary project and the mechanisms of social control. The dual economy model received a fatal blow in the summer of 1993, when the dollar was legalized as a medium of exchange, but its propensity to segment markets as a mode of governability has continued to the present in a way I will analyze in what follows.

A second common element in this period was the existence of a relatively open political climate. Of course, this was a limited opening that never contemplated seriously the existence of an organized opposition and cut off tolerated debate short of any questioning of principles such as the single party, Fidel Castro's leadership, and continued confrontation without compromise with the United States. But it was nevertheless an unprecedented stage that incorporated much of what was best in Cuban thought and society.

In some cases, this climate of openness was stimulated by the state itself. In fact, the Rectification campaign was accompanied by an invitation to deformalize political spaces and in its final stage produced the convocation to a public debate around the draft program of the Fourth Congress of the Communist Party.[5] The role of the state was also evident in the promulgation in 1988 of a more flexible and modern penal code; in the constitutional reforms of 1992; in the new electoral law the same year; in the liberalizing economic measures of the summer of 1993, such as the legalization of the dollar; in the liberalization of the archaic emigration policy; and finally in the legalization of some civic associations and domestic nongovernmental organizations under the terms of a restrictive regulatory law in 1985.

In particular, the constitutional reforms of 1992 produced changes in

---

5. According to the official call for this congress, its aim was "to promote a consensus that has as its basis the recognition of the diversity of criteria that can exist among a people and that will strengthen itself by means of democratic discussion in the heart of the party and the Revolution, above all in the search for solutions, in the examination of alternatives to attain objective socioeconomic goals, and, in general, in a reflection oriented to perfect the society in which we live" ("Llamamiento al IV Congreso del Partido," in *Cuadernos de Nuestra América* [July–December 1990]).

almost two-thirds of the articles, and although many of these changes had to do with the economic sphere (property rights, decentralization of foreign trade), others affected—at least in principle—some of the core principles of the constitution of 1976: for example, the proclamation of the nondenominational character of the state and the prohibition of any form of discrimination against religious believers, the suppression of allusions to democratic centralism and unity of power, the suppression of the strictly class-based definition of the social foundation of the state, and the establishment of direct elections for parliamentary seats.

But in general, these initiatives tolerated but did not encourage new forms of political and economic agency, and their effects began to diminish as the political leadership overcame the causes of its own perplexity. A good example of this is the *via crucis* suffered by the new Electoral Law of 1992. The substitution of the old electoral system, which permitted only indirect election of representatives, by one based on direct election of deputies had been a constant demand in the public debates taking place around the time of the Fourth Congress of the Communist Party in 1990. And, as previously noted, this was a demand that was taken into consideration in the constitutional reforms of 1992. The subsequent Electoral Law sought to incorporate the demand, but in a way that limited its democratic character, among other things by permitting only one candidate for each electoral position. The designers of the law were more concerned with closing off the possibility of undesirable candidates than with offering Cuban citizens the opportunity to choose between various candidates, a basic principle of any democratic election and one that had prevailed vigorously in local elections since 1976. In 1993, when the first elections were held under this singular new law, the Cuban leadership hastened to clarify that the system was a provisional one, adopted in light of the country's state of emergency. Five years later, during the second round of elections, it was pronounced the most democratic electoral system imaginable. What in 1993 was seen as a necessity had been transformed into a virtue.

The crisis of the early nineties inevitably began to impinge on the conduct and dynamic of the political class in two major ways: (1) the possibility of a meltdown of the regime stimulated ambitions within the political class for a succession of leadership; (2) the climate of uncertainty precipitated contradictory reactions that had their most notable public expression between December 1993 and May 1994, when the leadership had to decide if the crisis was to be faced fundamentally with extra-economic measures (expropriations, police control, mass mobilizations) or with new economic measures based on prices, taxes, and business incentives. From 1986 onward, an instability in the membership of the main political bodies of the country, particularly the Political Bureau of the Communist Party, is evident. Between 1975 and 1986, the Political Bureau showed a surprising stability in its membership, which was made up at that time of thirteen plenary members who were also members of the Council of State, the major collective decision-making organ of state power in Cuba, and who, in general, were appointed from the "historical" cadre closest to Castro from the days of the insurrection or from leadership positions in the party apparatus. The only relevant figure in the Political Bureau who had experience in the economic area was a person closely tied to the Soviet Union and its agencies of cooperation. This was, without doubt, the period of greatest continuity and concentration of political authority in the hands of an elite that directly controlled all institutions.

In the Third Congress of the Communist Party in 1986, however, over half of the members of the Political Bureau, many of them "historical" leaders, were removed and replaced by provincial cadres and representatives of mass organizations. The next reconfiguration of the Political Bureau in 1991, which was carried out in the wake of the Fourth Party Congress, produced another renewal of more than half of its membership. Again, there is a departure of "historical" figures and an accentuation of three types of candidates: provincial leaders, economics ministers and functionaries, and military officers. Of the twenty-five members, only three could be considered "historical" figures, four were party functionaries, four were officers (one of them was the architect of the armed forces' system of business enterprises), five were involved in economic affairs, six were provincial leaders, and three represented other activities. Fourteen members of the 1991 Political Bureau were also members of the Council of State.

In one way, this renovation of leadership can be considered a positive outcome, to the extent that it evidences a will to regeneration on the part of a political class that was subject to electoral scrutiny only in a very indirect way. But if we look more closely at the characteristics of the Cuban regime, we would also have to admit that the changes brought about in 1986 and above all in 1991 reflect the natural instability of leadership in a period of crisis. It is relevant, in this regard, to look at the continuity of the membership of the Political Bureau as a whole since 1986: With the exception of four cardinal figures (Castro himself, his brother Raúl, and their close associates, Juan Almeida and José R. Machado), only three persons (two military officers and one provincial leader) have remained in their positions. Moreover, at least two members of the Political Bureau, both of whom were considered rising stars in national politics and, in one way or another, championed a discourse of renovation, were later relieved of their positions.

The current Political Bureau, configured in 1997 and designated to function until 2002, confirmed the pattern of composition of the previous one but reduced the number of members replaced to one-quarter. In addition to the four cardinal figures previously noted, there are now five military officers, four representatives from various ministries of economics, six provincial leaders, two party functionaries, and four political leaders of diverse sorts. Eight people now simultaneously have or had a seat on the bureau, the Council of State, and the ministries: two "historical" figures, two economic figures, and two state functionaries, including the once promising Chancellor of State Roberto Robaina, who effectively disappeared from the political scene at the close of the century. But in 1997, the situation to which these renewals of leadership responded had changed substantially.

In 1995, the Cuban economy began to grow for the first time since 1990, and it has continued to do so, albeit in very irregular spurts. This gave the political class a chance to overcome its own perplexity and embark on a complex balancing act between its social commitments and the exigencies of an economy determined now, both in its public and private dimensions, by its relation with foreign capital and the world market. This emerging model of accumulation has as its basic premise the subordination of sectors of the national economy to the rules of the market, with the resultant implications for Cuban life, such as the extension of market mechanisms to the assignment of resources, the principal role of foreign investment in the most dynamic sectors of the economy, the superexploitation of the labor force, and the co-optation by the political class of an emerging technocratic-entrepreneurial sector that has been gaining influence in decision making and cultural and ideological production. In strictly political terms, the new economic situation brings with it a new schema of governability characterized by a strong mechanism of sociopolitical control that is beholden as much to the exigencies of reproduction of power as to the new model of accumulation. A number of diverse economic measures liberalizing the activities of foreign capital, a new hardening of the penal code, two new laws for the defense of national sovereignty (known outside Cuba as the *leyes mordazas*, or gag laws, because of their limitations on permitted criticism of the regime), a reorganization and modernization of the state apparatuses for capture and control of finances, an offensive directed since 1996 against an already emaciated civil society and the spaces open for public debate, and the intense mass mobilizations that have inundated the streets and public squares of the island since 1999 correspond to this phase of recomposition.

Accumulation, Society, and the State

As many observers have noted, Cuban society today is in a process of transition to significantly greater diversity. This process has different sources and implications for the country's social dynamic. In more than one sense, it is the result of the social conquests of the Revolution that raised the levels of education and social awareness of the population and opened up new opportunities to those sectors of the population traditionally subordinated, such as women. It is also the result of a generational turnover, with the entry into the public arena of age groups whose socialization occurred in different periods. But no balance sheet of the current situation can overlook the fact that the dominant factor behind this increased diversification has been the extremely rapid colonization of social relations and everyday life by the market, and, consequently, the process of social restratification determined in the last instance by the relations of persons to different types of property, economic areas, and consumer circuits. In the wake of globalization, Cubans are beginning to experience the displeasures and pleasures of now being actually, and not only symbolically, Latin Americans.

A key point to take into account in this respect is the impoverishment of the majority of the population. The deep economic crisis that the country experienced between 1990 and 1994 reduced substantially the levels of personal and social consumption, even where there was a political will to maintain the free provision of education and health services. Although the state has maintained a subsidized "basket" of essential foodstuffs for each member of the population, it has been calculated that in 1998, ordinary Cubans had to purchase, in dollarized markets, 60 percent of their protein needs, 50 percent of edible oils, and 30 percent of their caloric intake, despite the fact that wage and salary levels in pesos have remained almost static, at levels corresponding to the heavily subsidized markets prior to 1989.[6] What is striking about the current situation is not only that the economic recovery has

6. Armando Nova, "La nueva relación de producción en la agricultura," *Revista Cuba: Investigaciones Económicas* (January–March 1998). When I refer here to "dollarized markets" I mean not only markets where only dollars are accepted but also those where the price levels have attained relative parity with dollar values, even when the medium of exchange is the Cuban peso. In this sense, the only markets that are not dollarized in Cuba are those of everyday services provided by the state and the subsidized food basket system.

not resulted in a corresponding renewal of state subsidies but rather that the greatest reductions in these subsidies have occurred precisely as the economy began to recover from its prostration.[7] In other words, the decline of subsidized markets is not an effect of the crisis but an outcome that is consubstantial with the new economic logic.

Although we do not have full statistics about the magnitude of poverty in Cuba (and in fact the studies that have been produced emphatically deny its existence), it is fair to assume that a significant part of the Cuban population lives today in a situation of poverty or relative impoverishment and marginality. A survey recently taken in Havana (where the standard of living is higher than in the rest of the country) revealed that 14 percent of households were surviving on incomes of less than 50 pesos a month per capita, and 43 percent of households were surviving with incomes less than 100 pesos a month per capita, that is, at levels that are evidently insufficient to purchase even minimal dietary requirements much less other primary living expenses. Of the households surveyed, 77 percent declared that they had insufficient income to cover basic expenses.[8]

To the relative impoverishment that has affected a majority of the population and the outright poverty suffered by particular sectors we need to add other indexes of social diversification and stratification produced by differential relations to property and markets. All ordinary Cubans participate as a matter of course in a variety of activities of survival and resistance that range from a generalized corruption in everyday transactions to the acceptance of money transfers from émigré family members—transfers that the official propaganda had at one time condemned as antinational and had urged the population to abjure as a demonstration of patriotism (and which now, of course, increase the internal influence and role of these émigrés). It is important to add that we are not talking about a politically innocent social differentiation, because we are witnessing a process of fragmentation, weakening, and alienation of precisely the social sectors that constituted the social base par excellence of the revolutionary project.

7. A study of a local municipality performed under my direction revealed that between 1996 and 1998 the sale of subsidized food "baskets" declined 50 percent, in spite of the fact that some of the prices of the articles included had in the meantime slightly increased. Although there are regional differences in the distribution schemes, there is no reason to think that this is an exceptional case. See H. Dilla et al., "Los agobios de la industrialización periférica en un municipio cubano: San Juan de las Lajas," in *Mercados globales y gobernabilidad local*, ed. H. Burchard and H. Dilla (Caracas: Nueva Sociedad, 2001).
8. Omar Everleny, "Ciudad de La Habana: desempeño económico y situación social," in *La economía cubana en el 2000* (Havana: CEEC, 2001).

In sharp contrast to this process of impoverishment is the notable enrichment achieved by a very small minority of the population through speculative activities in the black market, or in the reduced spaces available for domestic private enterprise, or in association with foreign capital—a phenomenon that has substantially increased the levels of social inequality. Here, as noted, one witnesses the rapid emergence of an entrepreneurial-technocratic elite whose principal obstacle to consolidating itself as a caste or class resides in the continuing fragmentation of the market, but which possesses a high capacity for ideological and cultural production. Here, too, the available data are scarce but suggestive. Around 1996, for example, reports of the National Bank of Cuba indicated that 13 percent of bank accounts made up 85 percent of all savings. Only two years earlier, the same proportion of savers controlled only 70 percent of savings. Another study based on a survey of households reported that while the lower fifth of the population received 7 percent of total national income, the upper fifth of the population enjoyed 58 percent. Cuban society continued in the nineties to be the most egalitarian society in Latin America in terms of individual income and consumption, but it was more unequal in these respects than some developed and underdeveloped capitalist societies.[9]

The increasing differentiation and stratification of Cuban society is a basic aspect of governability, its forms and methods, and the complex role of the state in elaborating it. The Cuban state has adopted a firm position of defense of the social consumption of the population that has attenuated the effects of impoverishment and for the most part avoided economic marginality or exclusion. By doing this, the Cuban state has retained a basic principle of any state: the universal commitment to social prosperity, a principle worth remarking in an international context characterized by its neoliberal renunciation. Likewise, the state has defended the feasibility of its role as owner and direct provider of goods and services, another praiseworthy stance in the miasma of antistatist rhetoric that predominates today in world politics. All this supposes additional costs and headaches for the state in fiscal and administrative terms, but these are costs that are inseparable from its function of responsibility for the common good. However, this positive will loses efficacy and credibility when it is subsumed under an aspiration to a form of bureaucratic power that seeks to penetrate every nook and cranny of society and, with the exception of its relations with sectors

9. Lia Añé, "La reforma económica y la economía familiar en Cuba," in *Reforma económica y cambio social en América Latina*, ed. M. de Miranda (Cali, Colombia: TM Editores, 2000).

dynamized by foreign investment or strongly corporative, that continues to attempt to reproduce the "command" model operative two decades ago, when the economy, the society, and the international context were radically different. Consequently, the state has to assume an overwhelming number of demands that it can satisfy only precariously at the price of political and economic irrationality. At the same time, it also stifles the unfolding of individual initiatives, contracts the spaces of freedom and tolerance, and limits the quality of democratic participation.

By renouncing a systematic political reform, one that—even with preventive measures against U.S. intervention built in—would have amplified the space for public debate and provided for the inclusion of the existing diversity of Cuban society, the Cuban leadership has opted instead for a simple aggregative policy compatible with its political inertia. By means of this aggregation it attempts to respond to direct economic pressures and to the demand for the inclusion of the emerging entrepreneurial-technocratic sector, as well as to the social demands of the general population. This situation explains many paradoxical features of contemporary Cuban reality, such as the generation of differentiated, fragmented policies on civil rights (in relation, for example, to emigration rights, wage and salary levels, or access to information); the marches and countermarches of the economic reform projects; large-scale popular mobilizations such as those that accompanied the Elián González affair; and finally the paradox of a political discourse that claims against the hegemony of neoliberal economics a space for choices at the global level at the same time that it anathematizes that space in the domestic sphere, all in the name of "perfecting" socialism. As a result, Cuban society today is undergoing a level of political exclusion or marginalization that is greater than the level of economic and social exclusion, which, as noted, is narrowing the social base of the system. But this narrowing is happening in a way that is quite different than the one imagined in the apocalyptic predictions of the fall of Castro created by the Right, and it is compatible in the short run at least with systemic continuity and paradoxically even with the vibrant mass demonstrations that have inundated the country in recent years.

Is the Social Base of the System Narrowing?

In 1994, the year in which the economic crisis affected daily life most dramatically and of the exodus of the *balseros*, the well-respected Gallup Poll conducted a survey in the streets of Havana, asking people about their degree of support for a list of political positions. The result was that 48 percent of the respondents described themselves as "revolutionaries," 11 percent as "communists," and another 11 percent as "socialists," while only 23 percent were opposed to the system.[10] This last piece of data is conclusive: Only a minority of the population maintained an antisystemic spirit. What is not clear, however, is the force of the distinction a Cuban might make between being a revolutionary, a socialist, or a communist. The last two terms are probably indistinguishable in ideological terms and represent a sector strongly committed to the system. But one would have to admit that the majority's preference for the term *revolutionary* offers at least a suggestion of doubt, especially since there were more militant choices offered by the pollsters. In this sense, to be revolutionary could mean recognizing the social and patriotic conquests of the Revolution, a definition antithetical to the negation of those conquests by counterrevolutionaries, or simply the fact that in the last 150 years of Cuban history there has been a tendency to identify political virtue with the condition of being a revolutionary.

In 1993 and 1998, national elections in Cuba were held under the auspices of the new electoral law discussed above. In both instances, without permitting oppositional propaganda, the government launched an intense campaign not only to get a high level of voter participation but also to assure that the electorate would vote in a "unified" fashion for the candidates whose names were listed on the ballots, on the grounds that only in this way could one vote for the nation, the Revolution, and socialism. The electoral data are quite similar for both cases. Of more than 8 million potential voters, 88 percent gave a unified vote; the level of abstention was minimal. The remainder—some eight hundred thousand (10 to 12 percent of the electorate)—either did not vote, submitted blank ballots, voided their ballots, or did not vote "unified." There is not sufficient evidence to think these negative votes were all necessarily in opposition to the regime. If we count those who annulled their ballots or submitted blank ballots (a more marked act of protest), the number of negative votes would reach some three hundred thousand (4 percent of the electorate), a minority with little overall significance.

Do these results signify, on the other hand, that the majority of persons who voted "unified" in these elections represents a spectrum of active consensus? This would be an unwarranted conclusion. For many citizens, there are more reasons to vote than to abstain: the relative ease of voting

10. *Cuba Update* (February 1995).

(it takes, on average, only ten minutes to vote in electoral stations situated close to households), a sense of civic duty, a desire to avoid social or political pressures, or, simply, routine. And so, too, there are good reasons to vote "unified," since the candidates whose names are listed on the ballot are usually people rooted in the neighborhoods with sufficient social recognition to be considered good representatives. But if we consult the available statistics on the number of persons who applied for visas to emigrate to the United States in 1998—some 732,000 out of the close to 2.5 million eligible to apply—then we can also come to the conclusion that a part of the electorate who voted "for the nation, the Revolution, and socialism" aspired to emigrate to the capitalist nation par excellence, the historical enemy of the Cuban nation, dedicated for over forty years to overthrowing the Revolution.

More than offering here an explanation of this paradox, my intention is to raise an issue that has to do with Cuban social psychology and its capacity for simulation in the face of power from colonial times onward. In a survey taken in 1997 among a small but in some respects representative sample of residents of Havana (137), Guillermo Milán found that 20 percent of the respondents demonstrated a total lack of confidence in the capacity of the prevailing political system to resolve the national problems, while another 26 percent had exactly the opposite opinion. Even more significant is the fact that 47 percent preferred to locate the solution of these problems in individual efforts without reference to the political system as such.[11] On this basis, it is possible to suggest the following hypothesis: Cuban society is beginning to experience a process of polarization of attitudes and behaviors. At one extreme is an atomized minority opposed to the system, while the other extreme is yet another minority, but in this case one that is effectively organized and characterized by an active ethos of consensus. In the center, the majority is made up of those persons who have opted for individual solutions, who are more nervous about an uncertain change than the vicissitudes of the present situation and at the same time are seduced by the expectations of enrichment that the market always brings with it, although very few have or will have adequate access to these opportunities.

The antisystemic sector is not growing significantly in Cuba for three reasons: continued emigration, which drains away discontented persons; the existing system of sociopolitical controls; and the chronic inability of the opposition to offer Cuban society a credible alternative program. But the

11. Guillermo Milán, *Los procesos económicos en la sociedad cubana* (Havana: Instituto de Filosofía, 1998), unpublished manuscript.

sector of active support for the regime is also a minority. One could even argue hypothetically that it is a remnant of the past, more liable than younger generations to accept charismatic leaders and requiring greater protection by the state, either because it depends on the state for its own continued existence or because it finds in its relation with the state optimal conditions for social mobility in the new situation of Cuba. But any political system can, in the short run, continue to reproduce itself with the active support of a minority, as long as the opposition is not organized and is unable to articulate a majority view. This is the Cuban case.

The most generalized social response to the crisis is not, then, opposition to the system or the regime, but anomie and simulation. According to the survey by Milán cited earlier, between 1990 and 1995, the number of suicides in Cuba remained at the very high level of twenty persons per one hundred thousand, a proportion that doubled for persons over forty years of age. In the same period, the level of violent crime (as reported to the police) soared 55 percent: There were 2 million delinquent acts, three hundred thousand of them involving the use of violence. A quarter of a million persons had been incarcerated, and a million and a half had gone through criminal proceedings of one sort or another. Another study shows that if we extract from the period of 1948 to 1958 a statistical baseline with a value of 100, the crime level in Cuba is 61 from 1981 to 1984, and 87 from 1985 to 1988, but this number rises to 169 in the five-year-period from 1989 to 1994.[12] Corruption in Cuba is a fairly generalized phenomenon, and the government has tried to limit its negative consequences in a variety of ways (including the signing of a pledge of honor by all state functionaries). But, generally speaking, widespread corruption in daily life is encouraged by a permissive environment that is, frankly, alarming.

Emigration is another formula for survival that, because of its frequently illegal character, also encourages anomic traits. Moreover, it is not distributed randomly but is concentrated precisely in sectors that are very significant for Cuban society. Between 1990 and 1995, some 142,000 persons emigrated from Cuba, 75 percent of them to the United States. The majority of these emigrants were men who were workers, approximately 30 years of age, and residents of the city of Havana. The migratory potential indicated in the applications submitted to the Foreign Interests Section of the United States in Cuba was 190,000 persons in 1994, 496,000 in 1996,

12. Ramón de la Cruz Ochoa, "El delito, la criminología y el derecho penal en Cuba," in *Revista Electrónica de Ciencia Penal y Criminología* (2000).

and 732,000 in 1998—out of approximately a quarter of a million persons in the current population of Cuba (over 11 million) eligible to apply, due to the restrictions U.S. immigration regulations and quotas impose.

A situation of this sort is perfectly manageable for a considerable period without affecting political continuity, even when this is accomplished by a fragile balancing act, often in circumstances that may erode governability. In this sense, the policy of the "hard nuclei" developed by the Cuban government has a certain rationality: strict control of the incipient civil society, repression of the very limited organized opposition, strengthening of or an increase in the public presence of police and security forces, segmentation of markets, selective and gradual co-optation of the entrepreneurial-technocratic elite on the basis of proof of political loyalty, and mobilization of the general population around a nationalism expressed not only in the face of aggression by the United States but also in the face of the dynamics of a global economy in which the Cuban government can portray itself as a bastion of human dignity. Nevertheless, the new decade poses for the Cuban political class a series of new challenges. The first of these, noted above, is that economic recovery appears to be possible only at the cost of a greater liberalization of the market and consequently an inevitable ceding of power to the market's agents, at the expense of the persistent desire of the political class to exercise near total control.

The second challenge is the future course of the U.S. economic blockade and hostility to the Revolution, which have endured for many decades, almost as long as the Revolution itself. Since the nineties, U.S. pressure against Cuba has redoubled—an example is the Helms-Burton Act of 1996, a measure as unethical as it is illegal under international law. Nevertheless, it is important to note that the Cuban political class has been very dexterous in the ways it has handled this external threat, either by diminishing its effects and bringing the United States to more than one point of impasse in its relations with the island or by using the conflict as an argument for the mobilization and maintenance of a consensus on nationalist bases. The primary stress factor today, in any case, is not the continuation of the blockade but rather the ever increasing awareness that we are passing through its final stages, as Cuba becomes an interesting market for U.S. businesses.

Cuban policy has been precisely to stimulate this interest on the part of U.S. businesses in order to produce a normalization of relations with the United States without prior conditions (the policy is also designed to give the regime political capital to use in whatever scenario of negotiation) and, at the same time, to exploit holes in the blockade, such as the Elián González affair, to amplify internal spaces of legitimacy, presenting these to the population as achievements of the Revolution and popular mobilization. But even if an ideal negotiation scenario were to present itself to the regime, the end of the blockade would mark also the end of a specific form of governability and would lead to a depolarization of the Cuban political system. This suggests precisely a scenario in which part of the political class—formed in a climate of confrontation and unable to act in new conditions—might have to accept retirement or replacement in the near future. Of course, this prospect does not omit the possibility of regressive movements politically, which can be dramatic, especially when we are faced with a U.S. administration that is run by an ultraconservative team bent on pursuing a global antiterrorist campaign with as yet unpredictable consequences.

The other stress factor in the current situation is the aging of the historical leadership of the Revolution and its inevitable disappearance from the public stage. The Cuban system does have regulative mechanisms to assure succession of power: One person, Raúl Castro, is at the same time second in command of the party and the state, and head of the strongest and most coherent state institution, the armed forces. But the Cuban political system is organized around a strong concentration of charismatic authority, and a good part of the active support the political process still enjoys is based on Fidelismo. This does not imply, however, that the retirement of the historical leadership will lead to political chaos. In Cuba, there exist sufficient institutional frameworks and actors to rearticulate—or at the very least to renegotiate ably—the changing scenarios of power. But this rearticulation or renegotiation will have to be carried out without the recourse to the charismatic authority that has been an invaluable factor of consent and unity for the political class during the last forty years. Inevitably, it will be necessary to imagine new ways of doing politics.

The Lessons of a Revolution

In opening up this final topic, I am aware that, as in most issues related to Cuba, I run the risk of falling prey to the polarization that characterizes both the Cuban political system and the academic enterprise dedicated to its interpretation, and also of being judged myself by the same measure. The theme of governability in Cuba is in a sense the theme of the continuity of the project of national liberation and socialist orientation that has remained in power for more than forty years in spite of the brutal hostility of the United States. There is no space in Cuba for a crisis of governability that does not imply a systemic replacement. But a systemic replacement does not necessarily have to pass through a crisis of governability. Today that process of replacement is already happening and takes the form of an increasing subordination to the norms of the world capitalist economy and the creation inside the country of organic agents of this process who are and will continue to be the main beneficiaries of the new economic policy of adjustments and market liberalization. It could be said that this has been the only possible option, and in many ways that is true. But it is also true that the Cuban leadership has stifled the emergence of those autonomous spaces of popular organization in the economy and politics that could have shifted responses in the direction of the preservation and development of the socialist features of the system.

This conclusion would seem to support the idea that socialism no longer has opportunities in a world that is more capitalist than ever before. But in reality it is a question of something else. The possibilities of socialism that came into being in 1917 failed in 1918, when the German revolution was defeated. Socialism in a single country, and then in the socialist "camp" formed by the geopolitical expansion of the Soviet Union or semi-developed countries on the periphery of capitalism, was condemned to failure, among other reasons because of the counterrevolutionary siege to which it was subject. This siege not only impeded access to technologies and capital resources that were vital for its survival, but it also exacerbated nonsocialist features of these systems, above all the authoritarianism unfortunately ensconced in the proclamation of the dictatorship of the proletariat and democratic centralism. When Rosa Luxemburg reminded the Bolsheviks that freedom was only such when it applied to people who think differently, she was articulating an essential principle of socialism, democracy, in the face of men who defended an essential principle of politics, the conservation of power. The defeat of socialism was above all a political-cultural defeat. Its defeat was simply its nonrealization as an alternative. Socialist strategy will be viable only when it acquires a global dimension that is also profoundly democratic and pluralist.

Even if we assume that the Cuban Revolution should accept its bankruptcy in a shameful manner, and that a capitalist restoration is inevitable, none of this should be interpreted as a loss of forty years of history for the Cuban nation, as the right wing of the émigré community and the internal opposition tend to proclaim from their isolated positions. On the contrary, these have been forty years of unprecedented social, political, and cultural achievements that history, always more receptive than its participants, will know how to validate. And for those of us who continue to believe, as I do, in the superiority of the socialist option, they will also be a legacy, as contradictory as it is suggestive.

Havana–Santo Domingo, August 2001

The Island, the Map, the Travelers: Notes on Recent Developments in Cuban Art

Antonio Eligio Fernández (Tonel)

Translated by Kenya Dworkin

Ours has been defined by Michel Foucault as "above all the epoch of space."[1] Inspired by this idea, Edward Soja invites us to participate in "a practical theoretical consciousness that sees the lifeworld of being creatively located not only in the making of history but also in the construction of human geographies, the social production of space and the restless formation and reformation of geographical landscapes."[2] Soja proposes a "spatialization of the critical imagination," an imagination spread out in space that serves as a counterweight to the possible excesses of merely accumulative history, without disdaining temporal contexts.

In the spirit of Soja's invitation, I would like to rethink recent developments in Cuban art, developments that not only concern space as defined

A slightly different and earlier version of this article was published in the exhibition catalog *CUBA: Los Mapas del Deseo* (Vienna: Kunsthalle Wien, 1999).

1. Michel Foucault, quoted by Edward Soja, "History: Geography: Modernity," in Simon During, *The Cultural Studies Reader* (London and New York: Routledge, 1993), 136.

2. Soja, "History: Geography: Modernity," 136.

boundary 2 29:3, 2002. Copyright © 2002 by Duke University Press.

by particular cities (Havana, Miami, Mexico City, New York) but that also, in some way, effect territorializing operations as they attempt to define their own critical maps.

Recent Cuban art, created and located primarily on the island, frequently has been called "new."[3] From an equally historicist point of view one could substitute "of the eighties" for "new." Both labels identify a certain sequence of events, a conjunction of circumstances whose initial location was Havana. We could also say, perhaps once again privileging time over space, that this sequence has been occurring from the end of the seventies to some time (or place) not yet specified in the nineties. In this Cuban "Big Bang" of sorts, the art of the eighties was careful to demarcate its territory, undoing and re-creating frontiers as well as circuits in the process.

Its cartography proposed new contours for the island, destroying the nation's frontiers in favor of a transcultural conglomerate, in order for Latin America and the Third World to have a place—a place that was, moreover, now also the "West" and not the "non-West."[4] An ambitious map such as this would have room for, as Gerardo Mosquera put it at the time, "a new international cultural order, a new perspective of universality that would take into account the interests of all peoples, in opposition to a Manhattan, island-made cosmopolitanism."[5]

3. The term "new Cuban art" was almost certainly coined by Gerardo Mosquera, to define a process of change that was occurring in the art produced in Cuba from the end of the seventies on. See, for example, Mosquera's essay "New Cuban Art: Identity and Popular Culture," in *Made in Havana* (exhibition catalog) (Sydney: Art Gallery of New South Wales, 1988). Luis Camnitzer used the phrase as the title of his book on the same subject, *New Art in Cuba* (Austin: University of Texas Press, 1994), and it has also been used in exhibition titles: for example, at the Whitechapel Art Gallery, London, 1995 ("New Art from Cuba"), and at the Contemporary Art Gallery and the Morris and Helen Belkin Gallery, British Columbia University, Vancouver, Canada, in 1997 ("Utopian Territories: New Art from Cuba").
4. In 1976, the Ministry of Culture was established, with Armando Hart as the minister. From that moment on, there was a growing emphasis on the notion that Cuba belongs to the West. This was meant to imply that other kinds of ties were weaker, such as the relationship with the Soviet Union and the socialist countries in Eastern Europe, or with Latin America. See Luis Báez, *Cambiar las reglas del juego (entrevista con Armando Hart)* (La Havana: Letras Cubanas, 1983), 34–36. These ideas influenced not only institutional politics but also art theory and criticism. An example of this appears in Gerardo Mosquera's essay "New Cuban Art: Identity and Popular Culture" (see note 3), which references Hart's idea, relating it to the diversity of components that play a role in Cuban culture, and explaining that "Non-Western culture is our culture, but Western culture is also our culture" (36).
5. Mosquera, "New Cuban Art," 36.

Florencio Gelabert Soto (b. Havana, 1961). *Immediately Geographic*, 1994. Mixed media installation.

Geocultural strategies of indisputable transcendence, such as the Havana Bienal exhibitions, would be employed in working with just such a planisphere, for negotiating spaces such as these. The aerial and maritime routes to navigate Cuban "new art" would have to be drawn. This would occur once the Cuban avant-garde initiated its campaign to conquer always stiff-necked and distant metropolitan centers such as Venice, Paris, New York, and Düsseldorf.

Curiously, once this vast territory was defined as "multicultural," and its capital situated in Havana, Cuban artists began to turn their attention to a smaller and earlier map: that of their own island, the map of Cuba. It became popular to look at the small map at the end of the eighties; paradoxically, it quickly took on the appearance of the latest fashion. To it would be added an often irreverent flirtation with other symbols more or less sacred to the idea of the nation: the flag, the national shield, portraits of heroes and political figures.

The obsession, sincere or feigned, with the elongated contours of the largest Antillean island could be explained in a variety of ways. One would be to focus on the fact that Cuban art at that time entered an intense and problematic dialogue with the revolutionary government. This intimacy, even if motivated by dissent, did not allow art and artists to escape the influence of rampantly nationalistic discourse exuded by the regime. Great geostrategic maps, on which all roads led to Havana, convinced artists that they, too, should undertake some small measure of messianic protagonism. There was nothing strange in this reaction, in a place where one lived in and created a city bent on taking in and binding together all Third World culture (film, literature, plastic arts),[6] and that simultaneously offered itself as a forum for conferences on more worldly issues—for example, the Havana meetings on the foreign debt crisis in the underdeveloped world.

Ever since then, the repeated use of the map or image of the island has functioned as a graphic emblem, a kind of mark chosen by consensus, collectively promoted by the artists themselves. More and more exposed to the market, the artists of the eighties intuited the tactical convenience of reaffirming a group cultural identity in the use of certain motifs. This posture could also have been stimulated by a perverse logic in which a group ends up in fact seeing itself in the manner it is perceived by others, homogeneously. Of course, the latter—the others "outside" the scene—retain the power first to perceive, and then to label.

In the same way that Cuban art and artists were increasingly being noticed and cataloged as *tokens*—an unavoidable outcome, even when there was the will to avoid it—there was a reaffirmation by them of iconographic homogenizing mechanisms. The map as mark, an easily recognizable symbol, would be a surface symptom of the phenomenon of *tokenization*, one among many "postcolonial" paradoxes.[7]

On the other hand, the formal reiteration of the island's silhouette was also presented as the crystallization of a specific "insular consciousness," an insularity, in this case, taken as synonymous with an isolation deeper than that created by relative geographic solitude: an insularity seen as dis-

6. In the interview mentioned in note 4, Armando Hart lists the most important events that would, among other things, serve to consolidate Havana as a cultural mecca. Some of these are: the International Ballet Festival, the New Latin American Film Festival, the International Book Fair, and the International Guitar Festival. Since the interview is from 1983, it predates the First Bienal, which took place the following year.

7. On this point, see Gayatri Chakravorty Spivak and Sneja Gunew, "Questions of Multiculturalism," in During, *The Cultural Studies Reader*, 193–202. At a particular moment in this dialogue, Spivak observes: "In fact, tokenization goes with ghettoization . . . when you are perceived as a token, you are also silenced in a certain way because . . . if you have been brought there it has been covered, they needn't worry about it anymore, you solve their conscience" (196).

tance from everything and everyone, as an extreme precariousness of communications. Opportunely, this interpretation stands with one of the pillars of contemporary Cuban political ideology: the idea of a harshly besieged and blockaded country, of the walled fort, subject to an inescapable tragic destiny.

It is not that by playing with the map of Cuba the "new artists" mean to invoke an insularity that is so dark and claustrophobic. This sense of insularity has its clearest antecedent in the wracked and bitter vision of the island and the surrounding sea produced by the great Cuban writer Virgilio Piñera, who was cited more than once during the eighties.[8] In his long poem "La isla en peso" (The island on balance; 1943),[9] Piñera describes a suffocating, grotesque panorama, a landscape where the erotic and the scatological alternate. "The water surrounds me like a cancer,"[10] says the poet, later exclaiming, "No one can leave, no one can leave!"[11] The poem unfolds like a terrible inventory of kitsch, banal folklore, hostile nature, and foul odors. Its somber tone, with smatterings of black humor, differs greatly from the simple, usually unproblematic (even if irreverent) cartography typical of representations of the island in the "new art."

Notwithstanding, there is a background on which the elements of this peculiar triad are connected (the triad of the map of Cuba in new art; of the island in Piñera's poem; and of the somber ideological image of the blockaded fortress). It is as if, beyond the will of both artists and politicians, in the weave of acid metaphors expressed in the poem, art and political ideology converge, joined perhaps by the effects of what might be called an intangible "epochal unconscious."

That background is the geopolitical space of the Caribbean. There the obstinate autarchy of Cuba, an island if not finally resigned to at least "proud" of its perennial dramas, coincides with the deformed, truncated, inexpressive images of an icon (the map) transformed into a graphic onomatopoeia, an absurd interjection. Piñera's verses also feed off of a morbid absurdity and cruelty. The islands (of art, of the poem, and the actual one that floats in the Caribbean) now exist as stereotypes. They are empty spaces, cracks in the landscape, placed there to welcome expectations, to satisfy the desires of those who name, who label, who perceive.

8. Some of the "new" Cuban artists who reference Piñera are José Bedia, Ibrahim Miranda, Sandra Ramos, Tania Bruguera, and I.
9. Virgilio Piñera, "La isla en peso," in *La vida entera* (Havana: UNEAC, 1969), 25–42.
10. Piñera, "La isla en peso," 25.
11. Piñera, "La isla en peso," 32.

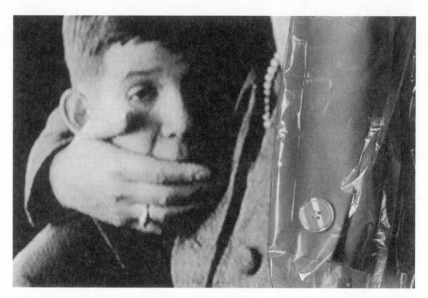

Eduardo Muñoz Ordoqui (b. Havana, 1964). *Untitled*, from *Banishments Series*, 1996–98. Ilfochrome photography.

In schematic terms, one could say that the strategic maps drawn by Cuban cultural politics in the eighties proposed something like the creation of a new "center" from the "periphery." A consolidation of a "pan–Third World" zone was attempted, often with success. The first link in this process would be the Latin American and Caribbean conglomerate[12]—a Caribbean carefully filtered through political ideology, however, as we will see in a moment. Politicians responsible for culture, critics, intellectuals, and artists found common cause in this agglutinating effort, despite the fact that the motivation and hopes of each group were, albeit complementary, not identical.

For different reasons, it was important for the politicians to maintain the level of cultural protagonism that the island had achieved in the international scene. One cannot forget that Cuba began the eighties by presiding over the Movement of Non-Aligned Countries, deploying its troops in various African nations, and convoking in Havana marathonlike meetings to discuss the socioeconomic problems of the Third World. Consciously or uncon-

12. This is cited in the Hart interview noted earlier: "We should strive for a strong unity in the Latin American intellectual movement, which is a prelude or antecedent of our own, of our future unity in all camps, political or otherwise" (Báez, 62).

sciously, for Cuban intellectuals and artists to promote the role of Havana, and to do it with the firm support of the country's institutions, meant essentially bringing to Cuba and to themselves the attention of their foreign colleagues. By means of these colleagues, as the artists and intellectuals soon were able to see for themselves, the cameras and microphones of the international press would arrive. Cubans became identified as an *Other*, distinguishable from the countless other *Others* caught in the ebb and flow of the inclement tide of multiculturalism.

Yet equations are never quite this simple. To speak of "center" and "periphery" as if they were fixed entities, exactly alike or completely foreign to each other, is more than problematic. James Clifford, in a beautiful text that explores the idea of cultural travel, has formulated the following sensible questions: "Why not focus on any culture's farthest range of travel while also looking at its centers, its villages, its intensive field sites? How do groups negotiate themselves in external relationships, and how is a culture also a site of travel for others? How are the spaces traversed from outside? To what extent is one group's core another's periphery?"[13]

These queries lead me to consider Cuban art and artists in motion, transporting themselves, being transported, crossing each other, getting mixed up. After all, to speak of maps is already to speak of exploration, travel, and travelers. As Antonio Benítez Rojo has observed: "Antillean insularity does not impel us to isolation but rather, on the contrary, to travel, to explore, to search for fluvial and maritime routes."[14]

In terms of vital space and mobility, Cuban "new art" was for a time— only for a time—a local sport, practiced in Havana's urban space. It was from this space that this art nurtured itself; it was toward this space that it was directed, with no other goal than to be noticed, commented upon, and enjoyed in the cultural circuits available in this city. To participate in this sport implied residence on the island as "natural." This was one of the "rules of the game." With the expansion of frontiers it was possible to aspire to mobility in other spaces, but even if one traveled and exhibited abroad, being "here," on the island itself, in Havana, was a determining factor in one's measure of success, a benchmark in the trajectory of one's work.

At some moment it was inevitable, with so many comings and goings, that this "interior" (the island art scene) would become contaminated by the

13. I cite from his essay "Travels," in James Clifford, *Routes* (Cambridge: Harvard University Press, 1997), 25.
14. Antonio Benítez Rojo, *La isla que se repite* (Hanover, NH: Ediciones del Norte, 1996), xxxii.

Antonio Eligio Fernández (Tonel) (b. Havana, 1958). *Desired Country* (detail), 1994. Installation. Polychromed clay and plaster objects.

"exterior" (the foreign art scene). The "periphery" became the "center"— another kind of "center," of course—beginning in 1984, when the First Bienal of Havana was inaugurated. The Havana Bienal did not delay in negotiating its differences with the aggressive cosmopolitanism of that other island— Manhattan. In 1986, Keith Haring, Leon Golub, Nancy Spero, and many other North American artists brought their work to Havana, in a show that ran parallel to the Second Bienal (the works they exhibited were subsequently donated to Cuban cultural institutions).

The maps designed in Cuba during the febrile stage of cultural internationalism conceived the "center" as foreign territory, at once attractive and alien, a space to be conquered. So what was happening at the "margins" of that "center"? The margins eventually might have a place in the center, too, although not if they defined themselves as unfriendly, politically hostile enclaves. In the midst of this geopolitical conundrum it was possible to cede a bit of territory to the other side—understanding its oppositional character to be, above all, a lamentable consequence of history and national cultural destiny. Thus is the case with the parcel of territory granted by the Bienal to the Manhattan mainstream in 1986. It was also possible to grant other parcels to "marginal" zones of the "center" on an equal basis, for example to Puerto Ricans and other Latin Americans in the same cosmopolitan Manhattan, or its borders: Juan Sánchez, Pepón Osorio, Liliana Porter, Luis Camnitzer, and others. In this manner, Havana, invested with all the power of a new "peripheric center," created its own system of tokenization, naming and selecting those who would speak in the name of certain minorities.

All this is understandable, in my opinion: It has an "organic" aspect, if you will—in any case, the feel of something that is always attentive to the subtleties and ebb and flow of more crude political realities. The situation gets more complicated, becomes less comprehensible, when this principle of selectivity ignores certain "uncomfortable" phenomena. Notably, this has been the case with the diasporic component of Cuban society and, by extension, of Cuban art. This is neither the time nor the place to discuss the Cuban diaspora, considered by William Safran to belong with the Armenian, Northern African, Turkish, Palestinian, Greek, and Chinese diasporas.[15] The historical, cultural, political, and demographic center of that diaspora is found in the United States, in South Florida, in Miami. Its ramifications are extensive; they reach Madrid and Caracas, San Juan and Mexico City, New Jersey and Paris.

Miami and Havana play out a unique history, a shared story of intense fascination and repulsion. They are two very different cities. Miami is the city of the automobile, the freeway, shopping centers. It has beaches, Art Deco, and many other things. Havana is an old city, creaky and old. It, too, has beaches, some Art Deco, and many other things. The two cities, touched by the warm current that flows from the Gulf, watch each other with an attraction that is poorly disguised. In Miami, that fascination is fed with large doses of nostalgia. The corresponding strategies in Havana range from illegal (and risky) immigration to the naïve envy provoked by images of Miami or the periodic visits of an already emigrated relative. There are many monuments to nostalgia in Miami, the most famous of them being "Little Havana." As Gustavo Pérez Firmat notes, "Since there are so many establishments in Little Havana that have their roots across the sea, one tends to think of this neighborhood as a mirror image of its Cuban original."[16]

With such specular similarities and overwhelming differences, the two cities, Havana and Miami, distinguish themselves by the energy with

15. William Safran, "Diasporas in Modern Societies: Myths of Homeland and Return," cited in Clifford, *Routes*, 247 ff.
16. Gustavo Pérez Firmat, *Next Year in Cuba* (New York: Doubleday, 1995), 84.

which they each have attempted, with some measure of success, to become "centers." I have already described some of the features that illustrate this project in Havana. Meanwhile, on the other side of the Florida Straits, one hears enthusiastic talk of "the development of a 'postnational' environment centered on Miami," something Orlando Patterson calls "the Emerging West Atlantic System."[17]

This all takes place in the Caribbean basin. Let us pause for a moment, then, to consider the Caribbean archipelago and, in particular, the ways it can be understood. Benítez Rojo underscores how "the Caribbean increasingly runs over the limits of its own sea" and "has the virtue of lacking limits and a center."[18] This author, an inspired cartographer, includes Miami in his list of the "repeating islands" of the Caribbean, situating it as part of an Antillean meta-archipelago. His map allows us to insist, albeit ever so slightly, on an inescapable problem in the current analysis of Cuban art and culture: the relationship between the "inside" (Havana) and the "outside" (Miami, for our purposes here).

We are faced with a question of limits, with spaces that are physically close that have opted to see themselves, at least in their public voice, as inexorably separated—parallel "exhibition" spaces, ostentatious in their differences and pretentious in the ignorance about each other they share.

It is not my intention to resolve, in a few paragraphs, the debate between the "outside" and the "inside" of Cuban art and culture. I know my own limitations too well to become involved in a matter as complex as this. I will attempt below, nevertheless, to show a relationship between processes of displacement shared by these "islands"—Miami and Havana—that otherwise appear to resist absolutely any sort of communicative flow. However singular or interrupted these processes may seem, their existence suggests the partial and limited character of the model of a rigid and insurmountable isolation mentioned earlier.

Before doing this, however, I need to mention two very important events whose effects extend over several generations of Cuban artists. One of these is the sudden, vertiginous mass emigration of the generation of the eighties, from Havana to Mexico City, and from there to Monterrey, Miami, or New York, which tapered off in the early nineties. The other relates to the changing balance in the "outside-inside" relationship, and how it influences art produced on the island today. The "inside," constituted by local

17. Orlando Patterson, "The Emerging West Atlantic System," cited in Clifford, *Routes*, 38.
18. Benítez Rojo, *La isla que se repite*, v.

Tony Labat (b. Havana, 1951). *Fight: Practical Romance*, 1981 (a year-long performance involving the artist becoming a licensed professional boxer). Keezar Pavillion, San Francisco, California.

institutions and spaces that functioned more or less smoothly during the eighties and a good part of the nineties, is now becoming increasingly an obsolete, run-down machinery, with few practical applications in the socio-cultural present, when artists are trying more and more to insert themselves in international circuits. The dialogue between art and local culture, particularly in Havana—a city abandoned by the previous generation but in which the artists who are most active in Cuba still live, albeit only seasonally—

has become almost unnecessary. This has implications for "successful" artists—that is, those who have been assimilated by the mechanisms of tokenization mentioned before and have achieved access to "outside" circuits with some regularity. It appears that it is toward this still vast and stiff-necked "outside" that the scale is tipping, at times because of sociocultural pressures that are hard to resist. One of these pressures, for example, is the existence of a real or potential market for Cuban art "outside" the island that is much more tempting than the relatively weak internal art market.

One asks who, in the territories covered by these maps, are the displaced and displacing artists? Artists in whose work ideas concerning confusion, travel, uprooting, processes, encounters, and movement are prominent. Artists who emigrated, now returning to their native (and now foreign) land. Someone like Ana Mendieta, back in Havana in the early eighties, tracing a path between Miami, Iowa, New York, Jaruco, (re)connecting to a changing and tumultuous Cuban art scene, influencing us in that process: "She gave us [Cuban artists] a sense of rigor, of an artistic and professional ambition that was unknown in the Cuban scene, at least at that moment." Changing herself, letting herself be permeated by Cuba: "We gave her [Ana] a vivid and intimate sense of identification and belonging to her cultural roots."[19]

Ana was following a personal path and simultaneously establishing a connection between spaces that previously hardly ever communicated with each other. With her body, or more precisely from her body, she would discover new territories, would gain a capacity to move beyond her own limits. Returning to New York from one of those trips to Cuba, Ana wrote these lines, in which the desire for Cuba turns into a physical, carnal will to become one with the land:

> And so,
> as my whole being is filled with want of Cuba
> I go on to make my mark upon the earth
> to go on is victory.[20]

Several years after Ana's terrible death, other artists of the diaspora would repeat her daring gesture of redefinition on their return to Cuba. Ernesto Pujol was one of the first. Installed on the island, he reconsiders

19. Flavio Garciandía, personal communication, by letter, to the author, 1998 (unpublished).
20. Ana Mendieta, cited in Robert Katz, *Naked by the Window* (New York: Atlantic Monthly Press, 1990), 170.

his emigrant condition while simultaneously disarming the affected gravity of insular machismo. He pokes fun at machismo, insisting in his work on a disquieting, conflictive sexuality. Eduardo Aparicio is also an artist of the diaspora, which influences a significant part of his work. As an individual, and because of the nature of his art, Aparicio is one of the few figures directly linked to the Miami scene who has tried to establish contact with the island's reality.

The history of exchanges, of crossing or parallel trajectories in one direction or another, is an open and continuous process. In this process are inscribed figures whose artistic destinies are inseparable from the portents, the poverty, and the grandeur of the process itself: for example, Carlos José Alfonso and Juan Boza, who arrived in Miami in the early eighties as a result of the Mariel exodus. It was there, in Florida, and not Havana, that Alfonso and Ana Mendieta met, became friends, confidants, and copractitioners of *santería*. Another very recent chapter of this history was played out by the generation of the eighties, which was displaced, with few exceptions, to Miami, New York, San Juan, and beyond. The flow remains constant: Many Cuban artists travel today in one direction or the other, to and fro, causing the idea of an "inside" and "outside" to become even more fragile and dysfunctional.

In a way, the artists, including myself, who take that freedom of movement for themselves express a transgressive desire, a combative spirit that is seen sometimes in the conceptual structure of their work, other times in the heterogeneous materials they use, in their technical solutions, in their use of space. The essential attributes of this art are eroticism, the appeal to sexuality, manipulation of the body, ideas of decadence and the ephemeral, poverty, and, of course, allusions to emigration. It is an art that is unmapped, whose frontiers, whose limits in any dimension, are yet to be drawn.

Austin, 1998–Havana, 1999

The Cuban Literary Diaspora and Its Contexts: A Glossary

Ambrosio Fornet

I propose to approach the theme of the literature of the Cuban diaspora from the perspective of a literary critic committed to the cultural project of the Revolution. I will do so by means of a glossary that, starting with the term *diaspora* itself, includes, in alphabetical order, *exile, identity, language*, and *nationality*. Each one of these terms refers in turn to a semantic field whose intersections and ramifications, whenever possible, I will try to point out. I will not avoid the danger of contradiction, because what seems to me to be more important at this stage, in which we have only begun to explore the terrain, is the possibility of opening up a collective reflection on the future of our literary criticism. In this future—which has already begun to take shape—is inscribed the need to incorporate the literary production of the diaspora into the horizon of expectations of our critical reflections, that is to say, into the internal trend of Cuban literature. I warn the reader that I have many questions to ask and few answers to give.

An abbreviated version of this essay was read at the conference on Cuban literature of the diaspora, organized by the Centro Cultural de España in Havana, 27 September 2000.

Diaspora

Diaspora is a term marked by the dramatic history of the Jewish people, above all from the third century B.C., but today—by extension, as the dictionary says—it is used to indicate "the dispersion of human individuals who previously lived together or formed an ethnic group." In this sense, we can speak of the "African diaspora" as one of these phenomena of massive displacement that is close to us. But the term has not been traditionally part of our arsenal of concepts and metaphors, perhaps for the simple reason that there were two others—*emigration* and *exile*—not to mention the slave trade, that were firmly entrenched in our historiography. I myself for years resisted using *diaspora* because it seemed to me that to do so would mean, first, taking it out of context, and second, that this would serve only to occlude the connotations of the traditional terms, especially those of a political nature. The question of political connotations, however, was what finally made me adopt it, because I became aware that its "semantic neutrality," so to speak, facilitated its insertion into a terrain—that of literary criticism— where it was necessary to work without preconceived ideas, without prejudices. Besides, today the Cuban diaspora is a hybrid of exile and emigration, to which we would have to add unclassified displacements, from the sociological point of view, such as the so-called Peter Pan children, forced by their own parents to emigrate while still young.

Although it sometimes takes dramatic forms—the case of the Mexican wet-backs, the Dominican *yoleros,* the Haitian boat people, the Cuban *balseros*—within the demographic crisis of the modern world, diaspora is a "natural" phenomenon, the simple consequence of injustice on a planetary scale, a law of gravity in reverse that makes the underdogs, with no other recourse than to trust their luck, desperately seek a way of falling upward. This constant migratory flow poses problems related to national and cultural identity, problems that completely subvert our ideas on this subject.

Naturally, the Cuban diaspora is concentrated in the United States and especially in Dade County, one of the sixty-seven counties in Florida, in which the city of Miami is located. Of the 2.5 million inhabitants residing in the metropolitan area of Miami, some eight hundred thousand—more than one-third—are Cubans. The "Hispanic" (to use the American phrase)[1] character of the Miami area is reinforced by the presence there of some

---

1. In literary and artistic circles the term *Latinos* is preferred to *Hispanos* or *Hispanics*. Those who argue that this population forms such a heterogeneous conglomerate—given its national and class precedence, its level of education, its legal status—are correct that

seven hundred thousand additional Latin Americans and some five thousand Spaniards, which results in a total of approximately 1.5 million Hispanics. In this regard, only Los Angeles and New York compete with Miami. Indeed, on a national scale, there are already more than 30 million Hispanics in the United States—half of them Chicanos concentrated in California and Texas—and it is estimated that within five years Hispanics will be the largest minority group in the country, and that within ten, their numbers will exceed 40 million. It is possible that by 2020, one in every four North Americans will be of Hispanic ancestry. It would be equally foolish to exaggerate, on the one hand, or to underestimate, on the other, what these figures represent for the possible development of an editorial market for literature in Spanish or by Hispanics in the United States. Among other things, this demographic explosion has resulted in the boom of Latin American studies and Departments of Spanish in North American universities, as well as the gradual opening up of the mass media and advertising toward this not to be disdained new clientele, which in the decade of the nineties was already spending annually $200 billion on services and consumer goods and which had begun to transform itself into an active electoral force.

Placing ourselves as literary or cultural critics before a phenomenon of these dimensions, we run the risk of losing a sense of proportion and not seeing beyond our noses. We could then fall into a "Miami-ization"—if you will allow the term—of our perspective. And we know well that in the literary field, the map of the Cuban diaspora greatly exceeds the territory of a given city or country. Cuban writers reside, or their works are published, in Iowa and Chicago; in Mexico; in Venezuela and Ecuador; in Spain, Sweden, and France. The question is, then, To what extent do their works respond to the influence of these respective markets or literary environments, with their corresponding traditions, trends, and linguistic codes?

Exile

When I read in the *Diccionario etimológico* of Corominas that *exile* had been a "rare term until 1939," it seemed a partial observation to me, to which should be added "in Spain." But I soon recalled that in Cuba, too, during the whole of the nineteenth century and the first third of the twentieth century, one spoke preferably of *banishment* and *emigration*, not of exile. It

---

to group it like this under a supposed common denominator, the language of its ancestors, does not help in understanding the true nature of the whole.

was probably only during the Machado regime in the twenties that the term came to be more widely used, and it was commonplace to hear or read that this or that revolutionary, fearing for his or her life, had had to "go into exile."

Since the advent of the Revolution in 1959, taking into account the political positions of both sides—those in favor of and those against the Revolution, those outside as well as those within Cuba—it is clear that we are confronted with a serious paradox of an ideological and semantic nature. Exile—or its variants—forms part of a *revolutionary* tradition that among us refers back to the times of Varela and Heredia in the early nineteenth century and extends to Martí at its end. Indeed, some symbols of our native land—the single star on our flag, the palm trees—are, as we know, nostalgic images of an exiled poet. Paradoxically, then, for the exiled Cubans of today—and not only the most reactionary, known among us as "the Miami mafia"—it is difficult to claim possession of this tradition without taking it out of context, or, as they often prefer in order to avoid the problem, denying that *this* is a revolution and not a simple game of power. Accordingly, they always speak of "Castro" and never of the Cuban Revolution. In other words, the semantic weight of the term *exile* is no longer the same; an ideological inversion of the word has been produced which, for different reasons, changes it into an uncomfortable or inadequate reference, within Cuba as well as abroad. It is not surprising, then, that in a survey done in 1995 in South Florida, only 34 percent of those interviewed defined themselves as "an exiled Cuban," while 61 percent preferred to see themselves as "Cuban American."[2]

In order to accept—as I do—that what took place in Cuba after 1959 can be qualified as a revolution, one has to be convinced, first, that a profound social transformation was produced here which benefited the popular classes, and, second, that if 1902 inaugurated a process by means of which Cuba ceased to be a Spanish colony only to become a neocolony of the United States, 1959, on the other hand, meant the total rupture of this process. It is useful to recall, in this regard, the anguish of Jorge Mañach and other Cuban liberals who were faced with the grim reality of a country that was not succeeding in constituting itself as a nation because it had been left without collective ideals. With this I want to say that the debate between the supporters and adversaries of the Revolution should not be around the theme of identity—who is the *most* Cuban, what are our respective levels of

2. ANSA Cable, Miami, 24 November 1995. Rob Schroth, who conducted the survey, felt that "the mentality of the exiles was fading to be replaced by a sentiment of greater affinity with North American culture."

cubanía (Cuban identity)—but around the theme of our expectations. Let us acknowledge that both sides are equally Cuban, but our respective projects of nation building are different.[3] Can we at some point settle these differences without the *mediation*—we know this word very well—or the intervention of the United States? I personally doubt it. And this, for me, means that every discussion, even in the terrain of culture, will always end up suffocated—for tactical reasons—or marked by our respective political positions. Only objects are totally objective. I believe that what a hostile critic or another who is a supporter of the Revolution thinks of such novels as *Las iniciales de la tierra*, by Jesús Díaz, and *El color del verano*, by Reinaldo Arenas, will inevitably be, as they used to say when I was young, "tinged with partisanship." Ideological conditioning is so strong, and to avoid it completely so difficult, that we must take for granted that in 99 percent of the cases, when we speak of literature, we are speaking not only of literature.

Nevertheless, today the ideological fields are not so well defined as they once were. In 1959 and 1960, my generation saw some of our classical literary figures "go into exile"—Mañach, Novás Calvo, Montenegro, Lydia Cabrera, for example[4]—but we also saw that others placed themselves once again, or were not long in positioning themselves, in the vanguard of the literary movement that followed the Revolution, as was the case with Guillén, Carpentier, Lezama, Marinello, Roa, Cintio Vitier, Eliseo Diego, Fina García Marruz, Virgilio Piñera, Feijóo, Onelio José Cardoso, Pita, to mention only a few (and to which should be added a brilliant rear guard that included Navarro Lima, Regino Pedroso, and Tallet). Others, on the other hand, remained in a discreet internal exile, namely, Chacón y Calvo, Dulce María Loynaz, and—for many years, before finally leaving the country—Labrador Ruiz and Agustín Acosta. The two pillars of Cuban anthropology and historiography—Fernando Ortiz and Ramiro Guerra—remained in Cuba and died here. The young writers of my generation, with very few exceptions, incorporated themselves enthusiastically into the tasks of creation, promotion, and diffusion of literature opened up by the Revolution.

I believe the first writer to "break" with the Revolution, in a some-

3. I dealt with this and other related themes in "Soñar en cubano, escribir en ingles: una reflexión sobre la tríada lengua-nación-literatura" (Dream in Cuban, write in English: A reflection on the triad language-nation-literature), *Temas* (Havana), no. 10 (April–June, 1997).

4. Gastón Baquero, in spite of being the author of "Palabras escritas en la arena por un inocente" (Words written in the sand by an innocent person), was still not the great poet he would later become, and his links to the old regime were too fresh in everyone's memory for us to regret his precipitous departure.

what strident way, to be sure, was Guillermo Cabrera Infante, who, at that time, moreover, had not yet published his famous novel *Tres tristes tigres* (Three sad tigers). I will not give the chronology of those ruptures, which did not always coincide with the different migratory waves, but I do want to note that very soon the positions of the exile and the emigrant began to intermingle in this process, and that to try to mark the boundary between them one used to ask if the person who had *gone*—or had not *returned*—had publicly assumed a political position hostile to the Revolution. In such a way, it used to be said, around 1980, of Edmundo Desnoes and Antonio Benítez, for example—as earlier with Severo Sarduy or Calvert Casey—that they had "remained" abroad but that "they had not made any declarations," which placed them *in front of us*, so to speak, but in a kind of political limbo. It was a grave error not to attempt to keep this limbo linked to the literary movement inside Cuba. It was a time when we believed ourselves to be 100 percent right, and things seemed so clear. We could behave as if the Cuban diaspora had nothing to do with us, as if it did not form part of Cuba's history. Meanwhile, abroad, new Cuban writers, about whom we knew nothing—nor did they, if truth be told, know much about us—were making their appearance, and by the end of the 1980s, one could speak of a body of literature that included not only poems and essays but also novels, and that had nothing to do with the literature produced by the first or "historical" generation of exile that proliferated up to 1971. It would be Reinaldo Arenas, the most illustrious of the Mariel exiles, who, after 1980, would retake the agonistic model of the so-called anti-Castro novel written in exile and give it new life in works that were as counterrevolutionary as those of the "historical" exile, but at an incomparably superior literary level.

Today we know a bit more—although still superficially—about this group of writers and their work. I anthologized the poetry and prose of Cuban writers of the diaspora previously unknown here in a special issue of the journal *La Gaceta de Cuba* (2000). Other writers are being published and studied in our literary journals and at symposiums, in anthologies, in doctoral dissertations.[5] A critical study of the short stories of the diaspora in the

---

5. The magazine *Unión* has been systematically publishing texts and critical reviews of the literature of the diaspora. *Correo de Cuba (Revista de la Emigración Cubana)* has started to do the same for commercial reasons. Examples of this work have been included in compilations and panoramas such as *Estatuas* (Statues of salt [1996]) by Marta Apes and Marilyn Bobes, and *Las palabras son islas* (Words are islands [1999]) by Jorge Luis Arcos. Ricardo Hernández Otero directed the project "Literatura y emigración cubana contemporánea" (Literature and contemporary Cuban emigration), whose results were presented

nineties, perhaps the first of its kind in Cuba, recently appeared.[6] Our publishing houses have published half a dozen books by diaspora writers, several of which have been awarded literary prizes in Cuba.[7] What I want to emphasize, however, is that the category of "exile," given its political connotations, may no longer be all that useful for characterizing the work of the Cuban diaspora. Think of the case of Eliseo Alberto. After *Informe contra mí mismo*, which could be considered a typical novel of exile, he published *Caracol Beach* and *La Fábula de José*, which are very far from being texts that are politically marked by hostility to the Revolution. The same could be said for numerous works written outside of Cuba by authors who share neither our projects nor our ideology.[8]

Identity

A specter is haunting the First World: the immigrant. The bright metropolitan spaces are full of *border crossers*, multitudes who cross dividing lines of all kinds—geographical, social, cultural, linguistic—trying to find a point of equilibrium between what they are and what they want to become, between the desirable and the possible. Around them—the eternal *minori-*

---

at the Institute of Literature and Linguistics in Havana in May 2000. Nelson Cárdenas completed his thesis, "Archipiélagos: Explorando la identidad cultural en una novela de la diáspora" (Archipelagos: Exploring cultural identity in a novel of the diaspora) (Faculty of Arts and Letters, University of Havana, 2000), on René Vázquez Díaz's novel *La Isla del Cundeamor*. Juan Antonio Garcia Bareiro touches on the theme of the films of the diaspora in "El cine Cubano sumergido" (Submerged Cuban film), *Antenas* (July–September 1999). Désirée Díaz's thesis, "Memorias a la deriva: El tema de la emigración en el cine cubano de la década del noventa" (Faculty of Arts and Letters, University of Havana, 2000), is also about the theme of exile in film, but this time as it is represented in films made and distributed in Cuba itself.

6. Zaida Capote Cruz, "El cuento cabano del exilio: panorama de la década del noventa" (The Cuban short story in exile: Panorama of the decade of the nineties), *Extramuros*, no. 3 (June 2000).

7. See Jesús J. Barquet, *Escrituras poéticas de una nación: Dulce María Loynaz, Juana Rosa Pita y Carlotta Caulfield* (Havana, Ediciones Unión, 1999); Sonia Rivera-Valdés, *Las historias prohibidas de Marta Veneranda* (Bogotá/Havana, Ministerio de Cultura de Colombia/Casa de las Américas, 1997); Lourdes Fernández de Castro, *Espacio sin fronteras* (Bogota/Havana, Casa de Las Américas, 1998).

8. As part of a species of internal exile, it would be appropriate to mention some works by authors who reside in Cuba and who have been published abroad but not in Cuba—and not necessarily for political reasons—as is the case of the novel *Mariel*, by José Prats Sariol, and the short stories in *Trilogía sucia de la Havana*, by Pedro Juan Gutiérrez.

ties—is generated a semantic field whose categories seem to dominate cultural studies today. Indeed, never has there been so much talk in the metropolises of frontiers, boundaries, borders, margins, peripheries, interstices, crossings, hybridity, displacements, ethnicity, multiculturalism, and, of course, identity.

Identity is the nucleus—sometimes absent—around which all the other notions are organized. It incarnates one of the paradoxes of the era, similar to the one that made Unamuno cry out, tormented by the advance of collectivism, "Mi yo! Que me arrebatan mi yo!" (My I! They are confiscating my I!). For the first time in history, the expansion of capitalism and the fantastic development of the electronic mass media make it possible to think of the viability of a planetary culture: everywhere the same ideas, the same tastes, dreams, myths, patterns of behavior, the same lingua franca. Perhaps it is the horror at the growing danger of this uniformity that has led to an intensification of the claim to national and cultural identity in so many places, including some which in days gone by were imperial and colonial metropolises. Today there is only one country that, because of its economic, technical, military, and cultural power, can colonize the rest, carrying out what at the beginning of the twentieth century was called, still with a certain unease, the *Americanization* of the world. In such a situation, it is normal to be alarmed. At the same time, what sense will it make in the modern world to close oneself off in the old ghettos of nationalism and the illusory fortress of an immaculate identity? Duality is imposed as destiny on millions of people who live it dramatically or in resignation:

> Este pasaporte es personal e intransferible [writes Enrique Sacerio-Garí] y sera sancionado *Dual Citizens: a person who has the citizenship of more than* quien permita su uso por tercera persona. Es válido por 2 *one country at the same time is considered a dual citizen*, años y prorrogable por 2 años, 2 veces. El extravío de este *A dual citizen may be subject to the laws of the other country* documento sera notificado a la Dirección de Inmigración . . .[9]

In other words, national spaces are becoming fragmented: Turks in Berlin, Moors in Madrid, Algerians in Paris, Pakistanis in London, Mexicans in Los Angeles . . . What is the real map of national identities?[10] And as

9. Enrique Sacerio-Garí, "Documento, ver 2.0," in *Poemas interreales* (Madrid, n.p., 1999), 154.
10. Doreen Massey, cited by Federico Álvarez, "Espacios y tiempos reales e imaginarios

for cultural identity, it is obvious that it is determined not only by ethnicity or place of origin but also by other factors—gender, class, social status—linked to the formation of the subject. The metaphor of a *kaleidoscopic* identity has been proposed to define this kind of fragmented and, at the same time, multidimensional being.[11] To complicate things even more, in the United States, there is often discovered among members of the second generation of exiles or immigrants an ethnic and cultural consciousness in its infancy, which forms part of what Víctor Fowler calls "liminal identities":[12] young people born in Los Angeles or New York who declare in English—the only language they know well—that they are Cubans or Dominicans.

In the face of dilemmas of this sort, those of us who believe that the nation—and the forms of being derived from it—still has some tasks to accomplish, at least in the underdeveloped countries, are obliged to question the place of enunciation of discourses on identity. When we speak of frontiers, diaspora, identity, periphery, multiculturalism, *where* are we speaking from? Are we on the inside, on the outside, or on the fence? Are we part of the problem, part of the solution, or simply spectators of the drama? I think there is a need to seriously confront these questions—and their implications—in order to keep the debate on identities from becoming a dialogue of the deaf.

Language

Sonia Rivera-Valdés, a Cuban writer who lives in New York and whose novel *Las historias prohibidas de Marta Veneranda* won the Casa de las Américas prize here in Cuba, says (in Spanish), "I write in Spanish because I enjoy doing so and because I want, if one of my stories ends up in a bookstore in Artemisa where my father and grandmother were born, any boy or girl who goes in and takes it off a shelf to be able to read it without the need to have it translated [that is: without the need for intermediaries]."[13]

---

en el arte" (paper presented at the International Conference on Architecture, Mexico, 1997).

11. Iraida H. López, "A través del caleidoscopio: La autobiografía hispana contemporánea en los Estados Unidos" (doctoral thesis, University of Havana, 1998).

12. Víctor Fowler, "Identidades liminares," *La Gaceta de Cuba* (Havana), no. 5 (September–October 1998).

13. Sonia Rivera-Valdés, "A vuelo de pájaro. Notas sobre esta vida de trabajosa definición," in *Conversación entre escritoras del Caribe hispano*, ed. Daisy Cocco de Filippis and Sonia Rivera-Valdés (New York: Centro de Estudios Puertorriqueños, 2000), 99.

This desire to sustain a direct dialogue with the reader, where the only mediation is the text itself, is, in my opinion, the decisive factor in literary nationality. The bilingual or multilingual writer can write in the language he or she prefers, but the immense majority of his or her potential readers are obliged to read in the native language.[14] When we speak of literature— poetry and narrative especially—is the element of *authenticity*, which we tend to attribute to the originals, not the replicas, important? Is it the same thing to read a work in its original language or in a translation—however good the latter may be? But at the same time, one also has to ask if, in the modern world, the categorical declaration I have just made—that language is the decisive factor in literary nationality—can be sustained unconditionally.[15] If we believe that the concept of nation continues to be important, the answer would be no, except in the case of countries whose languages are confined to their national frontiers. On the other hand, when it is a matter of multinational languages—Spanish, for example—it is the binomial copula language/nation, and not just one of its members, that allows us to declare that a work is Cuban, Argentinian, or Mexican. Something similar could be said in the case of multinational states or multilingual nations. And what of other factors, such as the citizenship of the author, the theme of the work, the cultural context in which it was produced, in which it circulates? We can say of certain texts that they belong to the world, to the universe of the Spanish language, to Hispanic American literature as a whole; but if we wanted to be precise, we would have to ask one final question: Would a historian of national literature—do there *exist* historians of national literature?—feel obligated to include these texts in his or her history?

When it is a question of literature, translation brings more problems than it solves. Language is not a simple sequence of signs that can be mechanically substituted by others based on equivalences, as anyone who has tried to translate a joke, a poem, or a colloquial phrase knows. Lin-

14. The decision about which language to write in is not an easy one, which explains why, among writers, the tensions inherent in bilingualism are often highlighted in their work. See, as recent examples, Gustavo Pérez Firmat, *Cincuenta lecciones de exilio y desexilio*, and Ariel Dorfman, *Rumbo al Sur, deseando el Norte*, which is significantly subtitled *Un romance bilingue* (a bilingual romance).

15. Bear in mind that I speak of *literary* nationality. Historians such as Hobsbawm question the legitimacy of the identity of language and nation—"that mystical identification of nationality with a certain platonic idea of language"—because, in their opinion, it is distant from the daily life of the nation's inhabitants. See E. J. Hobsbawm, ed., *Nations and Nationalism Since 1780: Programme, Myth, Reality* (Cambridge: Cambridge University Press, 1990), 57.

guists have already told us that the signifier has a signified, but this signified acquires "meaning" only when it is placed in a context capable of embracing not only the text itself but also its cultural and historical referents. In the end, of course, the context "is the world," as George Steiner hyperbolically declares. Taking *Madame Bovary* as an example, Steiner postulates that its context "is the immediate paragraph, the previous and following chapter, the entire novel. And it is also the state of the French language in the moment and place in which Flaubert wrote; it is the history of French society, ideology, politics, colloquial expressions," and all the "implicit or explicit references" that gravitate onto the text.[16] So then, if language refers not only to signs but to things, and not only to things but to an entire experience of the world, the fact of writing in one language or another, or the decision to appeal to certain languages—math or Esperanto—in order to ensure comprehension, cannot be a matter of indifference. It is odd that this point is made by someone such as Steiner, whose mother (he tells us) "had the habit of starting a phrase in one language and ending it in another," and in whose home in Vienna three languages were spoken—not including Hungarian, which was spoken only by the servants.

For us, however, the situation is more complex. For us, it is not only a question of monolingualism or multilingualism, but of authors and readers coming from one or the other side of the diaspora, beginning from different experiences and even different cultural contexts, that is, from distinct—and almost always opposite—ideologies and worldviews. Technically they share a language, but in general, as is customary to say metaphorically of those who do not succeed in reaching agreement, "they speak different languages." This happens above all in the terrain of politics. Can politics be placed in brackets when the parties on each side turn to speak of literature? I don't know. But I believe that in the terrain of culture, our task consists of finding the words and the tone to make dialogue possible.

Nationality

Needless to say, when we refer to the nationality of a particular literary work, we are not alluding to the birthplace of the author, much less his or her country of citizenship. The language of the work, on the other hand, does turn out to be an unavoidable reference. Steiner's observations draw

16. George Steiner, *Errata: El examen de una vida* (1997), trans. Catalina Martínez Muñoz (Madrid, n.p., 1999), 33.

attention to the network of significations and meanings to which a particular language refers. The semantic field generated when I say "te quiero," "je t'aime," or "I love you" involves the body of a culture with its insinuations and admixtures. We have only begun to reflect on this phenomenon, because it did not become an urgent issue in Cuban literary criticism until the appearance in English in the United States of a group of novels by Cuban American writers: *Raining Backwards* (1988), by Roberto G. Fernández, who until then had written in Spanish, *The Mambo Kings Play Songs of Love* (1989), by Oscar Hijuelos, and above all *Dreaming in Cuban* (1992), by Cristina García. The question of the nationality of these texts or their authors brought in its wake a second question related to language: Is it possible to express the sense of belonging to a country in a foreign language? Can a male or female author born in Cuba claim a space in Cuban literature writing in a language unknown by the majority of Cubans? This is a matter, I believe, of two different questions that demand two different answers. Let me introduce here a discussion between three characters—Alicia, Francisco, and Catalina—in Gustavo Pérez Firmat's novel *Todo menos amor*, which is set in the United States. There is a moment in which Alicia asks Francisco to change the topic of conversation, and Francisco, annoyed, replies that he says what he feels like saying, because, "We are not in Cuba." And Alicia commits the imprudence of replying that Cuba has nothing to do with it, that it is not important at that moment:

> –¿Que no tiene importancia? [exclama Francisco]. ¿Cómo no tiene importancia? ¿Vietnam es importante y Cuba no es importante? ¿Las papas bien doraditas son importantes y Cuba no es importante? ¿Todos esos cuentos marrulleros que tú haces son importantes y Cuba no es importante? Oye lo que te voy a decir: Cuba *siempre* es importante. Cuba es lo *único* importante que hay. Lo que no tiene que ver con Cuba no me interesa.
> –Por favor, Francisco, no te pongas así [terció Catalina].
> –Olvídate de Cuba—insistió Alicia.
> –Tú podrás olvidarte de Cuba—rugió Francisco desde el borde de su asiento—, pero yo no. Estas hablando de mi vida. ¡De mi vida![17]

> ("What do you mean it's not important? [exclaims Francisco]. How could it not be important? Vietnam is important and Cuba isn't? French fries are important and Cuba isn't? All those mendacious

17. Gustavo Pérez Firmat, *Anything but Love* (Houston: Arte Público Press, 2000), 102.

stories you tell yourself are important and Cuba isn't? Listen to me: Cuba is *always* important. Cuba is the *only* important thing there is. What doesn't have to do with Cuba doesn't interest me."

"Please, Francisco, don't be this way" [adds Catalina].

"Forget Cuba," insists Alicia.

"You can forget Cuba," shouts Francisco from the edge of his chair, "but I can't. You're talking about my life. My life!")

Permit me to confess that I set a little trap for the reader here in order to place the problem of the relation of language/nationality in a new light. The passage I have just cited comes from Pérez Firmat's recently published novel *Anything but Love*; actually, the names of the characters are Alice, Frank, and Catherine, and what we have here is a simple version in Spanish of the original English text. The question then follows: This Frank, who spoke in this way in English of his relationship with Cuba, is he Cuban, or, rather, does he have the right to call himself and be considered Cuban? Is the possibility of using this character in a reflection on Cuban identity something that should be rejected out of hand as irrelevant?

But the *theme*—or to be exact, the *topic*—which for some constitutes an important factor in determining literary nationality, is a premise that does not stand up to scrutiny: The great tradition of Cuban poetry, as has been pointed out more than once, was built on an Aztec pyramid and a Canadian waterfall, and it would be difficult to persuade anyone that Alejo Carpentier's *El reino de este mundo* (The kingdom of this world) is not a Cuban novel but a Haitian one, in spite of the fact that it is about the Haitian Revolution. On the other hand, while it may well be that camels are not mentioned in the *Koran*, as Borges believed, any philologist worth his salt would find in its verses a thousand reasons quite apart from these melancholic ruminants to declare that it is a text of Arab origin. In short, what does not seem wise is to generalize and, even less, to speak in absolutes. If we are going to talk seriously about the literary discourse of the diaspora, if we want to know in what way it resembles and differs from the literature that is produced here, we must begin by trying to understand what is most specific to it, including its own historical and cultural contexts, which are not our own.

A Traveler's Album: Variations on *Cubanidad*

Víctor Fowler

In the first snapshot, I am listening to a rock concert in a tiny club in Providence that functions at the same time as a café, art gallery, and playhouse; the lead guitarist (a Peruvian) sings with equal energy in English and Spanish. He segues from the mythical "Jailhouse Rock" to a hard version of "No se tu" (I Don't Know You), a bolero recently made popular by the Mexican Luis Miguel. The audience, almost totally Anglophone, enthusiastically applauds the performance by the group, which also includes a Colombian bass player and a Philippine drummer. My friend Bob Arellano has taken me to this concert. A Cuban born in the United States, a specialist in hypertexts and a fan of rock and country music, he was anxious to show me this place, which is important in the city's alternative culture scene. At the end of the set, we go over to congratulate the musicians, and my friend (who also plays guitar and wants to produce hard rock sung in Spanish in the United States) starts negotiations for a subsequent concert with the group. He is fascinated by this vogue of taking songs from parents and grandparents, songs that have been part of the continental Latin American imaginary for generations, and inserting them into the musical rhythms of the present. I listen to him

boundary 2 29:3, 2002. Copyright © 2002 by Duke University Press.

say that this kind of creative adaptation is a good thing for Latino culture in the United States, instead of a simulacrum of some sort of "ethnic" sound as a means to gain a niche in the market.

In the second snapshot, now in Boston, at the end of one of my lectures, a young man approaches me. He wears on his lapel a pin with a small Cuban flag. He is a representative of the youth wing of the Cuban-American Foundation in that part of New England and the grandson of a certain Colonel Barquin, who in the fifties had been the leader of the most important conspiracy within the army to depose the dictator Batista. We chat, he promises to bring me books the following day, but nothing impresses me more than that small pin on his lapel.

The third snapshot corresponds to New York. In this one appears Luis, a young Cuban photographer, also born in the United States, who utters a phrase that still astonishes me: "When I return to Guanabacoa!" This astonishes me, first, because Luis was born in the United States, has never been to the land of his parents, much less Guanabacoa, and thus refers to, for him, an entirely imaginary place; secondly, because, with a will to identity that seems to me almost magical, he gestures and dresses exactly as a street kid in the real Guanabacoa would today.

In the fourth snapshot, I am back in Providence. This time, a group of art students, all of Cuban origin, are introduced to me; they tell me that there are, all told, a dozen of them in the city and that they recently founded their group in the Casa de España at Brown. They want to invite me to a special welcome meal, for which they promise to serve black beans, a dish their parents taught them to prepare.

The fifth snapshot takes place in New Orleans, in a tiny movie theater where the film *Bitter Sugar*, by the Cuban émigré director Leon Ichaso, is being shown. There are no more than twenty people in the audience, and before the first half hour is over, one of the two North Americans present (the other is the female companion of the friend I am with) shouts out that we are looking at imperialist garbage and walks out. The reaction to the film is quite cold, dispassionate, including the weak applause at the end.

The opposite occurs in the sixth of my snapshots. This time, I am in Miami, at the premiere of the opera *Balseros*, with a libretto by María Elena Fornes, about the Cubans who risk their lives on flimsy improvised rafts to cross the Florida Straits to get to the United States. Here, the public inundates the theater with its enthusiasm. However, there is an element that adds a certain extra-artistic tension to the occasion: For the first time, Fornes uses as a theme in her work the "Cuban situation" itself; thus, those in the know attend convinced that they will witness, at last, the librettist's "definition," or, what amounts to the same thing, an artistic statement linked to a political exorcism, a test. Just as the performance is about to start, into the theater walks a figure who symbolizes in his person what is about to be performed: Basulto, the leader of Brothers to the Rescue, the organization that arranges flights over the Straits to locate the rafters. The tension eases as the applause multiplies. In a matter of seconds, we have witnessed the apotheosis of a human destiny, that of the librettist, Fornes. In the following days, Miami magazines and newspapers abound with positive reviews of the opera, highlighting its artistic quality. This detail is not a simple one in a city such as Miami, or in relation to an opera such as *Balseros*, in which what is specifically "Cuban" is diluted by a desire to place the odyssey of the rafters in a mythical and universal dimension. There remains then the question: What would have happened without the providential presence of a tutelary figure such as Basulto? What demands would have been made on the author? Or, in what other way might her story have been read?

In another, different snapshot, I am with a friend in a small café in Hoboken. We are being served by Dominican waitresses, and when we realize that they are staring at us, we make a gesture of perplexity. By way of explanation, one of them says to the others: "How pretty those people speak!" I would not use the word *pretty*, rather *differently* and perhaps *too much*, since we have spent hours talking about nothing at all, just to hear another *habanero*, or native of Havana, speaking under the snowfall.

My snapshots could be multiplied with images of rumba players in Central Park in New York or of the refined dishes of the so-called New Cuban cuisine served at the Yucca Restaurant in Miami Beach, but perhaps the ones I have offered here are sufficient to suggest some variants of "what is Cuban" in the United States, as seen through the eyes of a visitor from Cuba.

The traveler cannot avoid behaving as a kind of hybrid of a narrator and an anthropologist: the one capturing details, the other verifying structures, since he is obliged to come up with a minimum, "operative" understanding of the space in which he will temporarily insert himself. The need for that minuscule repertoire of data is the universal condition of every new experience of socialization, but it becomes paradoxical when one inserts oneself as a foreigner within what is supposedly identical, since I am confronted, in this case, with having to "adapt" to a territoriality I have been taught to consider as my own. The traveler has no need to remind himself that he is in another country; he has been accustomed since childhood to separating the United States from Florida, and Florida from Miami, Hialeah, and Calle Ocho, Eighth Street, the center of Cuban Miami. After all, who lives there but "the Cubans," our friends from infancy, neighbors, acquaintances, relatives? No doubt this is a monstrous oversimplification of the experience accumulated by Cubans dispersed in almost every part of North America, but it is not with realities that we configure images of the unknown but rather with that contradictory sediment formed by letters, travelogues, film images, newspaper clippings, politicians' speeches, and the like. For this reason, for those of us who live in Cuba, the existence of a Cuban in the United States, in another place that is not Miami, is almost an accident, with all that the word connotes. Bearing in his unconscious this oversimplification, the traveler cannot help but continuously find himself entangled in the most dissimilar ambiguities; what he observes is certainly the same, but, at the same time, entirely different.

We speak of Cuban communities, those of the Island and its offshoots, where identifications are produced primarily around histories and politico-ideological symbols welded together into a kind of protective armor; it does not matter if, in this fusion of personal history, macrohistory, and ideology, the moment of the fracture "really" came about with the rejection or acceptance of the fact of the Cuban Revolution, since the quotidian accidents that we call reality assume the task of articulating what happened so that the history will be read in this way. In this regard, Miami is exemplary, since the posture of vehement anticommunism that the community projects aggressively, above all in the mass media but also to the recently arrived inhabitant "of the Island," fragments into innumerable pieces as soon as we begin to penetrate the ideological armor. Few things have astonished me as much as listening in the United States to reluctant apologies from people I knew in Cuba who had made half true or misleading statements to the U.S. immigration authorities in order to justify a status as victims of political persecution, which they never in fact had in Cuba. This detail is relevant not only for what it tells about the pedagogical side of the Cuban diaspora—the transmission and learning of its norms of civility and successful acculturation—but also for understanding what the diaspora values as "Cuban": that perpetual mise-en-scène in which the present mixes with memory and reality with fiction, and in which, to repeat, the politico-ideological operates, beyond its proper meaning, as a kind of protective shell around the exile communities, so that it also becomes truth, a space where the national essence is signified as much by the aggressiveness of the little Cuban flag pin on the lapel of the young man in Providence as by the gentility of a meal shared with friends, or the resistance implicit in rock sung in Spanish or in a way of dressing "like" they do in Cuba.

If one way of thinking about this liminal *cubanidad* structuring itself in the experiences of the diaspora is that prolonged residence outside of the country of origin "propels" members of an immigrant culture to integrate themselves into the mainstream of the culture of the country that took them in, the reverse may also be true. Take the case of my friend the *rockero*: His sublation of identity within a larger context, signified by his self-identification as part of U.S. Latino culture, is predicated on the fact that his passport for his recognition within that culture is given by his original and permanent, and, one might say, "resistant," condition of his being Cuban. In other words, only from his national origin, from his parents, is that elaboration of a rock tune sung in Spanish within the hegemony, as it stands to reason, of English in the United States meaningful; his act, then, is a movement of rebellion and linguistic reaffirmation of an identity still too close in time to the moment of the rupture to unread itself in the identity of a U.S. "Hispanic" without fragmentations. Not accidentally, during their performance, the members of the group, including my friend, made clear to the audience their country of origin. Here it is important to note the importance "Hispanic" (that is, Latin American) cultures in the United States have acquired in recent years—meaning that the fact of being Latino is no longer, for the most part, a shameful stigma but an identity associated with images of success.

From another angle this issue of the place of origin shows itself to be crossed by fiction. Take the case of my photographer friend; his notion of what Guanabacoa is, is encouraged and fed by what his family transmits to him about it—that is, most probably an image incongruent with the reality of the place and carefully freed of contradictions. We are talking about here an imaginary reinforced by things as dissimilar as family letters or memories of Cubans belonging to diverse migratory waves; that is to say that memory is a contract susceptible to being changed with the passage of time and not, as we tend to think in a simplified way, a rigid and congealed entity. The congealing of memory, the old theme of those who identify themselves with a lost Cuba of the past, although marked by antirevolutionary ideology, is also an act of cultural resistance, of self-preservation of identity; even actions that, to a naïve or jaundiced observer, might appear ridiculous, like the festivities and gatherings of the Organization of Municipalities in Exile (there is something strange in seeing in the *Miami Herald* an invitation to a party for former residents of neighborhoods such as Guaimaro or Marianao), are moments of transmission and strengthening of identity. On the other hand, one wonders what idea of the Cuban is present in the young man who shows his identity in the obvious, almost obscene symbol of a flag on his lapel, since identity here, more than a matter of culture, places itself on the terrain of the ideological, with a strong class-based component. In this case it speaks to us of a sector dispossessed by the Revolution whose references to the country are articulated by an ideological counterdiscourse in which the figure of the Cuban people is an abstraction that masks what really needs to be "saved": the private property confiscated by the Revolution. Not a simple matter, this.

In an apartment in New York City, which I later learn was bought with drug money in the eighties, a violent discussion erupts about the future of Cuba. Someone shouts that Cuban wealth should be given back to its legitimate owners because it is a moral question. It is strange listening to talk of morality in this apartment; sick and tired of the combative tone almost every gathering of Cubans assumes, I remove myself to the kitchen, where I receive an even better lesson in a phrase: "The poor get together to discuss how to attain middle-class status, the middle class get together to discuss how to become rich, and the rich get together to decide among themselves where to ski on Saturday." These are the words of a wealthy Cuban woman who was in the kitchen because she, too, was tired of the shouting. Some time later, in Miami, at a party whose guests include various representatives of historically prominent Cuban families, someone comments about a television program on which Fidel Castro appeared talking about a cheese he received as a gift. Once again, passions boil up, and it is considered a moral scandal for Castro to mention the word *cheese* when the Cuban people can't get cheese. For me, the amoral cynicism of the woman in the New York apartment is more interesting than the sentimental moralism of the guests at the Miami party, her feeling of alienation more interesting than their feeling of implication and their complex of blame.

The case of the young men in Providence determined to show their culinary talents making black beans for me links with something I suggested before: The exile-diaspora is also a pedagogical project, by which I understand an ordered and reasoned articulation of experiences to transmit a precise cultural heritage. The fact that a Cuban food paradigm—black beans— is preserved, even with enough force, moreover, to allow for the construction on top of it of the idea of New Cuban cuisine, is something that in the first instance we owe to oral transmission in families (to mothers and above all to grandmothers). But it goes well beyond that: Books, magazines, television programs, radio shows, school events, restaurant menus, anything that can articulate a fragmentary memory of the country of origin had to join together in a set of quotidian stimuli associated with that mythical space and time of before, the Place. But a pedagogy actually capable of interpellating three generations of subjects needs by force to have been transformed into a project of permanent education, abandoning the refuge of a transparent didacticism in order to invade the totality of life. What I am interested in highlighting here is that it is not a question of an educational plan elaborated at a conference table but rather of elaborating minimal conditions for the coherent survival of the community as it is.

We can imagine the culture of the exile-diaspora, metaphorically, as a kind of wide umbrella, under which fit the most diverse manifestations of what was lost: producers of popular culture (musicians, comedians, chefs), owners who give their businesses the same names they had in Cuba or who decorate their walls with scenes of the landscape left behind, journalists who have made a career out of recalling details of the prerevolutionary period . . . The dimensions and forms this culture can attain make the traveler feel sometimes that he is experiencing a hallucination. In one more snapshot it is almost noon, and I find myself in the home of a friend in Hialeah. A phone call comes through from another friend who has just returned from Cuba a couple of hours earlier and who now uses the telephone to gather together her small army of close friends. She invites my friend and I that same night to a special dinner: *tamales* brought over, frozen, from Havana. Not the ones made with corn that you can get all over Florida, nor those sold by vendors in the streets of Havana today, almost always dry and hard, but the authentic Cuban *ayacas*, delicate and soft, which have traveled from the hills of Santiago de Cuba to a table in North West Miami. What is more: Our hostess did not even have to go to Santiago to get them; instead, to make the offering even more sacred, her family sent the *tamales* on to Havana, knowing that they had no better gift to offer. Gift of the poor, open door to a dimension in which what is Cuban becomes almost religious. Doesn't the word *religion* perchance come from the Latin verb *religare*, to reunite? Beyond making fun or excessive nostalgia, what is certain is that we are witnesses to the sharing of prodigious *tamales*, cigarettes, cigars, rum, and symbols. The hallucination, or the educational project, I insist, is permanent. Some years ago, it was a fad to bring Cuban parrots to Miami; some months ago I listened to someone who decided to bring with her from Cuba a little bird (I don't recall whether it was a canary or a mockingbird) as a souvenir of her stay. These are facts in the face of which, for the most diverse reasons, politics and ideology are blind, but which culture assimilates in order to multiply its density.

The severe crisis into which the Cuban economy plunged at the beginning of the nineties extended even more the basis for the cultural operations we are dealing with, since it coincided with the stabilization of Miami as the bridge city for Latin America. I refer to the role Miami now plays as a trade and financial center for Latin America, and, beyond that, to the prior conditions of economic solidity and reliability that were necessary for it to assume this role—a long process of development in which Cuban exiles played a major role. This circumstance translates into a steady increase in the incomes of Cubans living in the United States, in a capacity to spend that runs parallel with the opening of spaces for a market economy on the Island. It is no surprise, then, that a significant part of that money ends up spent or invested (through family members who still live there) in Cuba. No one knows the exact magnitude of the flow of money from the diaspora to Cuba, since the fluctuations vary according to political circumstances, but whether it be travelers who use Mexico or the Bahamas as their trampoline or those who fly to the Island directly, what is certain is that a contact between the diaspora and Cuba that can be interpreted as a permanent updating of cultural origin is ongoing. By introducing into the discussion the question of money, it is possible to uncover new forms of that pedagogy I have been talking about. The present economic crisis of the Island has generated a veritable avalanche of commodified identity markers of *cubanidad*. Beyond symbols and obvious cultural capital (books by important writers, works of art, furniture), an underground market of "what is Cuban" has been slowly organizing itself, aimed mainly at North America.

What started at first as the purchase of jewelry by the Cuban state, whose proceeds the grateful owners then used to obtain consumer items (luxury goods or primary necessities), has been extended to include a surprising variety of items, to the point that it is hardly possible anymore to specify exactly what these commodified "identity markers" can be, given that they involve an infinity of objects and materials of the past: old school flags (La Salle, Santo Tomas de Villanueva, Edison); graduation albums; special editions of *El Diario de la Marina* or *El Mundo*; place settings; letters of manumission or contracts for the purchase or sale of slaves; original photographs of historical leaders and social luminaries of all types; manuscripts; autographs; electoral posters of the old political parties; fin de siècle erotic postcards; broaches; stamps—anything and everything that contributes to memory. There are already cases of families in Cuba who operate as "guardians" of the possessions acquired by their relatives "in the North": houses, motorcycles (most of all the famous Harley-Davidsons), antique jars, "stylish" furniture, classic automobiles, and thousands of other things that will be, in the hypothetical future of reunification, expensive status symbols. These immobile and nonproductive investments are accompanied by others that adopt the modality of "collaboration." Conceived primarily as the direct transfer of liquid cash for the improvement of family incomes on the Island, collaboration has extended itself toward the impulse to invest in the small businesses that more or less survive at the margin of the state; there are quite a few cases of such businesses operating with equipment and materials sent from "over there," or which have been set up literally as small transatlantic family partnerships with the obligation of submitting accounts to and generating profits for the investors in the United States. This is an interesting new development. In the first place, it establishes Miami as the utopian capital of the Cuban diaspora; in the second, it confirms the city as a sort of parallel economic and cultural capital of the Island. In the Cuban cultural imaginary today, Miami is more important than Santiago de Cuba: It functions as a kind of sub-Havana.

I am going to introduce a new scene related to Miami. It takes place in a bookstore, where *The Aguero Sisters*, the most recent novel by the Cuban American writer Cristina García, is being launched. I am surprised that there are so few young people among the more than three hundred persons who are attending the event, and I confess that there is also something chilly emanating from this perhaps excessively well-dressed crowd: "the historical exile," a friend explains to me. At the end of what seems more like a church service, I talk with another friend, and she also is surprised by the audience; it is unusual for the "historical exile" to give such clear support to a book by a Cuban American writer published originally in English (language continues to be a barrier that marks a generation gap), much less a novel that deals with the theme of Cuba without spilling over into invectives against Castroism.

But there is a way to sharpen what happened at the book launching if we see it as involving a situation of struggle for identity in which, unconsciously, there was an attempt to make an "appropriation," a displacement toward an idea of "what is Cuban" marked in this case by anti-Castro ideology. In the dialogue with the public after García's presentation, there was a question that pointed in this direction, but the author, who evidently had anticipated it, answered diplomatically, without allowing her presentation to be transformed into a political statement, meaning that she imposed an agenda of negotiation of identity marked by a community of culture. Between the book reading and what I said earlier about *Balseros*, there are both differences and an interesting commonality; the public was much more aristocratic at the book reading, a more familiar cultural vehicle than a minimalist opera, but both events were tests of political correctness and "definition."

There have been at least two fundamental experiences that have broken any rigid approximation to the dynamics of the Cuban culture in the United States: the Mariel exodus (1980) and the crisis of the *balseros* depicted in the opera (1994). What I want to suggest is that when the number of immigrants soars abruptly in a short space of time, as happened in both these cases, there is a parallel intensification of the social interpellations designed to reinforce the notion of having an identity, in this case, the Cuban one. Although it refers to a different circumstance, let me offer a relevant example. In 1994, a Cuban who was a professor at a North American university approached me to talk about a moral dilemma he was then facing. We had become friends, and he was embarrassed by his upcoming participation in a public event of the university, where he had been asked to speak, ex cathedra, about the American government's embargo of Cuba. In this particular case, the invitation presupposed an explicit anti-Castro posture; in an environment in which his academic colleagues came from many different countries, he was sought as a speaker precisely because of his condition as a Cuban, that is to say, as an "expert."

I want to emphasize here that nameless, institutional pressure exerted on my friend as a metaphor of the social pressures that, in any given moment, act as conditioners and stimuli in reinforcing identity. We have to multiply, even to the point of blurring together, the immense variety of influences that make up what I am describing here as a pedagogical project, a pedagogy that continuously reminds you who you are and classifies you within the confines of a particular place, a pedagogy constituted not so much by a single-minded and therefore self-contained plan but rather by the sum of infinite flows of ideas, attitudes, images, speech acts, chaotic at the same time as they are masterfully articulated in a kind of micropolitics. I am in a Cuban bakery in Miami. I find displayed for sale pastries which disappeared many years ago in Cuba itself, yet which those my age still can recall. One initial way of reading this situation, within the mythology of triumphant exile—the images of the good life "over there," "abroad"—is to awaken the memory of the magnitude of the suffering and deprivations that for decades the inhabitant of the Island has had to endure. In this case, the obscene wealth and economic power of the United States are transposed into the frame of an ethnic utopia, resulting in the erasure of important connections, since suddenly it is made to seem that such culinary abundance has nothing to do with the toil of Mexican *braceros* in the big farms of California, not to mention the peasants who produce bananas in Central America.

If from a perspective critical of the mythology of triumphant exile it is easy to uncover some of the silences that accompany similar enthusiasms, what is also true is that there is in them a cultural gesture related to the conservation of the identitarian universe of "what is Cuban" in conditions of separation from the country. The same thing occurs when we enter one of those pharmacies on Calle Ocho in Miami, in which it is still equally possible to ask for Scott Emulsion as a bottle of Jacoud Potion, a bottle of Milk of Magnesia as an elixir of paregoric. The sensation of strangeness or déjà vu here is derived from a completely abnormal political situation: the presence and future of the Cuban Revolution. What distinguishes the Cuban diaspora from the current migratory waves from other Latin American countries toward the United States is the fact of the Revolution, meaning that, in hypothetical historical conditions that did not include the immense transformation of 1959, the cultural relationship of Cuba with the emigrants would have been much less traumatic than the one we live today: The presence of pastry extinct years ago on the Island or of medicines that young people in Cuba have no knowledge of would not have the value of confirming the superiority of exile they now enjoy, but rather would be seen as the gestures of cultural resistance and affirmation they in fact are, that is, as strategies of defense of identity. If we consider as at least possible a major change in the policies of the United States toward Cuba, a change that may imply the reestablishment of commercial relations, lines of credit, business concessions, and normalization of immigration policies, we can also anticipate that it will be accompanied by a cultural encounter between two communities who remember, imagine, and yet do not know each other.

On three occasions, as in a déjà vu again, I participated in an identical situation in restaurants in Miami. The waiter—a Cuban—asked my companions (all white) if they enjoyed the meal but ignored me (just?) because I'm black. The interesting thing is that the waiters who treated me this way are all young "recent arrivals" (these are the kinds of jobs they can get); four or five years ago, when they were still in Cuba, they probably would not have read the world in such clear-cut racial terms, or they would have avoided showing that they did. Add to this the conversations in which someone speaks of the number of blacks, according to a video he or she saw, living these days in classy Havana neighborhoods such as Regla (not to speak of Miramar or Country Club). In yet another hallucination, someone condemns the Revolution for the repression gays suffered in the UMAP prison farms in the sixties; minutes later, when I make an effort to explain that we are living in more tolerant times, this same person is scandalized and reiterates his condemnation of the Revolution because so much attention seems to be dedicated to homosexuals and lesbians in the art and culture produced on the Island today.

The cultural collision I am anticipating will greatly exceed the expectations of those honest intellectuals who are willing on both sides to revise the catalog of intellectual creations produced by all kinds of Cubans. The collision will involve literary, artistic, and intellectual work, but it will also expand to include such issues as the differences in the concept of private life, neighborhood solidarity, actual forms of class status (and not the fiction or mirage that the lifestyle a high official position in Cuba today can provide). The attentive reader will perceive that I have just introduced a trap in what I write; perhaps it is time to decenter the hegemonic character that Miami has in the collective imaginary as representative of the Cuban experience outside of the Island, in order to acknowledge that we belong to a diasporic culture which also includes the hundreds of exiles who ended up in Australia, the thousands who find themselves in Puerto Rico, Spain, and Venezuela, or in the most recent settlements in Mexico, those who decided not to return from the countries of the former socialist bloc. To acknowledge, as well, the new centrality which, in the current, mainly "economic" emigration, previously "empty" countries such as Italy, France, Germany, and, once again, Spain, have acquired. A future in which the pressures for negotiating Cuban identity originate from all these locations is equally as probable as one centered on Miami.

The weight of the North American academy and the duration of the private war of the U.S. against the Island are facts that, in their combined effects, work to obscure our knowledge of the styles of *cubanidad* in other geographical locations. We have documented work on rumba in New York City's Central Park, but we do not know if Cubans in other places negotiate their identity through rumba. It is still possible to put aside, as being of an order of magnitude not worth considering, the evidence of these truly crossed identities, but it will not be so twenty years from now. How will we talk then of these "Cubans" in distant geographical places, where the pressure of the conflict is decidedly less? A friend told me of meeting, in Sydney, I think, a Cuban Australian cousin studying journalism. My friend, based in Miami, told me of his surprise at witnessing, in literally the other half of the world, conflicts of identity typical among Cuban Americans in Miami who belong to what Gustavo Pérez Firmat has wonderfully called the "one and a half generation," that is, children born in Cuba but brought up in the United States. The solution my friend proposed to his cousin, which seems to have borne fruit, was, "Produce a magazine on Cuban issues," which would be the equivalent of "go back to your roots."

We are talking about a bidirectional, pendular, agonistic, at times tragic, at times tragicomic, process of intercrossing. An enormous black man in the Miami airport was selling rechargeable lamps for those traveling to the Island, just in case they had forgotten them and wanted to buy them for their relatives in Cuba (because of the power shortages) before boarding the plane. His response, when faced with my surprise, was instructive: "Friend, I'm dragging a chain that reaches all the way back to Santa Clara." He was speaking of his sister, who lives in Santa Clara, to whom he sends the money earned from his sales. One man from my own neighborhood in Havana who left in the eighties when he was eleven years old asked me how his old playmates were, and if his neighbor's house was still painted the same color. Our age difference is such that I don't even know for sure who he is asking about, and I never in fact noticed the actual color of this house, which I walk by almost every day. What sense does it make to remember the color of a wall? What space does it occupy in a person's life? Another friend, this one from Queens, cried, thinking that he could die far away from Cuba. Yet another in Jersey City started to shout and swore that he could not take it anymore. His wife, also in tears, assured me that if she had known that living far from her family was like this—her present life—she would have stayed in Cuba, even if there was nothing more than flour to eat. These stories of pain can be complemented on the other side, in Cuba, since the separation left gaps that nothing in the future can fill. I traveled on one occasion with a vague address to a New York neighborhood to try to find someone about whom there had been no news in eighteen years. His mother, in Cuba, who asked me to do this, recalls the very last words of his final conversation with her: "Let me look at the game, and I will call you later," because that afternoon the Yankees were playing, and then she knew no more. I have also known mothers who for ten years did not even open the cards their children sent them from abroad, both imbued with a stoic, partisan discipline, one in the sternness of her revolutionary faith, the other crying with the sealed envelope in her hand.

The tragedy of the traveler is to discover the opposite shore of pain, to complete this image which he can never renounce, just as he cannot renounce the new dimension his questions attain. I've been told that a writer I admire, on touching the sands of Miami, shouted and cried like a child. I've been told a truly scary anecdote about a great goddess of song: She sang in a cabaret/bar in Panama, and, when the rest of the band left, she remained alone on stage in front of the piano playing around on the keys and repeating one word: "Cuba!" The force of the notes grew as she repeated something that was already agony: "Ay, Cuba!" The third person in these connections is me, crying, inconsolably, in a crowded New York subway train listening to a cassette by Barbarito Diez. Damned Walkman. One needs to see pain in every creation, or something like that, Lezama wrote in his essay on Julián del Casal. That applies to the decision to abandon one's native land, even more so when political affiliations limit the possibility of return, because it obliges one to undertake something so vast as the reconstruction of the totality of the world, friendships, references, places, customs, symbols.

I recall strolling through Manhattan and, by chance, coming across the statue of a soldier—I believe at the subway entrance on 14th or 23rd Street—and wondering, "And this? Who the fuck is this?" Because in my country I would have known; reverentially or hatefully, the name would have meant something, as would the deeds associated with him. For both those of us who remain in Cuba and those who are abroad in the world, it is only by understanding the cultural, almost ontological dimension of our options— the epic task of maintaining a culture alive—that we will have something to dialogue about between us. The rest are the political passions that always divide and separate us. This is a task of resistance, which, in reverse, multiplies on the Island those who listen to the music of Célia Cruz or Willy Chirino, the viewers of Cristina's talk show on Miami TV, or the fans of the triumphs of Ordóñez and Duke Hernández in the big leagues. The identitarian function of this reception is crucial, because in fact Chirino pales in comparison with other salsa singers, as do Cristina in comparison with Oprah Winfrey and the historical importance of the Duke in the face of the home run records set by Mark McGwire and Sammy Sosa. Their popularity in Cuba— the fact that there are those who offer for sale all of Chirino's music, or those who rent, with spectacular profits, videos of Cristina's shows, and those who pass from hand to hand videos of the games pitched by the Duke or selections of the best fielding plays by Ordóñez—is best explained by the emotional content they all bear. They are all Cuban, meaning *ours*.

In this sense, culture is amoral, apolitical, anti-ideological. And paradoxical. One of the strangest sensations the traveler experiences is being part of a conversation between Cubans who have just arrived in the United States, with North Americans and Cubans who left at the moment of the triumph of the Revolution and never returned. It is a conversation in which positions of power change back and forth continuously, since what is valued is a deep knowledge of what is happening in the place of origin: In other words, the "still" Cuban and the one who has just come "from there" win. These are schizophrenic types who could just as easily end up fighting if the conversation becomes too political as enjoy themselves (now that the encounter has become cultural) telling stories of strategies of survival which the North American or the Cuban who "missed it" listen to, as if to a tale about Martians in Timbuktu, openmouthed and disbelieving. What can one say, after all, but that we admire each other mutually. For what we have managed to become under conditions that are not our own, for what we have to do to continue to live in Cuba.

I will close with a final snapshot, once again in Boston. At the end of a conference, an elderly couple approaches me. Both are retired teachers who left Cuba in the very month of the triumph of the Revolution in 1959, never to return. They ask the most unusual question I have ever heard: "Does the seawall, *El Malecón*, still exist in Havana?" Since it was clear that they were not suffering from some kind of mental illness, I am obliged to find in this question both the result of the enormous pressure of ideology to lacerate the present and the infinite capacity memory has to resist. Uncomfortable, liminal forms of *cubanidad* are forged by the immigrants in the amalgamation of ideology and memory, present and narration, mass media messages and inherited family traditions, assimilation and rejection of new cultural forms. On the other side, what is happening, although often with opposite ideological signs, with the dynamics of identity among those of us who continue to live in Cuba, is not so different. In 1988, I was able to see in the former Soviet Union enormous lines in front of a movie theater that was showing Donald Duck cartoons. In today's Cuba, a similar situation is entirely unthinkable, since we share with our migrations an immense repertoire of cultural productions ranging from fashion, music, blockbuster films, actors from favorite TV shows, intellectual figures, to name just a few. If Althusser used Hegel to teach us that subjectivity is constructed by means of an interpellation sent to us by the Other, Foucault shows us that the atomization of power does not erase resistance but rather disperses it. On this point, where there are no guarantees, we have no other choice but to oppose the metaphor of the clash of cultures with its reverse, dialogue and negotiation, confident that every trace of culture, however minimal, is capable of revealing the totality of its meaning, as in that moment in Proust where the taste of the madeleine raises up a universe of buried experiences.

To the Statue of Liberty

Fina García Marruz

Madam,
I find you somewhat past your prime.
Let's say I don't find you fresh,
Nor innocent.

In Siena
I saw a fountain they call La Gala,
Where golden gray pigeons congregate.
A semicircular rather than a round
fountain,
Backed up against a wall and surrounded
With small statues that seem more like dancers,
than goddesses.
A semicircular fountain
Which did not lack, however,
Its other half, in another part of the world
Which surely wanted to dance too.

boundary 2 29:3, 2002. Copyright © 2002 by Duke University Press.

A fountain they call La Alegre (the Happy One)
In a square the children know.

Madam,
Standing strong, arm raised,
Your great allegorical torch
we can see is disposed
To light up the world, on its own accord,
Without asking permission.

And I assure you
That this is not good, simply,
That it is not good. Put down
The torch for a moment,
And

      Think about it

              Madam.

Havana, 22 January 1995

Looking at Cuba: Notes toward a Discussion

Rafael Hernández

Translated by Dick Cluster

> Seeing an eye
> doesn't make it an eye:
> It's an eye
> because it sees you.
> —Antonio Machado

An old fable (Hindu or African, according to taste) tells of four blind monkeys encountering an elephant. The first describes the animal as "a flat surface, with wrinkles, and moving in and out." The second says "thick and cylindrical, with toenails." The third describes the elephant as "long and pre-hensile, with something like rings, and two panting orifices." The last proposes that it is "vertical and like a rope, but with hair." Each observer is being

This essay appears as chapter 2 of Rafael Hernández, *Looking at Cuba: Essays on Culture and Civil Society*, trans. Dick Cluster (Gainesville: University Press of Florida, forthcoming). Reprinted courtesy of the University Press of Florida. It was originally written in August 1993 and published in *La Gaceta de Cuba*, no. 5, September–October, 1995.

terribly faithful to its experience of the monster. Nonetheless, the species in question remains a secret to all four.

A growing market in experiences and perceptions about Cuba (travel notes, speeches, chronicles, editorials, news articles, essays, and even books) has developed in recent times. This renewed interest, in many corners of the world, has given rise to a veritable eruption of "Cubanology."[1] Some of its perceptions contain curious paradoxes. In this essay I try to present and discuss a brief sample of those paradoxes as seen from a Cuban perspective.

I am not unaware of the merits of the intellectual work about Cuba being done abroad, especially in academia. Emerging from a variety of ideological perspectives, this work has helped make the shortcomings of Cuban social and human sciences clear to us, thus serving as a stimulus. It has also contributed to the sum total of knowledge about Cuban problems. So the notes that follow should not be taken as an attempt to deny the intellectual value of Cuban studies outside our country. Nonetheless, many of those studies are linked to a process of ideological positioning and find their niches within a given marketplace. To that extent, they share some of the characteristics and paradoxes I am about to describe.

"To Be Credible, the Author of a Work on Cuba Must Be Outside the Country or Be a 'Dissident' within It."

According to this view, Cuban intellectuals lack their own perspectives and capacity for reflective thought. Either they are fainthearted or they are mere bureaucrats repeating official discourse. Dissidents, on the other hand, are a splendid species, the product of some mutation; they carry the banners of truth, integrity, and credibility. Yet if one carefully examines the list of writers about Cuba whose ideas receive the greatest distribution, one finds a peculiar logic governing this question of credibility.

For example, it may be that these authors served for many years as Cuban government officials, reaching high ranks in the civil or military bureaucracy or even in the intelligence service. Or they may simply have climbed the technocratic ladder, minding the economic p's and q's. Maybe they worked as journalists for the official media, or as experts in propaganda

1. I use *Cubanology* in a loose sense to refer to visions of Cuba, and not in the strictly academic sense. For a discussion, see Nelson Valdés, "Revolution and Paradigms: A Critical Assessment of Cuban Studies," in Andrew Zimbalist, ed., *Cuban Political Economy: Controversies in Cubanology* (Boulder: Westview Press, 1988).

or censorship, or they were true believers in the Soviet outlook, or orthodox Maoists, who, as professors, may have incorporated the dogmas of the
respective manuals into their academic work. Maybe they even informed on
colleagues who did not seem to them ideologically hard-line enough, or they
censored themselves to avoid trouble.

None of that impedes their being awarded the status of dissidents.
Once they set foot in the Gander airport, or they move to Miami or Luxem-
bourg, or they declare their "dissidence," then the River Jordan has washed
them clean. Overnight, they become independent intellectuals with the keys
to credibility in their pockets.

By way of contrast, the others—those whom some of the above had
labeled, not without scorn, as "intellectuals"—are not treated this same way.

These others may be people who, while identifying themselves as
revolutionaries, have faced many problems because they said what they
thought. For example, they may have had trouble making themselves well
understood in a meeting, because some opportunist twisted their words or
some extremist decided to make an example of them. Perhaps their relatives have gone North, and so, since the 1960s or since the Mariel exodus,
they have been living in Cuba with a considerable part of their family on the
other side. Perhaps they have been labeled "conflictual" or "hypercritical"
or "individualist," or even "revisionist" or "carriers of foreign influences." It's
quite likely that they may know more about José Martí, Antonio Guiteras, or
José Lezama Lima than the majority of those I have described above. Or
that some book, poem, essay, or article of theirs has been questioned or
censored, on account of which some of them have had to suffer ideological ostracism. Perhaps they have had to confront arrogance, sectarianism,
cowardice, and the power or the weakness of others—including those who
later left Cuba or changed their stripes.

If such a person lives and works in Cuba, then he or she is viewed
abroad as a functionary who is neither credible nor possessed of the ability
to express his or her own ideas. A Cuban who neither leaves Cuba nor joins
the organized "dissidence" is, according to established discourse of the outside, a personification of the state—a nonperson, in fact.

It is certainly true that, as Cuban intellectuals, we have not always
been able to do our job without problems caused by bureaucracy, censorship, or dogmatism. But the central question here is what concrete position
a given person has taken with regard to these problems, and in what political context. If self-censorship has been a way of playing under the rules of
the game set by the bureaucracy and its accomplices, it is no less true that

"taking the path of freedom" has been a perfect formula for gaining access to the international marketplace.

An examination of the personal history of many champions of credibility will demonstrate that, paradoxically, the identity card which certifies an intellectual free spirit is more accessible to escaped officials, repentant Stalinists, turncoat functionaries, ex-professors of dogmatism, and former straw men of cultural conformity than it is to those who always sought and fought for room to think and act on behalf of freedom, independence, and the progress of the nation, who have paid the price for this attitude without abandoning a political commitment that they had consciously assumed.

It is obvious that, although many accept such a Manichaean view as valid, the alternative to "officialist" is not exactly "dissident." In terms of the market, though, the mutant labeled "dissident" is valued more highly than a species which has become endangered in today's world, the "revolutionary." The former, not the latter, is awarded the attribute of legitimacy.

"Fidel Castro Is the Source of the Revolution and All Its Evils."

Recently, words like "left," "right," "conservative," and "liberal" have undergone a "semantic restructuring" or degeneration of meaning. The same has occurred with the term "dissident." Those who were always opposed, or became so very early, or were always clearly antisocialist, cannot be qualified as dissidents strictu sensu. Yet the historical opposition to the Cuban Revolution has set about adopting this so-called "dissidence," incorporating it into the broad contemporary spectrum of opposition to the revolution that stretches, in fact, from former members of Catholic Action to ex-Marxists. In the midst of their irreconcilable differences, their most common feature may be that they are anti-Fidel.

Why is this? What is it that all of them, in common, see in Fidel? What is his role in the Revolution? What is the meaning of the popular support that he enjoys?

As Theda Skocpol has pointed out, a revolution is more than the imprint of its leadership or the reflection of a revolutionary ideology. Besides being a factory that produces new politics, a revolution above all brings fundamental social transformation. Its energy is manifested in the political system and the ideological discourse, but it has its roots in civil society.

Like every true social revolution (the French, the Russian, the Chinese), the Cuban one includes several revolutions. Each social group involved in the revolutionary struggle has been able to see *its* revolution being carried out. For 150 years, after all, reformists and autonomists, annexationists and *independentistas*, had been clashing in the country's ideological arena. As in other revolutions, the triumphant leadership of this one was able to defeat one set of opposing or antagonistic sectors, while joining with others which represented a much greater proportion of the social strata of the population. This was not a question simply of the effectiveness of the leaders or the solidity of their ideological propositions but of the vast social interaction which revolutionary politics implied.

For some, the Revolution left its *élan* behind after the 1960s because it was no longer an adventure, a mystique, an epic whose objective was the destruction of the old regime and the unleashing of world revolution. Leaving aside the question of whether there were also epic moments in the '70s and '80s, I wonder: What has allowed the immense majority of the population to continue supporting the Revolution? Is it Marxist political thought? Liberation expeditions overseas? The Leninist party? All of these elements are part of the picture, inseparable from the process itself. But it must not be forgotten that, from the beginning, revolutionary policies and politics were supported because they signified a fundamental change in direction for the conditions of existence of the people, and a net improvement in their standard of living. During the '70s and '80s the revolutionary process achieved substantial gains in the conditions of material and cultural life of Cubans, including their social and national consciousness. This development has constituted a fundamental pillar of the Revolution all these years.

If politics is the art of winning internal and external support, broadening and unifying the social base, forging alliances, preserving the stability of the system, weakening opposition and foreign threats as much as possible, obtaining the respect of one's enemies, and even knowing how to achieve a certain halo of invincibility, then there are few leaders alive who have the political capacity of Fidel Castro.

Today, the political leadership must run a country that does not have the kind of consensus that developed in the early '60s. It is no easy task to govern with less consensus, in the midst of discontent, among the formidable difficulties of shared scarcity, ineffective ideological communication with the outside world, and U.S. arrogance. To steer the ship of state in the middle of these rough seas requires appropriate ideas about democracy and economic policy. But it also requires real authority—authority which can allow for readjustment, inspire a new generation of leaders, peacefully let go of old dogmas, maintain the continuity of the Revolution's essential social achievements and goals, reform the structures that were created earlier,

reorder the economy and the legal system, promote more effective mechanisms of governance, and at the same time carry out the delegation of power
required for the viable transition to a more decentralized and democratic
system. The one who can lead this process in the least costly manner, with
the least trauma for the social body and the most stability for the country, is
Fidel Castro.

This notion is not so odd, not so unique to Cubans, as it might appear.
The other side of the coin—that Fidel Castro is a factor acting contrary to
the change in Cuba that hegemonic North American interests hope to see—
reminds Cubans that those interests, the *others*, also appreciate the importance of his role.

"Cuban Socialism Consists of a Political System and an Ideological Discourse. Civil Society Has Been Suppressed."

The impression given by some writings on Cuba is that Cuban society
is dormant, which is to say that it hardly exists. They make it appear as if
Cuban reality were made up of "the government," "the Party," and "the elite"
on one side, and a passive multitude on the other. As if all the citizens who
think or have the capacity to act had moved to Hialeah or Coral Gables or
had enlisted in a "human rights group." This view is worthy of discussion
only because of how widespread it has become outside the island.

In the first place, the majority of Cubanologists do not generally
explain what they mean by "the elite." Does this include the million members
of the Party and Communist Youth? The local delegates to People's Power?
Or only the list of members of the Central Committee? Or maybe only those
on the Political Bureau? Does it include everyone who enjoys some kind
of privilege—for instance, possession of hard currency and the opportunity
to buy in special stores, as in the cases of musicians, artists, athletes, or
technicians who often travel abroad, or of those Cubans who receive dollars
from their relatives abroad? Or the members of the armed forces? Or those
whose annual incomes are many times greater than those of a worker—as
is the case for the great majority of Cuban private peasants, possibly the
richest in Latin America? Or those who make decisions, and if so where,
and about what? In the Council of State or in a corporation, in matters of
religion or of agriculture?

Cuba is not the transfiguration of a doctrine, nor the reification of a
totalitarian philosophy. It is a country. Little is written and even less is published about this real country, whether inside Cuba or abroad.

To do sociology about Cuban reality has not always been an option. Even now it is difficult—and more difficult still for a foreigner—to do field research. It also happens that, among those who come to Cuba to gather information, some end up collecting merely what they want to find, usually what they need to characterize the system as Stalinist or Fidel Castro as a figure down to his last days in power. Others complain that they are not given the information they need to write in a believable manner about an imperfect society. For whatever reason, the prevailing result is a sociology of images viewed from outside, which takes Havana for Cuba and takes the Revolution and socialism for slogans of the moment. Such banal assumptions denature what should be profound political sociology about Cuba today.

Cuban society cannot be sociologically reconstructed as a puzzle pieced together out of political discourse. In that way it is no different from any other country in the world. Cuban society cannot be inferred from the discourse of Fidel himself, and even less so from that of his less brilliant followers. At the same time, researchers must face the fact that this discourse does continue to have a level of resonance in the population, a resonance which it would be erroneous to discount as pure emotional reaction or a mere expression of necessity.

The tendency to underestimate Cubans' level of political culture[2] is reflected in the visions predominant outside. It is also reflected, in the form of a certain paternalism, in Cuban political discourse itself. We have a broadly literate population with very high levels of access to schooling (an average of over nine years). Cubans have known the U.S.S.R., Eastern Europe, and Africa better than any other people of the hemisphere and, as a whole, have read more books and seen a greater variety of films than the rest of the region. They are accustomed to paying close attention to what is going on in the world and to discussing everything from baseball to laws proposed for the approval of the National Assembly. All this begs a question: Doesn't that population have knowledge, maturity, and culture enough to face and understand the real changes that the country needs? In my opinion, it is precisely this political culture which makes the fundamental difference in Cuban society.[3] Yet our people is viewed as one with a strange incapacity

2. For a differentiation between *political culture* and *ideology*, see Haroldo Dilla and Rafael Hernández, "Cultura política y participación en Cuba," *Cuadernos de Nuestra América* 15 (July–December 1990).
3. This subject has been avoided by Cubanology in a nearly systematic fashion. Consulting the complete collection of the journal *Cuban Studies*, published for two decades by the University of Pittsburgh, will reveal that almost no one pays attention to the topic. Richard

to think with its own head, an absurd ineptitude to decide for itself what it most needs, and a desperate need for tutelary salvation.

In other countries, reference to civil society tends to mean the middle class, the intellectuals, the entrepreneurial elite, certain influential social movements and organizations, et cetera. Some of those conceptions are applied to evaluating the current situation in Cuba.

Thus, on the island, some have employed the concept of the middle sectors as the "soft underbelly" of society, identifying them with criticism and discord. Outside of Cuba, some use this same concept to define the supposed carriers of national salvation. I think that both groups are making the mistake of assuming that a social category definable according to salary levels or occupational categories possesses an ideological identity or constitutes a differentiated sociopolitical stratum.

The first group, those who demonize the middle sectors as possessed by the vice of discord, is simply trying to attribute to a portion of the society a capacity for questioning, which, as such, runs through the whole society. The second group believes those sectors to be the medium of a part of the Cuban bourgeoisie, which in the 1940s and 1950s could not take power or lacked the political courage to do so, which in 1959 or 1960 chose the lesser of two evils as between socialism and the North Americans, and which now sees in the middle sectors the spiritual heirs of reformism. Curiously, both perceptions reveal a singular point of convergence.

People devoted to the arts or sciences, professionals and technicians, constitute an important group within the whole Cuban workforce, a group with an unquestionable capacity to take part in the development of the society but quite heterogeneous within itself. They may have very different tasks, display different social behavior, and naturally have different points of view. For me, they do not constitute an ideologically differentiated sector of Cuban society and so are not the possessors of an exclusive role as "critical conscience." In other words, they are not the only ones called upon, by virtue of their capacities or courage, to identify and confront the country's problems.[4] Much less are they the reservoirs of dissidence. Cer-

---

Fagen's pioneering work in *The Transformation of Political Culture in Cuba* (Stanford: Stanford University Press, 1969) continues to be a lone exception which has not been updated either empirically or theoretically.

4. I share Cintio Vitier's outlook on the Eurocentrism implicit in this vision of intellectuals' exclusive role as culture's "critical conscience" in a confrontation with power, equidistant from all political positions, a vestal virgin of some sterilized objectivity—as opposed to the intellectuals (as in our Latin American case) who act in history with their criticism and

tainly, they are not any of these things to a greater degree than production workers, service workers, or those in other labor or educational sectors, in a country where, as the poet Nicolás Guillén said, everything is so mixed.

Let us take one objective indicator of social diversity: the Cubans who are leaving the country today. They don't, on the whole, reflect political dissidence, though they do reflect a degree of dissatisfaction and some very specific interests. They leave, in general, for family reasons and to gain access to a higher-level consumption market, that of the United States. Now, then, who are they? Fifty percent of those who emigrate are production and service workers (a group which represents 65% of the active Cuban labor force), 36% are administrators (only 7% of the workforce). Just 13% of the employed persons leaving are professionals and technicians (though the representation of this group in the Cuban workforce is a good deal higher, at 21%). The proportion of high-level professional emigrants is much lower today than it was in the '60s and '70s. In a more homogeneous society, as Cuba is in the '90s, there are more direct production or service workers migrating than there were in those earlier years. The immense majority of those who leave do represent the higher overall level of education in Cuba, however, naturally, they are not university graduates but people who have finished primary or secondary school.[5]

Paradoxically—and this is perhaps the paradox par excellence of Cuban socialist society—criticism, disagreement, and even demands are nothing if not the children of the Revolution itself at the level of civil society. Cubans truly consider themselves equal citizens, and not only in the text of the Constitution of the Republic. In other words, any Cuban—whether a black resident of Old Havana, a peasant in the Escambray, a youth walking in any city park or seafront, a retired person living in any apartment building, or a working mother who is head of her household—all these Cubans consider themselves capable of asserting this right, out loud, accompanied

---

their polemics, contributing to concrete social change and taking sides in favor of social justice and independence. See Cintio Vitier, "Resistencia y libertad" (Havana: Centro de Estudios Martianos, June 1992, mimeo). (A translation of this essay is included in this collection.)

5. These figures are based on studies of legal emigration in the years 1990–92, which also report that 92% of these emigrants are white, more than 60% are from Havana City or Havana Province, 55% do not work (that is, they are students, housewives, retirees); 5.7% of all migrants of working age are unemployed. See Ernesto Rodríguez, "El patrón migratorio cubano: cambio y continuidad," *Cuadernos de Nuestra América* 18 (January–June 1992): 83–95.

by a declaration of complaints about what the system, and especially the state, owes them as rightful members of civil society.

The question is: Should we regret having created these demanding citizens who (accustomed as they are to the munificence or even paternalism of the socialist state) think they deserve an adequate level of health and education services, social security, work opportunities, et cetera, in the midst of the current crisis? Or, on the contrary, should we congratulate ourselves on this level of political culture and social consciousness engendered by the Revolution, which is pressuring the socialist leadership today? This social phenomenon would pose serious difficulties for any project of "pure socialism" and isolation from the world at all costs. It would also pose serious difficulties for the return of capitalism to Cuba. Such an imposition would run the risk of unleashing great social tensions.

Indeed, what would be the reaction of these Cubans who, unlike the poor of Latin America and other regions, have become accustomed during more than thirty years to being *inside* rather than outside? What would they say if they were informed that the achievements of socialism have been the result of a mistake, of a historical aberration, and that the truth of the modern world is that their portion is almost nil? On the other hand, the majority of Cubans do not want to live egalitarianly poor. Workers in general legitimately aspire to salary compensation reflected in their level of access to the market. In terms of equal opportunity as well as in other dimensions of a new model, it would be tragic to renounce the main thrust of social justice, solidarity, independence, and freedom which makes up the nucleus of Cuban revolutionary ideas—and that is nothing but the natural fruit of Cuba's own history.

"Cuba Is the Same as Ever. It Is Just Going through a Process of Surface or Temporary Changes."

For some, the Revolution is an aberration, a monster of the dream of reason, so to speak. In fact, however, since the nineteenth century Cuba has rarely gone through three decades without a crisis of economic, political, and social change. These periodic crises have been characterized by strong ideas about renewal, progress, development, social justice, national vindication, and independence. The Marxist socialist outlook flowed naturally into this historical channel.

The difficulties of the current crisis often hide that long-term dynamic's stubborn consistency. Some outside observers seem to be discussing a present with no history, as if the future could be predicted according to the manner of those ancient cosmographies described by Borges, in which the world was still new. On our shores, some *compañeros* believe that the revolutionary leadership has a demiurgical power to shape social reality according to its desires. Both groups forget that this is not 1959. They underestimate the real political force of the Cuban people, the product of historical accumulation and—as discussed above—a unique political culture.

Popular support for the system is what gives it stability. Continued identification of the system with the interests of the population guarantees it support. In spite of the relative erosion of consensus in the last few years, what is most notable is how much that equilibrium has been maintained.

In fact, the system has already demonstrated an exceptional capacity for assimilation. Could such a brutal drop in levels of economic growth have been cushioned to a comparable degree in any other country of Latin America? Naturally, it's not much consolation for Cuba's population, confronting the overload of daily life, to know that Latin America has 200 million poor. Nor would it be prudent to conclude that its capacity for endurance is invulnerable or unlimited. People do not confront the hard things of life in peacetime the same way they do in war, nor do governments command the same political resources or instruments of power.

The Cuban people's endurance is joined to an expectation of change. The debate preceding the Fourth Party Congress—the deepest and widest process of critical analysis that Cuba's socialist society has known—expressed itself in favor of decentralization, economic efficiency, more popular participation in decision making, democratization of the country's political institutions (starting with the Communist Party itself and National Assembly), effective means of political representation (especially elections), and the struggle to end discrimination against religious believers and other sectors such as youth, women, and blacks.

Obviously, to the extent that economic difficulties and external pressures affect the space for internal debate, limit the decentralization process, and contribute to keeping us on the defensive, they do not favor the process of change. Democratic styles don't find a friendly climate in fortresses under siege.

However, that does not mean that solving the problems of the political system can be de-emphasized or postponed. Though the major effort is dedicated to the difficult task of supplying food and articles of primary need, this does not imply that the necessary restructuring of institutions and rectification of the system can be dropped. Survival tactics will not get very far without a political and economic development strategy suited to the new conditions reigning in the world. Classically, while the economy may seem to be determinant, politics really is.

The process of political reforms does not have to be based on certificates of good conduct issued by "international" institutions like the Carter Center or Americas Watch. Neither do the decentralization of the economic system, the opening of a space for certain forms of Cuban private initiative, and collaboration with foreign capital imply the implementation of neoliberal-style reforms that wipe out the state's role in the economy.

In fact, the July 1992 reform of the Cuban Constitution has opened the legal possibility of redefining the nature of property, including its private use in the case of "non-fundamental means of production," and of modifying the irreversible character of the socialist sector, as well as recognizing the form of property represented by foreign investments.[6] Similarly, while allowing private investments and a less administrative concept of state planning, the constitutional reform gave more autonomy to state enterprises themselves, which could point toward a system with both planning and more freedom in mercantile relations (Article 16).

In the terrain of politics and ideology, the majority of the constitutional reforms tended to open space for greater pluralism. First, the bases of the state were defined in terms of "people" and "workers," rather than a particular social class or stratum. Second, the lay character of the Cuban state was stipulated, explicitly proscribing any form of religious discrimination, thus excluding atheism as the official ideology (Articles 1 and 3). Third, the system of People's Power was broadly reformed, establishing (among other important changes) direct popular election of the National Assembly and the Provincial Assemblies, and fundamentally modifying the municipal and provincial administrative apparatus.

Finally, the reformed Constitution presents the Party as the vanguard not of one particular class but of the Cuban nation (Article 5). That implies a differentiation between political pluralism and a multiparty system. The fact is that none of the fundamental problems of today's Cuba would automatically be resolved by means of multiple parties. But the Cuban Communist Party does now face a challenge. One of the main hurdles it faces in the coming years is that of really making itself the Party of the Cuban

6. See Articles 14, 15, and 23 of the reformed Constitution. Subsequent references are also to this new version. For an analysis of the content of those changes, see Hugo Azcuy, "Aspectos de la ley de reforma constitucional cubana de 1992" (Albuquerque: Latin American Data Base, University of New Mexico, dossier, August 1992).

nation, welcoming various currents of thought which reflect the feelings of the people, without thus losing its strength, unity, and capacity to direct the country's development and the preservation of its independence and national sovereignty.

Might Cuba need more than one party in the future? I think that, independently of the preferences of Cuban revolutionary stalwarts, the answer would objectively depend on the capacity to meet the above-mentioned challenge. Of course, the political unity represented by the Party remains an unquestionable strategic necessity in the face of the constant threat which the United States poses to the sovereignty of the country. What would happen if this threat ended or were substantially reduced? In any case, a future and more democratic Cuba would not resemble the Cuba of the 1950s. It would be a Cuba that, while popular and pluralist, would not allow annexationist or autonomist parties, or business lobbyists; a system where politics would not become an electoral or parliamentary exercise far removed from the interests and needs of the population, much less a proliferation of special interests with money from Miami or Washington which could fragment and block the state actions needed to protect the overall interests of the country.

The real issue of democracy in Cuba (not democracy in the abstract, according to definitions in vogue in countries whose citizens barely bother to vote) is that of the capacity of the population to self-govern (in lowercase) and exercise control over the Government (in uppercase). It is not only about self-government and control in the *act* of choosing, but especially in the *process* of governing. If democracy is conceived as part of a social process in motion, not merely as a formula allowing parties to rotate the possession of power, then in meeting that challenge Cuban society—with all its failings—would have advanced further down the long and difficult path to democracy than any other society in this hemisphere.

Postscript

The chorus of foreign attitudes toward the Cuban situation that I've tried to describe (without ill humor, I hope) hides a diversity of motives. The majority of the members of that chorus see Cuba through a filter of received truths, commonplaces, and simplifications; they are the lovers of black-and-white distinctions. Then there is a familiar group of enemies, those who always knew that socialism here was evil and who now console themselves with the idea that it is finally coming to an end. Finally, there are those who once called themselves socialists and later renounced this mirage. They neither repeat set phrases nor rub their hands in expectation; rather, they await the end of socialism as a necessary part of their second thoughts. They watch the collapse with a certain bitterness, but at the same time they feel the relief of finding evidence that they did not make a mistake, while they gravely nod their heads at the stubborn reality in which the dreams of men crash.

In Cuba, those who believe in—as Fidel would say—"miracle formulas,"[7] whether monetary mechanisms or foreign investment, reflect a peculiar pragmatism expressed in the idea of a forced march toward who knows what. Those pragmatists are the other side of the coin of the uncompromising ideologues: Both lack new, clear, and distinct ideas about the possible future to which they aspire. The question is, how are current changes tied to that future? Above all, how can we rethink the system so that the future, as Martí would say, is not simply one in which the strongest prevail?

---

7. See the July 26 celebration speech by Fidel Castro in *Granma* (28 July 1993), 3.

In the Furnace of the Nineties: Identity and Society in Cuba Today

Fernando Martínez Heredia

The decade of the nineties, as a whole, and each year in it, has registered in Cuba a wealth of movements and returns, gains and losses, continuities and changes that the urgency with which we live makes it very difficult to analyze. In the midst of the crisis, the word *nation* has multiplied its presence. It is clear that one of the reasons for this is the disappearance of other certainties that govern the spiritual world of Cubans, not because of a substitution in the field of dominant ideas but rather because of the emergence of macrosocial relations different from those that prevailed before and the force of the cultural field related to them. *Nation* would be linked, then, according to the person, either to the symbolic field of a period of transition or to the symbolic field of a resistance to that change—linked, that is, to diverse affects, needs, interests, or sensibilities.

A quantitative analysis would verify what I am saying about the multiplication of the idea of nation, showing its distribution according to the variables selected: mass media, political discourse, film and theater, and so forth. A classification of current uses of *nation* would, without doubt, provide even more data. A historian might show, for example, coincidences with the

boundary 2 29:3, 2002. Copyright © 2002 by Duke University Press.

ideological weight the idea of the national attained half a century ago, during the period of the Second Republic, when the National Bank was founded
and *The History of the Cuban Nation* was published. But another historian
would immediately remind us that a transcendental event, the Revolution,
self-denominated as the socialist revolution of national liberation, enriched
and gave new and more specific meaning to the national question, thus ren-
dering the comparison improper.

My proposal is much more modest. In what follows, I will comment
on some aspects of the national in relation to the popular at the present
moment, or, more precisely, on the current vicissitudes of the concept. With
more suggestions and personal opinions than objective analyses and data,
I request for these lines the indulgence due to the genre of the essay.

1. Some Introductory Remarks

First point: The national implies always a class dimension. That is,
it implies that the nation and the social classes it contains are intimately
related, although this is not necessarily always apparent. One of the main
functions of the nation, in fact, is to cover up class domination. Nevertheless,
implies warns against the reduction of the national to the question of class,
because it denotes that it is a matter of relationship. The national has other
dimensions outside of the class one. In Cuba, the achievement of social justice and the end of neocolonial domination happened together—they could
only happen together—transcending, thus, the old nationalist discourses
and reformist ideas and practices. For this reason, we can characterize what
happened in 1959 a "socialist revolution of national liberation."

In the 1970s, the path was opened up for a second, very contradictory
stage of the process of socialist transition, which I will not try to explain here.
Suffice it to say that it was a period of extraordinary achievements, but also
one of deformations, impasses, and retreats. At that time, the consent of the
majority—the legitimizing force of the regime that claimed to stand for the
Revolution—and the ideology of the bureaucratized, authoritarian regime,
which was invasive of all spaces, coincided. This generated a tragic confusion. The ideology of the bureaucracy claimed to represent socialism and
a "class-based" vision, and came to see itself as the supreme dispenser of
qualifications, prizes, and punishments. It was a closed discourse, more like
a straitjacket than a force for creation and change. The deep devaluation of
the idea of socialism among us in the nineties has been all the more severe
because it is natural to confuse socialism with the bureaucratic ideology that
governed in its name. It is sad to have to listen today, from those who qualify

as "leftists," to dogmatic, outdated positions, authoritarianism, sermons, or simple stupidity.

In the face of the present, and looking toward the future, however, it would be catastrophic to forget the dimension of class. But this forgetting prevails in the majority of the references to and diverse visions of the national in Cuba today. It is understandable that it seems in bad taste to speak of classes, especially when the surviving priests of the bureaucratic ideology, with their rigid postures, seem to reinforce the reasons for rejecting old dogma. But this discourse no longer determines anything. In another direction, forgetting the existence, relations, actions, and ideologies of social classes is beneficial for the advancement of capitalist relations that are replacing those of socialist transition in Cuba today. In this instance, a tacit exclusion of the theme of class can be present without there being necessarily an agreement between those who practice that exclusion. It is essential to take up this crucial theme again from different points of view and in different ways in order to comprehend the current processes and trends of the Revolution and the motivations and interests in which they are inscribed.

The national exists—and this second point is fundamental—in the form of cultural manifolds and through cultural expressions. It is a question of collective representations, of symbols and the elaboration of codes, of the social construction of realities. This is how the nation is formed, how it articulates its contradictions, how it evolves, resists, struggles, and processes external impacts. National culture shelters and expresses a wealth of traits and elaborations peculiar to it, made up of the most dissimilar material and methods, the most diverse social groups, in successive and simultaneous deposits. This *process of cultural accumulation* is what operates in every historical era and conjuncture; in it are contained all the particular aspects and instances of national culture, with their complexes of relations and interactions.

Social domination promotes, discourages, hides, discerns, and arranges the order of the elements of national culture. It engenders fame and decrees forgetfulness. The already formed nation implies—along with a "national" economy and state—a dominant culture within a situation of cultural plurality, a dominant culture that subordinates in subtle or not so subtle ways the other cultural forms, just as the national state and economy subordinate social diversity and the economies of households and different social groups. Although permanence is a dominant goal of this subordination, each nation has a history, and the elements of the national change with the passage of time, as does the value given them.

But this is not a theoretical essay. Let me reiterate, then, a basic point:

Cuba is one of many countries in which the national is linked to colonialism and neocolonialism, that is, to the main historical forms of globalization of capitalism. We have been subalterns of successive waves of globalization, from the military, communications, services, and production colony created by the Spanish, to what is called today, to designate a new stage of capitalism, "globalization." The nation thus turns out to be a hope, a yearning, a difficult task that is taken up only to be abandoned, an agony and a struggle, a manipulation, at once something sublime and a place bound by shackles of steel. The nation is an instance "of everyone," because for all practical purposes we all are "black" or subaltern in the face of the foreign—of those foreigners who perceive as "black" or subaltern their own fellow countrymen—and because the world chain of domination that goes from technology to telecommunications and public opinion creates over and over again new subaltern "everyones," or separates or breaks up those who remain behind or to one side, but always from a place of creation that is foreign to us, that attracts and tempts us but also frightens, governs, and leaves us helpless.

Therefore, in the national appear—or are masked—the lack of self-esteem of the colonized; the national pride of those who fought so hard and did win some victories, as is our case; and a history of cultural accumulations. Likewise, in the national, the conflicts, subordinations, accommodations, negotiations, pressures, and struggles of social groups are revealed or hidden. In the postcolonial world, national culture is considered strategic, is mobilized, becomes a political issue. In truth, in the central capitalist countries this also occurs, but it occurs as if it were a matter of course, without risks or consequences, and therefore without the anguish of failure. (We recall that the much heralded Fifth Centenary of Columbus's voyage never appeared to include Canada and the United States.)

2. Identity and Social Change

National identity has been a basic determination in Cuban history for over a century. Like all forms of national identity, Cuban identity is the daughter of a very slow and protracted accumulation of characteristics taken, created, re-elaborated, or re-created from daily life, mythical materials, beliefs, artistic expressions, and the forms of knowledge acquired by different ethnic groups, their clashes, relationships, and fusions, from the local communities and regions that make up the country. It is, at the same time, the daughter of—and this is more specific to Cuba—profound political revolutions that upset the expected ("normal") reproduction of social life. From these revolutions comes the very name *Cuban*, the main elements of the national imaginary and numerous projects of "achieving" or "completing" the nation, in which radical tendencies have predominated.

Cuban national identity today is associated with the word *risk*—the risk of losing the society of social justice to which national identity has been linked for decades, the risk of losing socialism. And the risk of losing sovereignty as a people, as a nation-state. At first glance, this seems to be a single risk, but in reality these are two separately discernible risks. From 1959 onward, the Revolution linked the idea of the achievement of a sovereign nation-state with the most radical anticapitalist representations. National identity made socialism and social liberation its own, and vice versa.

The massive, organized, and sustained participation of the majority of the population in the Revolution allowed the successful implementation of revolutionary social changes. Radical representations of popular armed national liberation struggle, and of the anti-imperialism associated with it, were the decisive ideology of the triumphant insurrection; but this type of national consciousness was rooted, became massive and permanent, only because it was intimately associated with the ideology of social justice expressed in socialism and because it became fused with that ideology in the course of the revolutionary process. In the Revolution, the dominated masses freed themselves and multiplied their capacity for social change and for changing themselves; this libertarian impact marched side by side for some years with the form of revolutionary power. That union was successful in breaking down the limits of the possible and changing history. The social regime and the form of government in power in Cuba created by the Revolution have been maintained for such a prolonged period—through very different circumstances and internal changes—as a result of the great social cohesion that existed and that still persists today. The basis of this cohesion was a way of life based on the systematic redistribution of social wealth and a dominant egalitarian ethos, at once exemplary and widespread, and the links established between civil society and the political power of the state as the guarantor of this way of life and bearer of the national project, a project that was always perceived as something in process, in large part yet to be realized.

Social differences changed. Some lessened profoundly (for example, class differences), others were attenuated, some remained hidden. The idea of a nation of Cubans attained much richer and more complex dimensions than those before the Revolution. For more than three decades, nation and socialism were united, almost to the point of exclusiveness: Without the two, nothing or nobody was Cuban. The national symbols became those of Cuban socialism. Language consecrated this exclusiveness: Antirevolutionary Cubans were called "unpatriotic" (*apatrida*) or "mercenary." In the second stage of the revolutionary process, when Cuba became dependent on the Soviet bloc, national identity operated as a defensive wall in the face of "actually existing socialism" and the colonization "from the Left" it implied. In spite of the tide of sovietization, the regime itself continued to claim the national as its source and as part of its very nature, and made available to that idea of the national resources, advantages, and space. In daily life, in the "common sense" of the people, the national had a central place.

What we risk today is the *disassociation* between *the Cuban* and *socialism*: that is, the possibility of a transition that will leave us, like the majority of countries in the world today, in a situation in which national identity is not related to socialism. The consequences of the changes in the Cuban social structure in the nineties are, without doubt, fundamental. The differentiation of incomes has become widespread and leaves major social groups in divergent situations. Some increase their incomes by lucky circumstances, without improving their social status; others move up both the income and social status ladders; many thousands maintain their social prestige while their standard of living drops. The divergences still do not bring with them the formation of significant social pressure groups or new classes. The groups with higher incomes are still far from obtaining social legitimacy. But drastic changes have taken place in the relation of the social sectors to the sources of power, representation, and social mobility.

Other forms of difference have made their appearance, have come out into the open, or have intensified. Local authorities have acted in favor of new local forms of economic survival and restructuring. Thousands of informal associations have appeared and others already in existence have grown stronger. There is a real hunger for them. The system of state control designed to reduce or repress social initiatives of this type that was so prominent in previous decades has fallen apart and will be impossible to keep going. It goes without saying that the Cuban social fabric was always complicated. What characterizes the present is that (1) this fabric is becoming even more complex and diversified, and at a faster rate; (2) social diversity unfolds in the face of an egalitarian ideal of homogeneity, which reigned for decades; and (3) these new forms of social organization have new effects and greater incidence in society as a whole.

Cuba has been a Western, mercantilist, and liberal-individualist

country since the end of the nineteenth century, without a significant presence of pre-Columbian indigenous communities and with a dynamic history
and a population with high expectations. The Revolution was so profound
that it succeeded in throwing back, and even, in certain cases, eliminating,
previously dominant features; this happened with mercantilism, the profit
motive, and individualism and egoism. Now these features are coming back
strongly and are opening up space for themselves in a thousand ways. If
they succeed, there will emerge the split in consciousness between the quotidian and the civic, and private/family values and economic planning that is
typical of capitalist societies.

3. The Cultural War

Cuba is the bad example of Latin America, the moral vengeance of
the oppressed of this world, a proof that another way of life is possible.
Therefore, it will be too hard for the North American empire to forgive us.
But another, potentially greater danger threatens us, a danger that is widespread in the present-day world. The culture of developed capitalism has, in
the last few decades, deployed a combination of great maturity to integrate
or neutralize past challenges to its hegemony: a qualitatively superior level
of control of cultural production and consumption combined with an explicit
project of cultural domination. In this way, it efficiently dissembles the dead
ends into which it is leading people on a world scale, and the planet itself,
due to its inherent contradictions, which include the dominance of transnational and parasite capital, at the cost of sacrificing national or regional economic possibilities to the logic of superprofits, growing surplus populations,
impoverishment of the majority, and irreversible attacks on the environment.
Today, the cultural machinery of centralized capitalism offers all countries—
albeit in different forms and levels—a decisive form of *homogenization*. This
consists of numerous cultural, ideological, and spiritual features that appear
to repair at a symbolic level the increasingly deep fracture existing between
the lives of the dominant and middle classes of the central capitalist countries and those of the masses in the rest of the world.

The cultural production of homogenization makes up a whole world
system directed toward the neutralization, channeling, and manipulation of
the potential for rebellion that is latent in the advances obtained by humanity,
such as the growing consciousness of the need for tolerance—political,
ethnic, racial, gender—the demand for democratic forms of government, the
rejection of poverty—considered as a social rather than a natural fact—eco-

logical awareness, and so on. The goal of what is, in effect, a cultural war is to assure that those achievements do not turn against the rule of capitalism, that there be no resistance to its economic, ideological, and politico-military-repressive actions, and that everyone accepts the fact that wealth and human diversity are able to exist only in both a private and a public life governed by capitalism.

This cultural war can gain more and more ground in Cuba in the current conditions, which are dominated by the simultaneous crisis of the economy and most of the institutions, ideologies, and beliefs of the Revolution; and all of this within the iron cage of the need for Cuba's economic reinsertion into a world market dominated by capitalism. In my opinion, we will not be able to effectively resist the cultural war of supercapitalism by relying only on the convictions and experiences of our heritage of struggle, past achievements, affects, and ideas, and on the identities they formed. This heritage contains many strengths that are a solid cement of spiritual union, and it has many positive features that have marked in an indelible way the majority of Cubans, with variations across different generations. But it also possesses many features that constitute weaknesses in the face of the practical challenges of today and tomorrow. Besides, this heritage was already falling into decline or disrepute before the crisis of the nineties: Its partial connection to the ideology of bureaucracy, noted before, debilitates it morally in terms of its own declared values. And the enemy culture does not seek to impose itself on us today as the return of a Cuban past that was defeated by the Revolution; it is not the old counterrevolution. It comes, rather, as "progress," an adjustment to new circumstances, or "necessity." This disguise of a desirable or inevitable future makes it all the more dangerous.

The "popular" element of the national culture has been the most profound and effective form of resistance, but it has also weakened over the last few years. Large sectors of the population—those which have attained socially valid personal "development" (higher education, cultural sophistication, status, international "vibes")—perceive Cuban national-popular culture as "premodern." And these strata are among the most active in the country today. The process of homogenization stemming from global capitalism at the level of everyday culture—a global phenomenon, not exclusive to us—is an agent of the weakening of Cuban cultural density in general. The devaluation of our own culture has its roots in the frustration of individual expectations during the second stage of the revolutionary process, from 1970 to 1980. Today, the enormous economic crisis, the apparent lack of economic viability of the country, and the discrediting of socialism have produced a *national* frustration that is different from the experience of individual frustration; both, however, coincide in the present and can influence each other mutually. To the extent that "popular" national culture is identifiable as the root from which the political regime stems, it is also a victim of the wave of conservative ideas and sentiments washing over us today.

For homogenization to prevail in Cuba, it will not be enough that certain upwardly mobile urban sectors have the ability to satisfy needs and desires, such as having differentiated consumer levels based on spending power, private arenas for economic initiatives, new forms of social mobility, videos, facilities—that is to say, it will not be enough that these sectors be able to live like their peers in other peripheral capitalist countries, for example, Argentina or Haiti. In those countries, homogenization exacerbates already existing features, it "modernizes" them and brings them nearer to the formal models of social organization and individual behavior of the central capitalist countries, which are set by the mass media that shape public opinion and affect. In Cuba—and this is the most important and difficult thing to think about—homogenization would have to be capable of erasing needs and expectations that were deeply and broadly rooted during the revolutionary regime. It would have to come up against a cultural complex comprised of very diverse elements from very distinct time frames but fused in a profound, all-embracing, and defining process that gave it an anticapitalist, patriotic, nationalist, and communist-oriented character. In other words, to be successful, homogenization would have to dismantle the fundamental elements of the Cuban rupture with capitalist domination and the achievements and values that have become customary over the course of four decades.

4. Paths

One logical reaction—we were talking of risk—is to seek to preserve. I allow myself to wonder: Preserve what? Who? What for? What is at stake? What nation, what Cuban are we speaking about? If the present-day realities of social differentiation and divergence I alluded to are not taken into account, appeals to the nation, to Cuban identity, or to an abstract "people" will not be credible or of much use. I can say much the same of the past. It is vital to deepen our understanding of the past, to identify the "oversights," the silences present in national identity, silences that are closely related to the ways in which the dominant classes in Cuba's history have sought to rearticulate their hegemony in the face of the successive radical upsurges and the human and social disasters produced by their successive forms of profit making and depredation of the natural environment.

Nationalism, that exacerbated form of national identity, acquired among us a very special value with the Revolution. An immense pride in being Cuban was the outcome. The intimate link of Cuban nationalism with socialism and internationalism took the edge off the negative aspects typical of all nationalisms and contributed a great deal to shaping the motivations of Cubans. Today, however, that pride in being Cuban faces serious setbacks and, for certain cases and for certain social groups, is in crisis. This situation lends itself to a relapse into the lack of self-esteem of the colonized; but I believe that the frustrations of not having futures to attain are the main problem. The affirmation of the national is also resented because its search for "roots" tends to convert necessity into providence, creating a deus ex machina that justifies ideologically whatever happens.

The present-day nation-state continues to be representative of national identity for many reasons. The persistent identification of the Revolution with sovereignty and social justice works in its favor. The political power of the state—still decisive for the economy—struggles arduously to guarantee economic reproduction and growth, and, at the same time, to maintain the social pact that is the basis of the system. But the state has been deeply affected by the drastic reduction in its resources, by the profound defects it bears within itself, and by the very nature of the structural changes under way.

Cuban civil society can play a very important role in the socialist struggle. It can help decisively in the decentralization and rearticulation of society the nineties have made the order of the day, by lending them a sense of socialist character and organization. It is a positive development that organizations dealing with a variety of basic social questions, such as those of consumers, proliferate. And it would be a great achievement if the social organizations were, in turn, to influence the state economic enterprises by initiating new ways of sharing decisions and responsibilities in this fundamental field of reproduction of national life. Civil society can be the vehicle of social diversity, not only as a means for satisfying basic needs but also as an enrichment of a national identity that is linked to socialism, embodying as it does a diverse people that has experienced solidarity and possesses strong sentiments of postcapitalist community. Civil society can cover with its organizational and political cultures spaces being left empty by the state, not so much to compete with the state but rather to participate in forms of revolutionary power in which the state should also be instrumental. Perhaps in this way, the necessities imposed by the crisis of the nineties favor a process that should have been natural to all forms of socialist transition. The popular elements of the national culture can be an important factor in this endeavor, contributing to its effectiveness and, above all, to its legitimacy.

In the face of the kind of economic determinism that advises us to sit and wait—in effect, a philosophy of surrender to capitalism—the Cuban option is *to begin from the realities in which we live in order to force them to give better results than what can be expected from their simple reproduction.* This is possible only through conscious, organized actions that mobilize the social forces we can still count on, their interests, their ideals, and their project. A national identity that does not renounce the heritage of the past decades but that is capable of revising itself from within, without lies or cover-ups, would be an extraordinary force, because of the profound anchorage that identity has in the people and because of its capacity to lift us above narrow interests to prefigure utopias and to summon us to give a more transcendent sense to life and to the search for well-being and happiness.

Havana, September–October 1998

Signs After the Last Shipwreck

Margarita Mateo Palmer

> An island is a perpetual promise for the imagination. A promise which
> is met and which is like a reward after a long and tiring exertion.
> —María Zambrano

In 1994, in Tenerife, there was a conference of Cuban writers who
lived both on and away from the island, hosted by the Menéndez y Pelayo
International University, to discuss Caribbean culture. The dialogue, at first
cautious, became increasingly more fluid until it culminated in a ritual of
jingled black coins under a ceiba tree to the sound of the "calabazón," a kind
of conga drum that paraphrased in its rhythm a fragment of the paper presented by Antonio Benítez Rojo. During those days of 1994, the situation for
those of us who lived on the island was extremely precarious, and on top
of the dire economic necessities that besieged us daily there was the sadness of seeing family and friends opt for the difficult path of emigration. Not
long afterwards, this tendency would culminate in the so-called exodus of
the *balseros*, or rafters, which would take place that same year.

The popular joke that asks the last person who leaves Cuba to turn
off the searchlight above Morro Castle in Havana would acquire a special

boundary 2 29:3, 2002. Copyright © 2002 by Duke University Press.

connotation, more somber than funny, in the darkness of a blacked out city where so many destinies were debated in anguish. The feelings of loss, nostalgia, even of uprooting were also shared by those of us who remained behind as we became aware how the landscape of the city, the meaning of our customary walks, the emotional value of certain places changed with so many absences.

Meditating on insularity during that conference in the Canary Islands through the voice of the Spanish writer María Zambrano, brought to us by Gaston Baquero, one of the poets present there, I wrote the following lines, which belong to the long Latin American tradition of the utopia:

> Half-glimpsed in the mists of distance, since it is not found anywhere except in legend, there appears only to hide again in the sea, the Non Trovada (Not Found), the unforeseen island of the Canary Archipelago as sought after as it is imagined. Unreal and yearned for space where the dreams of visionaries—shipwrecked or not—converge, the island of doubtful existence shows itself only fleetingly in the distance to remain covered in the mystery which veils it, like the sign of the smallest opening towards the world of the unknown. Fugitive island, it seems to show us in its fleeting epiphany the possibility of a journey similar to the one undertaken by the old shamans of the American continent through the agency of their sacred plants.
>
> The Canary Island legend of the hidden island derives in good measure from the archetypical meaning traditionally accorded the insular: a refuge against the assault of the sea of the unconscious, a protected place of purity and stability in the face of the tide of instincts, a center of solitude and meditation where the ebb and flow of the mundane can transmute itself into the secret of the golden flower.
>
> But the myth of the inaccessible island also becomes confused with the story of the pilgrimages initiated to find it, thus reaching that point where the image impels history to incarnate it in an unforeseeable way. The long tradition that associates insularity with utopia— the island of the Fragrance, of the Siren, the Lucky Islands, the Fortunate Ones, Atlantis, Ultima Thule—constitutes a strong cultural heritage for the inhabitant of the islands, a heritage that also drives history onwards in a direction sometimes glimpsed by rationalists and delirious visionaries alike.
>
> The very nature of insular geography will always offer the vision of a horizon lost in the distance. Frontiers of water, the sense of limit-

lessness in the incommensurable presence of the sea, the hunger for space provoked by that plenitude of space that expands the sight: what is clear is that the sea, in its constant flow, awakes in us contrary longings. Meditating on insularity in *A Summer in Tenerife*, Dulce María Loynaz writes:

> The worst of the prisons is the one that stands near the sea. Because the sea, in a form of supplication similar to that suffered by Tantalus, offers the prisoner the widest of horizons, and through the untamable nature of its waves, continually suggests the idea of freedom.[1]

The sea is indeed an objective limit for the inhabitant of the islands or of the coast, but at the same time it suggests—in a paradox familiar to the islander—the notion of infinitude when the gaze is lost in an unattainable distance. This duality of the meaning of insularity—proximity and distance, enclosure and freedom, conflict and ease, concentration and expansion—will always point back to an awareness of distance—the physical tangency of the limit—which can be directed inside, seeking withdrawal in the face of the vastness of the landscape—"the insular being lives towards within" observed José Lezama Lima in his dialogue with the Spanish poet Juan Ramón Jiménez—, but also outwards, in an eagerness to break the isolation and to make up for by means of the journey or the imagination that other space that is not accessible to the islander. The gaze fixed on the horizon can lead to mirages, to a replacement of what is not there by force of the imagination.

Space of desire, sign of adventure, land of utopias, islands seem to reflect in the waters that surround them the stellar map transmuted into terrestrial possibility: a promise still not fulfilled, but sketched and converted into image . . .

Today, looking at the horizon of the sea from my city, always cloudless, without a single boat in the distance, where it is no longer possible to imagine, like Saint-John Perse, the sails of sailboats on the sea as on a sky, since for a long time sailboats have not crossed this seascape that is, nevertheless, populated by the invisible and fragile embarkations of the *balseros* fleeing to Florida, I think that the reward for a long hardship mentioned by Zambrano takes so long to come that it seems to be condemned

1. Dulce María Loynaz, *Un verano en Tenerife* (Havana: Letras Cubanas, 1994).

to not exceed its condition of promise: an illusion that disappears like the *Non Trovada* the closer we get to it, to linger on the horizon like a hope that reveals itself in its stubborn negation only to embody itself in the real.

If the final decade of the past century meant for Cubans an agonizing daily struggle for basic survival—in the desolate landscape of a city that seemed to collapse with every May downpour—today a change is apparent, a slight movement of recovery from a fall that seemed to have no end; but some cracks have also appeared—for example, the new and diverse social inequalities that seem to form an indispensable part of this recovery—in the project that for years encouraged us to renounce present comforts in the name of a time to come. What has also changed, then, is the nature of our gaze: The cracks, before imperceptible in the face of the vastness of the landscape, were always there, it was just that the eye, accustomed to looking at things in too grand a scale—so much so that it lost itself in the horizon—did not notice them. But that very dream, united with the force that naturally springs from injustice, superimposed itself on the desolate landscape that has accompanied for so many years a country blockaded and subjected to attacks of all sorts, most of which come directly from the most powerful nation in the contemporary world. This dream, then, helped us to keep swimming in the midst of the shipwreck, and not only with the goal of reaching the shore simply to die there.

If in the urban landscape of Havana the ruins have already begun to be removed or coexist, waiting to be restored alongside new buildings, the spiritual landscape, on the other hand, still retains the marks of intimate collapses: These downfalls cannot be raised up so easily since they form part of a scale of values that has been significantly damaged. Part of this damage comes not only from the overwhelming experience of misery, always reductive and spiritually impoverishing, but also from the loss of dreams and of the certainties on which those dreams had been constructed.

Nevertheless, when I was asked in an interview some years ago about the end of utopias and the negation of the future in the name of living in the present, I answered:

> I do not see anything alarming in this desire of wanting to exhaust the present and live it with all possible intensity. The full vindication of a now so many times denied in favor of a splendid but all too distant future does not seem to me to be a goal worthy of reproach. Here and now, not there and later. Especially when that later has come so many times in shadow and not in resplendent light.
>
> This does not imply a renunciation of the possibility of project-

ing the future but, more modestly perhaps, measuring with less arrogance our possibilities and, above all, not at the cost of converting the present into an endless succession of renunciations. To affirm individual tastes, to give a more deserving place to pleasure, to erode homogeneity, to recover the trivial, to, in sum, admit the heterogeneous—because the same was already admitted—, the pleasant—because the unpleasant was already subscribed to—, the immanently and pleasingly superfluous—because the boringly transcendental and profound were already accepted—, if only as ways of escaping an inflexible teleological order, to do all this does not necessarily imply ignoring the future, nor denying the project of social justice: rather it is a question of affirming it. . . . The issue of utopias is more complex. But utopias are not denied, rather the Utopiiiiias—spelled like this, with a capital *U* and the same intonation as in the joke about the husband who played dominoes while his wife . . . It is true that we have put the metanarratives under erasure, that we reject cities built of smoke, that we have turned our backs on unviable projects, but the possibility of imagining, dreaming, transforming, projecting what has been called a better world has not been closed down, although now it must be pursued in another way and with our feet more firmly planted on the ground.[2]

I would still subscribe to these ideas today, but with much less enthusiasm. If for most of us it is no longer a simple matter of survival, since we made it into the new century alive, and in one way or another found the means—unstable, uncertain, precarious, transitory, but in the last instance, effective—to find an individual solution that allows us to satisfy basic material necessities, nevertheless the new picture is not especially comforting. Limited possibilities of participation in decisions that affect national life, the reiterated homogeneity of a univocal ideological discourse, the continuing lack of information—not only about international affairs but also about our own insular reality—the repetition ad infinitum of old and new slogans, the impoverishing redundancy of a handful of political ideas produce a negative oversaturation and fatigue that do not stimulate reflection or creativity. If in the nineties a greater space for freedom of expression in the literary field was achieved, and currently texts are published that, ten years ago, it would have been unthinkable to see in print on the island, this space, at the moment, seems destined not to transcend itself.

2. Margarita Mateo Palmer, *Ella escribía postcrítica* (Havana: Editorial Abril, 1995), 52–53.

Beyond our own internal contradictions, the events taking place in the rest of the world, where increasingly the hegemony of the few is sustained by the misery and unhappiness of the many, do not leave much room for optimism. Nor would I want to lose sight of the fact that Cuba has never stopped being a part of this historically looted world that has seen its misfortunes increase in the course of the past century. So, although the island of utopia can seem increasingly distant and insubstantial, situated as it is in a world system increasingly hostile toward "the wretched of the earth," in which egoism is a condition that overruns possibilities for personal choice, I desire, as in the well-known poem by Aimé Césaire, to share my destiny with those who dwell, on earth, as if on the dark side of the moon: one, perhaps basic, way of not renouncing a dream of collective fulfillment, even when it is no longer possible to believe, socially speaking, in the redemptive explosion with which Césaire's poem concludes.

I return, then, to some lines of my own on Césaire written shortly after my trip to the Canary Islands, in an exercise of recovery of memory that may help me to recover my native island in its exact geographical location in order to superimpose it over the image of the utopias that seem to proliferate on this side of the world:

The Recovered Island

That I am twice yours: in the farewell and in the return.
—César Vallejo

The possibility of a return to one's native land after a long absence, during which a new affective and cultural world that compensates the loss has been constructed, but that, with time, becomes an island closed to the new codes of identity that now seem absolutely necessary for someone who has been born again in a different space, is a difficult and painful dilemma. The one who returns is no longer the same as the one who left, nor can his or her gaze on the recovered land be the same. For Aimé Césaire, who does not leave his island forever, but rather is temporarily absent from it, the return implies vertiginous changes: from a Paris of light and noise to a dark island, lost in the waters of the Caribbean Sea. The choice is heartrending, above all if the person who chooses to return has already suffered the uprooting involved in making an unknown space his or her own. Once this other space has been conquered—in the case of Césaire brilliantly—, to return is to look back in order to retrace a road already traveled and to renounce a path that could lead to new adventures.

The dilemma, then, appears when one decides to leave, not one's native land, but the distant land, and as one looks ahead the horizon feels closed off beforehand and one's hopes are mutilated, since the very space one travels toward is negatively marked:

> When dawn fades, fragile inlets reappear, the
> famished Antilles pearled by smallpox, the Antilles
> dynamited by alcohol, run aground in the mud of
> this bay, sinisterly failed in the dust of this city.[3]

The return implies then exposing oneself to the contagion of the sick islands and willingly renouncing a possibility of individual salvation for the sake of a sense of belonging that is also acceptance of the common destiny:

> To depart . . . I would arrive young and open in this
> country that is my own and I would say to it:
> "Embrace me without fear. If I only know how to
> speak, I will speak for you."
> And I would say to it again:
> "My mouth will be the mouth of your misfortunes
> which have no mouth to speak, my voice the
> freedom of those other voices that fall silent in the
> prison of despair."
> And returning I would say to myself:
> "And above all my body and also my soul, avoid
> crossing your arms in the sterile attitude of the
> spectator, since life is not a show, a sea of pain is
> not a stage, a man who shouts is not a bear who
> dances . . ."[4]

The reencounter then will be with the native land, but also with the most damaged part of the subject, with that dark side of his identity, which, from not being illuminated and ventilated on the surface would impede the curing of the self. A rite of purification and heal-

3. Aimé Césaire, *Poemas* (Havana: Casa de las Américas, 1969), 3.
4. Césaire, *Poemas*, 15.

ing that starts from the recovery of the most lacerated areas of the island-body and opens itself out toward the rest of the archipelago and the world, Césaire's poem raises itself up from degraded and abject materials in order to affirm a sense of belonging that, far from excluding these materials, prioritizes them to pose an image of the insular against the European vision of the islands as quiet spots of peace and the sign of utopias:

> What belongs to me, these many thousands of
> moribund creatures who rotate unceasingly in the
> pumpkin head of an island, and what is also mine,
> the archipelago bent like a desire uneasy at
> negating, one could say, a maternal anxiety to
> protect that most delicate tenuousness which
> separates one America from the other . . .[5]

In this unreserved acceptance, this anguished search in the abysses of a sick disassociated consciousness is the key for the subsequent liberation of the subalternized subject. The sick parts of the self are incorporated when, reaching bottom in its descent into hell, the subject will transmute the total acceptance of itself in the energy required to initiate an ascending cycle. Having overcome the most difficult tests, nothing will ever be able to damage again the self which has faced that which is most difficult, for it will be drawing strength from its own weakness. The journey from light to darkness, then, reconciles the poet with a knowledge that will make his self invulnerable and will allow him to ascend toward the dark center of the magnificent insular night, where he is fused with nature and attains the cosmic dimension of his liberation.

In his essay "End of the Century: Reflections from the Periphery," Hugo Achugar, paraphrasing Cioran, writes that "an immense dose of disillusion is needed to be able to live in the periphery without utopia," and he proposes a notion of the periphery as the space of utopian skepticism, meaning a place "from which to think about the world knowing that for a very long time we will not be inhabited by the gods of the contemporary Parnassus."[6] This disillusioned and passive vision, which seems to invite us to

5. Césaire, *Poemas*, 16, 17.
6. Hugo Achugar, "Fin de siglo: Reflexiones desde la periferia," in *Postmodernidad en la*

a sterile meditation, from the back seats, so to speak, on the performance taking place on the stage of history, is not, in my opinion, an encouraging alternative. I prefer to think that it is possible to develop from this part of the world a creative thought that articulates some dreams in a viable project and participates in an active way in attempting to achieve their actualization.

From this perspective, the disenchantment characteristic of postmodernity—which acquires peculiar characteristics in the current Cuban situation—reveals at the same time a hopeful sign when it allows for a lessening of expectations to more modest, but, for that very reason, also more viable scales, more capable of incarnating themselves in the real. As Norbert Lechner notes, "Disenchantment is, more than a loss of illusions, a reinterpretation of desires."[7] This reinterpretation of desires is, of course, conditioned by the objective possibilities that make it possible to measure the range of dreams. At the same time, the faith required for dreams to renew themselves—above all when one has had the bitter experience of seeing some of them transform themselves into nightmares—does not come alive by magic. As Graziella Pogolotti says, "Conviction is not a beautiful gift bestowed at birth by some fairy godmother. It is found in the debate between dreams and reality, won through the bitter toll taken by daily labor."[8] From this daily labor, counterpointed by the necessary contradictions of any process of renovation, should arise the projects that now are envisioned as evanescent.

After the shipwreck, the waters return to the monotony of a gentle rhythm. It is the moment of collecting the splintered remains of the boats, the remains that the sea returns to the shore, and of gazing once more at the horizon, naked above the now diminished fold of the waves, to find in the clear sky the signs that once again invite us to recommence the journey. In these circumstances, it is proper to look again at the maps that have not been destroyed by the storm, adjust the compass, and begin to draw the new cartography that will guide us on our way in the changed landscape.

periferia: Enfoques latinoamericanos de la nueva teoría cultural, ed. Hermann Herling-haus and Monica Walker (Berlin: Langer, 1994), 254.

7. Norbert Lechner, "A Disenchantment Called Postmodernism," in *The Postmodern Debate in Latin America*, ed. John Beverley, José Oviedo, and Michael Aronna (Durham, N.C., and London: Duke University Press, 1995), 148.

8. Graziella Pogolotti, "Art, Bubbles, Utopia," in *Bridging Enigma: Cubans on Cuba*, a special issue of *South Atlantic Quarterly* 96, no. 1 (winter 1997): 180.

Three Poems

Nancy Morejón

Translated by Dawn Duke

Those Who Go

They are going.
With no other recourse now, they are going
toward the night.
      Desperate,
A boat will come for them,
with no answer. Above,
the stars, with nothing to say.
And below our coastal patrol,
with its monotonous step,
will not end the nightmare.
For hours we have been looking at them face to face
through the iron grille of a make-believe garden.
It rains ink from the heavens.
They are going. They are going.

boundary 2 29:3, 2002. Copyright © 2002 by Duke University Press.

Something is about to be born.
They are going. They are going.
With larvae, with rats, with sea foam.
They are going. They are going.
Something is about to die.

NEXUS

Destinations . . .
was the first word
and already he didn't want to continue
with the rest:
Travel and travelers are two things I loathe—
and yet here I am,
about to tell the story of my expeditions.

That was how the manuscript began
Claude Lévi-Strauss
would later turn into
the vast introduction to *Tristes Tropiques.*
Sad tropics in stories about the poor world,
silent tropics, drunk with sun or fog.
. . . and yet here I am,
about to tell the story of my expeditions.

He stopped reading that first page
and rested his eyes
on an abandoned skiff at the pier.
There was a pale light,
as if he were not in Havana;
like the light of a tunnel
fleeing toward the Baltic Sea,
to meet soft, white Nordic snows;
like a black light
that would try to come out
almost any other dawn.
He walked along the Alameda de Paula.
He almost touches the dark masts of the harbor.
An enormous line of ships wishes him good morning.
His wandering soul had landed there, inadvertently,

next to the scows
and the little skiff
and a great drunken ship called NEXUS,
all balancing themselves on the water under the steady rain.

He walked along the Alameda de Paula.
It was a gray September.
A rice-like water
ran between the paving stones,
and he made out, in the distance,
the blue cap of that stevedore,
son of Tito and Brígida,
conceived on the turbines of Ciego de Avila,
Felipe Morejón Noyola,
agile sailor and proud black man
of undecipherable lineage,
carrying empty sacks
as he walked along the Alameda de Paula;
tying up ropes wet by the sea,
and more ropes wet by the sea,
along the Alameda;
oh, sad tropics;
whistling lost in thought in front of
a certain ship called NEXUS,
anchored in the memory
of the few passersby he could see.

But what matters now
are not the dreams of that stevedore
of the sad tropics;
what matters
is not the headless wandering phantom
who tries to take refuge in the doorway of the union hall;
what matters
aren't the thick eyebrows of Aracelio Iglesias,
king of the cargo hold and friend of the dawn,
walking along the Alameda;
what matters, oh sad tropics,
is not his colorless hat,
but rather his raised hands,

once more clamoring in a mute cry,
oh sad tropics.
over the oil stains,
which the waterline of the NEXUS
stretches between the waters.

Manjuarí

A little fish called a manjuarí comes into my dream.
Its sad eyes seem to want to ask me a question.
It swings its tail in front of my eyes, which are also sad.
What will become of us, manjuarí,
you who have come into my sleep
after crossing centuries and centuries,
centuries of centuries, amen,
and managing to endure,
avoiding arrows, traps,
and nets?
My eyes and yours asking
the reason for this encounter
and this moment which is better
though less brilliant than your scales
and your dreamlike, restless, eternal tail.
What does it matter how long this moment lasts
if the time of dreams
has propelled you toward me,
phosphorescent against the bitter cyclone
the exterminating angel brought
in the midst of the muffled bells of a shipwreck?
A polyhedron gathers us up in its light.
The two of us seeking the deepest seas of Cuba,
the great carpet of the Caribbean,
without a thought for the fisherman's silent boat
or the squadrons of armed ships.
Manjuarí, thank you for giving me wings,
and for having left the invincible silver of your body
to cover my feet.

Alien-Own/Own-Alien: Globalization and Cultural Difference

Gerardo Mosquera

1

There is a general concern that globalization will impose homogenized, cosmopolitan cultural patterns built on Eurocentric foundations,
which inevitably flatten, reify, and manipulate cultural differences. This fear
has serious grounds. There is no doubt that the transnational expansion of
our age requires languages, institutions, and international functions in order
to make possible communication on a global scale.

Globalization is possible only in a world that has been previously
reorganized by colonialism. What is feared most is a planetary radicaliza-
tion toward a homogenized international culture, launched from the United
States. Standing out is the powerful diffusion of North American pop culture,
whose inventiveness, dynamism, and networks of circulation and marketing
have spread its influence throughout the world. Already at the end of the
thirties, Clement Greenberg was saying that kitsch was the first universal
culture.[1] The consolidation of English as the language of international com-

1. Clement Greenberg, "Avant-Garde and Kitsch" (1939), in his *Art and Culture: Critical
Essays* (Boston: Beacon Press, 1961), 12.

boundary 2 29:3, 2002. Copyright © 2002 by Duke University Press.

munication on a global scale is causing great concern. Today, even dogs are trained in English, and it is said that they understand this language better than any other.

It isn't simply a matter of language, communication, and mass culture. These processes are also woven into "high" culture. When the fine arts are discussed in very general terms, people tend to use the terms *international artistic language* or *contemporary artistic language* as abstract constructions that derive from the type of art-crit English in which today's "international" discourses are spoken.[2] Both terms are highly problematic. Frequently, being "international" or "contemporary" in art is nothing but the echo of being exhibited in elite spaces on the small island of Manhattan.

By the thirties, a sort of language of modernism had been forged, the result of a paradoxical assemblage of the various ruptures produced by the historical vanguards. A stock of resources had been established, drawing from various tendencies that artists were using, combining, or transforming at will. The explosion of pop, performance, minimalism, conceptualism, and other orientations that were later called "postmodern" produced another rupture. But by the nineties, a sort of "postmodern international language" was instituted, prevailing over the so-called international scene even while its coinage as a dominant code denied de facto the pluralist perspective of postmodernity.

The extreme case is the figure of the international installation artist, a global nomad who roams from one international exhibit to another, his or her suitcase packed with the elements for a future work of art or the tools to produce it in situ. This figure, an allegory of the processes of globalization, represents a key rupture with the figure of the artist-craftsman linked to a studio in which the work of art is produced. Now the artists export themselves. Their work is closer to that of the manager or engineer who travels constantly to attend to specific projects and businesses. The studio, that ancestral, Vulcanian site linked with the artist, has become more a laboratory for projects and design than for production. Thus the physical link of demiurge–studio–work of art, which associated each of the three elements within a specific space and, furthermore, with a place and its genius, is broken. This type of artwork and methodology has a genetic relationship to the international postminimalist-postconceptualist language. With them, a kind of circulation based on biennials, thematic shows, and other forms of collective *global* exhibits is facilitated.

2. See Gerardo Mosquera, "¿Lenguaje internacional?" *Lápiz* (Madrid) 121 (April 1986): 12–15.

The exclusivist and teleological legitimization of the "international language" of art acts as a mechanism of exclusion toward other languages and discourses. In many art institutions—as among many art specialists and collectors—prejudices based on a sort of axiological monism prevail. In a catch-22, this circle tends to regard with suspicions of illegitimacy art from the peripheries that endeavors to speak the "international language." When it speaks properly, it is usually accused of being derivative; when it speaks with an accent, it is disqualified for its lack of propriety toward the canon.

Frequently, works of art are not looked at—they are asked to present their passports, which tend not to be in order, for these works depend on processes of hybridization, appropriation, re-signification, neologism, and invention as a response to today's world. This art is asked to present an originality related to traditional cultures—which is to say, oriented toward the past—or to show an abstract, pure originality toward the present. In both cases, such art is required to state its context rather than to participate in a general artistic practice that at times only refers to art itself.

The appropriation of modernism by the peripheries turns out to be interesting within this order of things. This appropriation signifies an active construction of modernism itself, diversifying its language, meaning, and aims. But we don't usually tend to consider a global modernism that reacts to different contextual situations. Thus, José Clemente Orozco is always discussed within Mexican muralism, never as one of the great artists of expressionism. In this subtraction of interpretation, the positions of the central powers, which confine difference to the ghetto, coincide strangely with nationalism, which encloses difference behind a wall.

Globalization, the postmodern opening, and the pressure of multiculturalism have moved us toward a greater pluralism. But in general, and above all in elite circles, globalization has responded less to a new consciousness than to a tolerance based on paternalism, quotas, and *political correctness*.

The new attraction toward otherness has allowed for a greater circulation and legitimation of art from the peripheries, above all as channeled through specific circuits. But too frequently value has been placed on art that explicitly manifests difference or that better satisfies the expectations of otherness held by neoexoticism. This attitude has stimulated the *self-othering* of some artists who, consciously or unconsciously, have tended toward a paradoxical self-exoticism.

The case of "international language" in art reveals a hegemonic construct of globalism more than a true globalization, which is understood as generalized participation. Today we have both exclusive mainstream circuits and hegemonic alternative ones, with their own mainstream and antimainstream establishments, the latter being also exclusive, although broader than their counterparts. Both legitimate their own field, and actively interact. Dominant major and minor circuits of museums, galleries, and publications (what we might call the "universalizers") construct the "world art scene," even without intending to. This system claims to legitimize specific practices without conceiving international or contemporary culture as a plural game board of multiple and relative interactions.

The rhetoric regarding globalization has abounded in the illusory triumph of a transterritorial world, one that is decentralized, omniparticipatory, engaged in multicultural dialogues, with currents flowing in all directions. In reality, globalization is not as global as it appears. Or, to paraphrase Orwell, it is far more global for some than for others—the majority. Even the Internet, the paradigm of free universal and individual communication, connects only a small percentage of the world's population. The speed of the avenues of optic fibers and satellites makes us forget the congested avenues of the megalopolis and the flight corridors, or the critical lack of avenues and highways in a large part of the world. Cyberspace may be a virtual paradise, a designer drug for escaping the global cybermess.

It should be obvious that globalization does not consist of an effective interconnection of the whole planet by means of an interwoven grid of communication and exchange. Rather, it is a radial system, extending from diverse centers of power of varying sizes into multiple and highly diversified economic zones. Such a structure implies the existence of large zones of silence, barely connected to one another or only indirectly, via the neometropolises. This axial structure of globalization and regions of silence constitute the economic, political, and cultural networks of the planet, motivating intense migratory movements in search of connection.

There has been little progress in South-South relations, other than shared economic recessions. Globalization has certainly improved communications to an extraordinary extent, has dynamized and pluralized cultural circulation, and has provided a more pluralist consciousness. Yet it has done so by following the very channels delineated by the economy, thus reproducing in good measure the existing structures of power.

The lack of South-South horizontal interaction is a colonial legacy barely modified. This situation compels the peripheries to undertake stronger efforts to establish and develop horizontal circuits that act as cultural life spaces. Such circuits will contribute to pluralizing culture, internationalizing it in the real sense, legitimizing it in their own terms, constructing new epistemes, unfolding alternative actions.

On the other hand, pluralism can be a prison without walls. Jorge Luis Borges once told the story about the best labyrinth: the desert's incommensurable openness, from where it is difficult to escape. Abstract or controlled pluralism, as we see in some "global" shows, can weave a labyrinth of indetermination confining the possibilities of real, active diversity.

We are living a postutopian epoch of reformism that seeks change within what exists, instead of *changer la vie*. But many transformations are taking place in silence. Some come out of a Lampedusan strategy of power establishments, aimed to change so that everything remains the same. Power today strives not to confront diversity but to control it. However, mutations also correspond to the international activity of new social and cultural subjects, postcolonial processes, massive urbanization in Africa, Asia, and Latin America, with its cultural and social implications, extensive migrations all over the world, with their cultural displacements and heterogenization, and other processes from "the bottom up."

To affirm cultural identity in tradition, understood in a sense of "purity," is a colonial heritage. It has led to disastrous cults of "authenticity," "roots," and "origins," above all in the years after decolonization, when the new countries attempted to affirm their identities and interests against the metropolises and their imposed Westernization. Now the tendency is to see identity performatively, according to how each subject *makes* contemporaneity. Wole Soyinka once said that a tiger doesn't proclaim its tigerness: it springs.

Candice Breitz has said, with regard to the realm of traditional culture in South Africa, "Social change can lead to the imbalance of certain African 'traditions' but inevitably new and dynamic forms will emerge in their place. Nevertheless, that doesn't mean that these traditions must or ought to develop along the same lines by which the West has defined its own progress."[3]

Paradoxically, the global world is becoming the world of difference. Globalization's aims of conversion and domination also imply more generalized access. If globalization seeks to convert the "Other," its availability also facilitates its use for the "Other's" own, different ends, transforming the international metaculture from within. If that metaculture retains its hegemonic character, the subaltern cultures are taking advantage of the metaculture's broadcasting capability to transcend local frameworks. Used from

3. Candice Breitz, "Why African Avant-Garde Artists Have Never Existed," *Atlántica* (Las Palmas de Gran Canaria) 11 (fall 1995): 60.

the other side, cultural globalization has allowed the dissemination of multiple perspectives and has itself undergone adjustments in line with these perspectives.

Furthermore, every process of homogenization on a large scale—even when it succeeds in smoothing out differences—generates other, new differences within itself, like Latin shattering into the Romance languages. This is evident in the heterogeneity that immigrants are producing in the megalopolises.

A truly global diffusion and evaluation of culture is possible only through a multidirectional web of interactions. We need to organize South-South and South-North circuits able to pluralize what we understand by "international art," "international art language," and the "international art scene," or even what is "contemporary." Equally important is the construction of international and contemporary art and culture in a true international way: in differences and *from* differences. That is, enacting difference rather than representing it, thus actively fashioning "international art language" in multiple ways.

The fact that artists from every corner of the world, including Cuba, now exhibit internationally reflects only a quantitative internationalization, but numbers are not the issue. The question again is whether we are contributing or not to the transformation of a hegemonic and restrictive situation into active plurality, instead of being digested by that situation.

It is necessary to cut the global pie not only with a variety of knives but also with a variety of hands, and then to share it accordingly. This is neither revolution nor political correctness: It is a need for all if we don't want an endogamic culture. The key point is who makes the cultural decision, and in whose benefit is it taken.[4]

2

In "Musique Nègre" (1931), the Haitian poet Léon Laleau laments his sense of alienation in trying to express in French—the language and culture in which he had been educated—his African roots:

4. Guillermo Bonfil Batalla, "Lo propio y lo ajeno: Una aproximación al problema del control cultural," in *La cultura popular*, ed. Adolfo Colombres (Mexico City: Premia, 1987), 79–86; and "La teoría del control cultural en el estudio de procesos étnicos," *Anuario Antropológico* (University of Brasilia), no. 86 (1988): 13–53. See also Ticio Escobar, "Issues in Popular Art," in *Beyond the Fantastic: Contemporary Art Criticism from Latin America*, ed. Gerardo Mosquera (London: Institute of International Visual Arts; Cambridge: MIT Press, 1995), 91–113.

And this hopelessness has no equal
To tame, with the words from France
This heart, which has come to me from Senegal?

Et ce désespoir à nul autre égal
D'apprivoiser, avec des mots de France,
Ce coeur qui m'est venu du Sénégal?

The meaning is more complicated if we think that Laleau's Africa, like that of negritude, came to be a substitutive illusion for the European illusion, or, rather, an invention, in an effort to construct Caribbean identity from components of African origin, participants in a syncretic culture.[5] These components were used to confront the Francophilia imposed by colonial domination, establishing a difference from the subaltern non-Western side. Of course, the invention is not enacted from the outside: It comes from a transatlantic Africanicity lived and transfigured as an active factor of Caribbean cultures. Laleau imagines an Africa as part of the West, although conflictual and subaltern.

In any case, the attitude of the poem is passive, allowing French to domesticate difference. Beginning in the late thirties, writers of negritude, especially Aimé Césaire, were concerned with forcing the European language to culturally express a hybrid context, where very active non-European ingredients could participate—those from Africa and Asia as well as those resulting from the transformations of European cultures in America. Césaire said that he had wanted "to make an Antillian French, a black French that, while remaining French, would bear the black mark."[6] This decolonizing operation gives a communicable voice to the excluded and to difference.

Shortly before Césaire, in the same epoch, Nicolás Guillén, of Cuba, introduced rhythms, intonations, sonorities, and airs of African ancestry into classic Spanish. Some of his poems, according to Alfred Melon and Desiderio Navarro, possess a phonic texture characteristic of Yoruba, Kikongo, Efik, and other African languages. Navarro concludes that "by speaking Spanish, the poet is also speaking in a black-African language."[7] Already the tonal

5. See Jean Bernabé, Patrick Charnoiseau, and Raphael Confiant, *Éloge de la Creolité* (Paris: Gallimard, 1989), 20.
6. Aimé Césaire, interviewed by René Depestre, in his introduction to Césaire, *Poemas* (Havana: Casa de las Américas, 1969), xx.
7. Alfred Melon-Degras, "Guillén: poeta de la síntesis," in his *Realidad, poesía e ideología* (Havana: Ediciones Unión, 1973), 25–61; Desiderio Navarro, "Sonido y sentido en Nicolás

character of the Bantú and Sudanese languages influences the manner in which we Cubans pronounce and intonate Spanish.

This phonic synthesis participates in the ideology of cultural *mestizaje* that lays the foundation for the idea of a Cuban national identity that Guillén's poetry helps to construct:

> We are together from far away,
> young, old,
> blacks and whites, all mixed;
> one ruling, the other ruled,
> all mixed

> Estamos juntos desde muy lejos,
> jóvenes, viejos,
> negros y blancos, todo mezclado;
> uno mandando y otro mandado,
> todo mezclado

This position coincides with that of the ethnologist Fernando Ortiz, who compared Cuban identity to *ajiaco*—a stew of very diverse ingredients, in which the broth that results from the mixture represents an integrated nationality, a synthesis.[8] The problem with the idea of cultural *mestizaje* is that it can be used to create the image of a fair and harmonious fusion, disguising not only differences but also contradictions and flagrant inequalities under the myth of an integrated nation. This is the problem with all notions based on synthesis, which tends to erase imbalances and conflicts. What remains to be seen is which ingredients each puts into the *ajiaco* and who gets the largest serving. Moreover, it is necessary to emphasize that, apart from the broth of synthesis, there remain bones and hard meat that never dissolve, although they support the substance of the broth. The paradigm of the *ajiaco*, as it refers to hybridization, would have to be complemented with that of "moros con cristianos" ("Moors with Christians"), a Cuban dish of rice and black beans cooked together, as a symbol of multiculturalism.[9] Both interconnect: They must be eaten together. And to drink? Perhaps Coca Cola. . . .

Guillén," in his *Ejercicios del criterio* (Havana: Unión de Escritores y Artistas de Cuba, 1988), 11–32.

8. Fernando Ortiz, "Los factores humanos de la cubanidad," in *Orbita de Fernando Ortiz* (Havana: Unión de Escritores y Artistas de Cuba, 1973), 154–57.

9. See Gerardo Mosquera, "Africa in the Art of Latin America," *Art Journal* 51, no. 4 (winter 1992): 30–38.

Another difficulty is that the model of hybridization leads to thinking about intercultural processes as a mathematical equation, a division and sum of elements, the result of which is a tertium quid, the outcome of the mix. This kind of model obscures cultural creation, which is not necessarily the fruit of the blend but rather an invention or a specific use of a foreign element.

To force French and Spanish to speak African is, in reality, to empower them, enrich them, make them capable of communicating other meanings corresponding to other experiences, often marginal. But here again there is ambivalence, because the European languages come out winning. These achievements are appropriated by hegemonic circuits and can be used, as anthropology was, to make the tools of domination more sophisticated. Such are the disjunctions in which cultural power is settled today. Beyond, there is French that ceases to be French, when it is transformed into the numerous Creole languages of the Caribbean. But French assures writers an international diffusion, which is very important in areas where very few people are able to read. The high level of illiteracy in countries such as Haiti forces writers to produce for export.

If Laleau experienced the European language as a ball and chain, and Césaire and Guillén proposed to transform it, there are other instances in which there is little anxiety over its use from a position of alterity. The Congolese intellectual Théophile Obenga proclaimed, at the beginning of the sixties, in his poem "Tu parleras," dedicated to Césaire:

the words are their words
but the song is ours.

les mots sont leurs mots
mais le chant est nôtre

This position eliminates the conflicts over the origin of the cultural instrument and stresses instead its use. But it maintains a separation between foreign language and one's own. Today, a dialogic relationship in which the imposed language and culture are experienced as "own-alien," as Mikhail Bakhtin states in his discussion of literary polyglossia, seems more plausible.[10] Hegemonic cultural elements are not only imposed but are also assumed, reversing the schema of power by the appropriation of the instru-

10. Mikhail M. Bakhtin, "De la prehistoria de la palabra de la novela," in his *Problemas literarios y estéticos*, trans. Alfredo Caballero (Havana: Editorial Arte y Literatura, 1986), 490–91.

ments of domination.[11] In this way, for example, the syncretism in America of African deities with Catholic saints and virgins, practiced by slaves who were forced to Christianize, was not only a strategy to disguise the African gods behind the Christian icons: It implied the installation of all of them at once in a new inclusive system.

All cultures always feed on one another, be it in situations of domination or subordination. Conscious and selective *antropofágia*, or cultural cannibalism (in other words, the critical assimilation of foreign elements to incorporate them into one's own organism), proclaimed by the Brazilian modernists in the twenties, has been a constant of Latin American modernisms. *Antropofágia* as a program is not as fluid as it seems, since it is not carried out in a neutral territory but rather in one that is subordinated, with an aesthetic practice that tacitly assumes the contradictions of dependence and the postcolonial situation. In the end, who eats whom?

The flow of culture cannot always remain circulating in the same North-South direction, fixed by the structure of global power, its circuits of diffusion, and the local accommodations to these. However plausible appropriating and transculturating strategies may be, they imply an action of rebound that reproduces the hegemonic structures, even as it contests them. It is also necessary to invert the flow—not by turning it into a binary schema of transference, defying power, but by endeavoring to pluralize by enriching circulation in a truly global direction.

In her poem "Not Neither," the Nuyorrican poet Sandra María Estévez oscillates between languages and identities, constructing a "de-alienating" option that operates through the displacements between disjunction and affirmation proper to this dynamic:

> being Puertorriqueña bien But yet, not gringa either, Pero ni
> portorra, pero sí portorra too Pero ni que what am I? . . .
> Yet not being, pero soy, and not really Y somos, y como
> somos Bueno, eso sí es algo lindo Algo muy lindo.[12]

This poem is untranslatable. Furthermore, it underscores the very paradoxes endemic to translation. But it also involves a statement in favor of bilingualism and biculturalism. The key word in the poem is precisely the untranslatable one: *portorra*, a term for *Puerto Rican/Puertorriqueña*, which

11. Ticio Escobar, *El mito del arte y el mito del pueblo: cuestiones sobre arte popular* (Asunción, Paraguay: R. Peroni Ediciones, 1987), 76.
12. Sandra María Estéves, *Yerba Buena: dibujos y poemas* (Greenfield Center, N.Y.: Greenfield Review Press, 1980).

is simultaneously deprecatory and affectionate. Estévez subscribes to and simultaneously unsettles Bakhtin's "own-alien" notion, turning it around to emphasize the "alien-own."

We are living in the Era of the Hyphen: The proliferation of prefixes and hyphens highlights the difficulties of inherited language for describing contemporary nonrevolutions. Rather than invent new terms, the existing ones are combined and recycled, in a spirit of readaptation, with meaning concentrated less in words than in the connecting dialogical, transfiguring space of the hyphen. But this also represents an interaction originating from within the rupture: The hyphen unites at the same time as it separates. In a fascinating book, Gustavo Pérez Firmat has gone so far as to summarize the Cuban American condition as a "life on the hyphen."

3

I will end with two open-ended metaphors, one optimistic and the other pessimistic. You can choose the one you prefer as a conclusion. First, the optimistic one. Upon their arrival in America, the Spaniards were obsessed for years with knowing whether they were on an island or a mainland. A historian from the nineteenth century, a priest from the Cuban village of Los Palacios, tells us that when Columbus asked the indigenous people of Cuba whether that place was an island or a continent, they answered him by saying that it was "an infinite land of which no one had seen the end, although it was an island."[13] Perhaps today's currents point us toward a globe of infinite islands.

The other metaphor might be useful to discuss the issues of globalization, difference, and power. The following anecdote was told to me by the Cuban painter Julio Girona, who settled in New York City in the thirties. Once, in the early sixties, he happened to be crossing a street where people were marching in a political demonstration. The police attacked, and amidst the chaos, a cop approached Girona violently. "Nigger, get out of here!" the policeman barked. Surprised, Girona answered: "I'm not a nigger." "Okay, but go away, you dirty *Portorican!*" replied the cop, threatening him with his club. "I'm not *Portorican*: I'm a Cuban!" the artist pointed out. But the policeman ended the debate beating him, while saying, "It's all the same shit!"

13. Andrés Bernaldes, "Historia de los Reyes Católicos," in *Memorias de la Real Sociedad Patriótica de La Habana*, vol. 3 (Havana: n.p., 1837), 128. Quoted by Cintio Vitier and Fina García Marruz, *Flor oculta de poesía cubana (siglos XVIII y XIX)* (Havana: Editorial Arte y Literatura, 1978), 63.

The Body and Its Politics in Cuba of the Nineties

Magaly Muguercia

The Body Was a Festival

There was a time when Cuba was a festival and the Cuban body proclaimed itself socialist. At that time I was thirteen. Fidel and his young bearded troops crossed the island in caravans from the mountains of the east to the other side and entered Havana triumphantly. Dazzled peasants, heroes and heroines of the sierra, poured into the city. The main headquarters of the dictatorship was converted into a school and called Ciudad Libertad (Freedom City). A white dove rested on the shoulder of the leader. Soon the people (workers, intellectuals, peasants, students, housewives) wore army fatigues. In long early mornings, girls and boys stood guard, with old Mauser rifles on our shoulders, over the sites conquered by the Revolution.

Then there was an invasion in reverse: Leaving the city for the countryside were tens of thousands of young literacy teachers who climbed mountains and hiked over fields instructing those who didn't know how to read and write; but at the same time, they also learned and were transformed by their passage into unknown territory. The neighbors didn't recognize them when, a year later, they returned to their homes, thin and mus-

boundary 2 29:3, 2002. Copyright © 2002 by Duke University Press.

cular, their uniforms reddened by the earth, garlands of seeds around their necks, and with an air of confidence mixed with sadness. Enormous and varied cultural crossings engendered in the Cuba of the sixties a democratic, egalitarian, dignified, and communal body. To march to the Plaza of the Revolution was another festival. Those millions of us who spoke there with our leaders created a stage on which it seemed that history was being made for all time. City people learned to work the land and to recognize trees, animals, and strange customs. Sunday after Sunday, sweating and crushed together in precarious forms of transportation, on the verge of asphyxiation, we left the city to cut sugarcane and weed fields. I was scrawny, sixteen years old, and middle class, and with my new friends, the happy knights of the people. We were stevedores in the ports and bricklayers in the new schools, built, as the poet said, "by the same hands that caress you." And the stevedores, the bricklayers, the peasants, and the guerrilla fighters soon installed themselves at the desks of the university. We threw everyone in our world into reverse gear: We the "educated" were thick-headed, and the "humble" moved about like kings.

At the end of those years, Che was killed, and then Allende, and three generations of Cubans cried without being able to hide our tears. In a brutal way, a part of us was lost that has been missing since then: the body of a fighter that we pictured torn apart by bullets, raped, or violated, its gaze perhaps suspended and helplessly exhausted.

And it was thus that the socialist body was set up; in this friction and disorder of diverse identities, in conflict and understanding, in tensions between diverse classes, races, ages, and sexes who, for the most part, shared the same project. In the deep memory of our culture there remains, I believe, the treasure of the ductile body, expert in risk, given to solidarity, blessed with Mackandal's gift of metamorphosis, and crazy enough to take deep breaths in a truck with no windows, the Sunday truck, or on a milk train or an overloaded cart, which taught us what every good actor and dancer knows: that the organic performance, the one that produces real action (and is not necessarily realist), arises when the most difficult path is chosen; that profound coherence, which is truth in the act, touches chaos at one of its extremes.

But time passed, and some part of that ductile socialist body with the stability/instability of a loose cord, of fear and joy commingled, froze. We were taught to sacrifice invention for the sake of a myth called "unity," or, rather, "ideological firmness." From the mid-sixties on, an incipient culture of dogma came to confuse participation with speaking in chorus. The rebels and critics, meaning almost every one of us, unwillingly began a new process of learning. We were taught that the worst sin was to commit an error (it was called a "historical error"). To err was prohibited. We socialist Cubans, who were ourselves a living historical error, the scandal of the manuals of Marxism-Leninism, were prohibited from committing errors! Popular mobilization slowly began to change character, and there was no longer that feverish interchange between heterogeneous subjects, but more an ordered and linear march toward the "goal," a subjection to the structure, a delegation of the power of the multitude to those in central authority. The dance began to transform itself. The minuet began to displace the conga.

This, however, sounds very clear-cut, but it wasn't that obvious. A Cuban is a very complex, divided being, never entirely satisfied. In Cuba, it should not be forgotten that during slavery there were runaway slaves. And in the national soul there is also a runaway slave. Many a socialist runaway slave is still wandering around out there!

This idea of a socialist *cubanía* (Cuban identity), not so easily decipherable, nor as univocal as some believe, could be associated with the notion of the compound body elaborated by the North American Marxist writer Randy Martin. According to Martin, the compound body generates social scenarios in which a multiplicity of differences interlace. This requires, therefore, a theoretical instrument that helps to think the physical constitution of complex social relations. This body is not single but multiple, not a being but a principle of association that rejects the categorical division between the self and the society, between the personal and the mediated, between presence and absence.

The compound body is always/already in movement. It is the work between the differences that constitutes it. This mobile body creates scenarios of adjustment, resistance, or subversion in the face of the dominant logics. It is our potential for obedience or revolution.

Every social process consists then, for Martin, in the incarnation (flesh, desire, strength) of this multiplicity, in the in-corporation of this swarm-like dynamic. The idea of a compound body offers a way of thinking about politics (and eventually socialism) in terms of the question Martin formulates for us: How is the difference between those united in the nation to be worked out? Put another way: How to mobilize the oppositional-creative potential of the body, and promote a democratic relation between differences in such a way that that overflow of energies constructs a project, achieves some level of totality and coherence? (Here I understand the word *project* in the sense of desire, mobilized toward the accomplishment of some kind of alternative sociality.) One would have to rethink socialism, which will be socialist only if it is democratic, as a mise-en-scène and an egalitarian coordination of diverse affiliations and cultures oriented toward liberation. The critical and creative movements of the compound body generate structure and authorities, and this puts the socialist state before the paradox that the only strategy that guarantees the democratic orientation of the project, that is, the strategy of stimulating the work of the compound body, is, at the same time, the one that relativizes the state's power of control and that, therefore, also weakens the sacred character every form of power tends to attribute to itself.

And the Crack Widened

It might be useful to put beside Martin's idea of the compound body Victor Turner's well-known anthropological concept of social drama. According to Turner, social drama occurs when the flow of life in the community is interrupted by a sequence of events that alters its normalcy. This "dissident" sequence channels desires and tries to introduce values distinct from the ones consecrated by the traditional order. According to Turner (I am paraphrasing), the first phase of a social drama would be the breach (or "crack") and consists of a dissident faction materializing some transgressions (violation of a taboo, protests, behaviors that in some way alter the norm). The crack, as it widens, sets off an alarm for the legitimate order. There is a sense of uneasiness. The second phase is the crisis as such, when the community is clearly divided in two, and the leaders of one or the other band recruit followers. Then fights break out, perhaps physical confrontations and violence. Turner notes that these processes, because they imply an intense destabilizing of the social order and of the codes that allow identification of the norm, give way to a special liminal parenthesis in the life of the community. This liminality is configured as a shifting frontier zone where each value remains momentarily suspended, and anything can happen. Oscillating practices and thoughts, which mix the old and the new, consensus and outrage, proliferate. The experience of the community is tinged with ambivalence and hybridization. From the appearance of the crack and its sequel of crisis, the traditional order multiplies the confirmative rites in order to remind the community of the sacred values on which it is constructed. In the third stage, reparation, the crisis is settled or loses intensity. The confirmative rites continue, possibly accompanied by rituals of punishment, for example, public trials to disqualify the rebel faction. The fourth and last phase (which does not always occur) is schism. If it does not succeed in imposing itself, the opposing band abandons the territory, physically or symbolically; it migrates, and in the other space it will try to promote its model of alternative sociality.

In the eighties, cracks and uneasiness were more and more evident in Cuban society. Three decades of relative stability had not transpired without consequences. The potent and cohesive body was born from the festival of the sixties. Twenty years later, something gray was clearly installed in the Cuban society: sovietization, dogma, authoritarianism. With the years, the socialist festival lost its shine.

In 1986, a character in the play *Accidente*, by the Escambray theater group, said, "Lately, we have dedicated ourselves to producing steel and we have stopped producing human beings."

That same year, 1986, the Cuban state launched the so-called process of rectification of errors and negative tendencies, whose ultimate objective seemed to be a broader democratization of Cuban socialism. It was in the midst of this process (we will never know where it would have taken us) that an amazing break in the history of the twentieth century transformed all Cuban political scenarios. The Berlin Wall fell in 1989, and the Soviet Union liquidated itself in 1991. Overnight, Cuba lost 80 percent of its markets, and we were left alone, with no oil, no allies, no foreign currency, and no possibilities for imports or exports. The country, basically dependent on imports, was on the verge of collapse. A much broadened Council of State, presided over by Fidel, met daily throughout 1992 and 1993, and decided the means of distribution of the scarce material resources that remained. The survival of the country depended literally on what the most recent ship brought in its hold. This was so exactly—and dramatically—the case, that I fantasized at the time an image I can still conjure up today: an office furnished in mahogany, a very large window looking over the roofs of Old Havana, and in the background the open sea, placid and blue. From the window Fidel looks at the port with binoculars and identifies the ship that is just dropping anchor. Then, always standing, and being observed by his ministers of state, he picks up the telephone and gives instructions. He exchanges plain words with each minister, who are all very tense. Some stand. He is like Lenin at the Smolny Institute, taking the pulse of the nation, on the eve, in this case, of a catastrophe. In 1992, Cuba could acquire only a third of its usual imports, historically concentrated in food supplies and oil.

The crisis that Turner speaks about was precipitated. A high-stakes social drama began, which, as I write these pages, has not yet, in my view, ended.

In 1991 and 1992, the Cuban population lost weight in a disturbing way, and a serious epidemic of neuritis affected the vision and motor skills of thousands of people. Today, this strange illness still persists in Cuba, without being pandemic, and the state has kept in place preventive measures to fight it. Its outbreak, around 1991, is attributed to the sudden deterioration of nourishment, which touched all sectors of society, combined with the extraordinary increase in the physical expenditure required for day-to-day survival (something analogous to war situations or concentration camps, which was how much of the medical literature consulted at the time by Cuban researchers reported it). It goes without saying that the birthrate fell sharply, and since then this indicator (1.3 babies per family—who could be the .3?) has remained constant.

Of course, the United States hastened to reinforce its blockade. But what is also true is that the tragic destabilization that the potent and cohesive body of the sixties underwent at the beginning of the nineties had antecedents. Already it suffered from fissures and maladies. For decades, an endogenous dysfunction had been installing itself in the Cuban social body, which taught, and continues to teach today, the public and the private sides of our being to live separately. Frictions, sometimes very painful and always paradoxical, began to develop between the immense creative potential of the people, encouraged by the Revolution, and the structures implemented by the state. This dysfunction operated in diverse arenas—political, economic, ideological, cultural, and spiritual. Not by chance, a significant number of characters in Cuban drama and dance of the eighties committed suicide or went crazy on stage or used their naked bodies to make subversive statements. Art, in its anticipatory character, incarnated the drama of this body, on the one hand potent and cohesive, on the other divided, impaired, sometimes desperate and fragmented, subject to a profound conflict with itself.

During the first half of the nineties, theater and its public, more numerous than ever, provided a space for complex critical reflection about visceral questions of belonging and identity that, in the midst of the evident crisis, official discourse, deliberately simplistic and resistant to any kind of unauthorized problematization, left abandoned. It was in this context that a new slogan began to appear in Cuban society, apparently justified but underneath consciously disqualifying all critical thought: "This is not a time for theories."

I recall, among the dozens of performances of this period, *Fast Food*, a dance solo by the great artist Marianela Boán. The public was gathered outside a well-known theater, waiting to enter the auditorium. Suddenly, the dancer came through the doorway and displayed her thin body, which seemed to the onlookers to be charged with a strange excess of energy. She carried a dinner plate and a metal spoon, rough, prisonlike utensils, which, of course, were empty. The choreography borrowed something from those sterile objects. Her body, that of a virtuoso dancer, broke up and recomposed itself fleetingly in a minimalist combat that posed strength and assertion against tiny, microscopic movements. And this incandescent body executed at the end the horrendous, impeccable act of eating its own fingers. This final gesture concentrated all our energies, all our greed and our courage, as we watched. Pale, in black leotards, without makeup, her performance said: hunger. We all had different hungers, but we accepted the offering of her vigor and her rigor, played out on the very threshold between street and the stage.

The Deflated Bicycle

As in *Fast Food*, projected at the beginning of the nineties with incredible intensity was a socialist body that, concentrating its energy to the limit, acted in all ways imaginable in order to survive, many times with exemplary dignity. And this body, which today is no longer famished, since the country has succeeded in initiating a slow economic recovery since 1995, continues to find multiple strategies of resistance; but it cannot fully mobilize its socialist, critical, and communal potential. It does not always make the history it desires.

In 1990 and 1991, bicycles inundated the city and transformed the landscape. Distances and time changed entirely throughout the country. One went to work or to the theater by bicycle or on foot. I recall having arrived, like almost everyone else, dead tired and on foot at a performance of the *Ópera ciega* by Victor Varela in 1991. A year and a half later, in 1993, under similar circumstances, I attended the subversive *Niñita querida* by Carlos Díaz, and *Manteca*, and many other theatrical or dance performances, which we went to as if to church, seeking to take communion, on our uncomfortable, rickety possessions.

Millions of people climbed onto heavy Chinese bicycles in 1990, but, while still popular today, they aren't quite the phenomenon they were back then. In 2000, with the introduction of new economic measures that have dollarized the economy and encouraged foreign investment, there are more private and business vehicles in Havana now than in the last forty years, but public transportation continues to be inadequate, as it has been since 1989. The self-employed plumber who carries his family of four on his Chinese bike, the brilliant doctor, the engineer who is also a Popular Power delegate (one of the best), the clerk, the actress, the teacher, the researcher, my good friend (who rides 40 kilometers each way every day, which his skeleton supports good-naturedly)—all continue to ride their bikes. I would say that it is not for the love of sport that these Cuban bicycles keep rolling. The precious energy of many people is squandered under the same tropical sun that puts the satisfied tourist to sleep on our beaches. Covering dozens and dozens of kilometers each day, for more than ten years now, Cubans have become ecologists in spite of themselves. Recently, a curious new professional has been added to the caravan of bike riders: the bicycle–taxi driver (*bicitaxista*), who charges in dollars, who often has a university degree, and who, using sheer muscle power, takes the same delighted tourist of the previous scene, now wrapped in the arms of his girlfriend for hire (*jinetera*) for a ride along the Malecón, through Miramar or Old Havana. False ecology. This body produces evil. I would say that the Cuban bicycle of the nineties contaminates.

Our Hand Hurts from Waving Good-Bye So Much

Traditional historiography scorns the quotidian. Because, in fact, it can't capture the everyday, as it was. It can't re-present it. Nevertheless, there are rhythms, tensions, attacks, and convolutions—vibrations of the body that make history. Therefore, I will relate my own experiences of August 1994 on the long Havana coastline, on the wharfs of the old idyllic Almendares River, on the white beaches to the east of the capital. That summer, we swimmers had to move to one side in the water to get out of the way of the rafts of the *balseros* setting out toward the open sea. Very young navigators or whole families abandoned the island on these precarious vessels. Responding to the maneuvers to destabilize the regime plotted in Washington or Miami, the Cuban authorities did not interfere; it was all the same to them. They allowed the *balseros* to depart on their own terms and at their own risk. And our hands hurt from waving so many good-byes. We wished people we didn't know a favorable wind, people exposed to death, separated and vulnerable, beyond any political position. A whirlwind of scarcity, disillusion, and illusion threw them off the island, their skin daubed with grease against the sun on those mythological rafts, made from anything, totally picturesque and pathetic. I made myself stay there in the water, watching the *balseros*, so as to experience the concrete materiality, the blood pulse of belonging to a country, the cement that binds the nation. Brotherhood, anguish, sand, tears, profound silence, blue sky. From that moment on, in the theater performances of the nineties, actors and dancers raised their hands in farewell and gazed for a long time at the horizon. The Cuban of the nineties was always going away. His or her soul remains divided in or outside Cuba. And I say *soul* because I can't find a better way of naming this hand that hurts us and feels like it will fall off from waving so many good-byes.

The Flying Cat

The copulation of the cat with the marten
Doesn't engender a cat
With Shakespearean and star-spangled fur,
Nor a marten with phosphorescent eyes
It produces the flying cat.
—José Lezama Lima

In the nineties, there was a need for rituals. I will mention only the most recent: the parade of millions of people along the Malecon, mobilized in all parts of the island to demand the return of Elián González, which went on for seven months. All of you know the story.

I quote the testimony of a Havana father: "My boys, 16 and 17 years old, who are in high school in Havana, attend staged meetings and marches dressed in T-shirts that endlessly repeat, depersonalizing, automatizing him, the face of a boy. My children march in military fashion surrounded by their teachers while someone, loudspeaker in hand, repeats to them the only slogan allowed, which they must shout only at the moment when he orders them. The person with the loudspeaker insists on the pause so that the slogan can be heard clearly: 'Save / Elián.'"

The return of Elián to Cuba on 28 June 2000 ended the most gigantic and protracted ritual of "loyalty to fatherland" ever to take place on the island. But there have been others, on other occasions. Recently, I heard on Chilean radio that Cuba's Council of State conferred on Elián's father the Order of Carlos Manuel de Céspedes for his extraordinary efforts in bringing his son home.

In the mid-nineties, for the first time anyone could remember, Fidel wore civilian clothes. Forty years of olive drab uniforms fell under the weight of the inevitable mixtures of the liminal, ambiguous, and frontier zones set loose by a social drama.

Today, the rituals of pairing the cat and the marten are many in Cuba. The latest, most visible example is the meeting of Fidel and Pope John Paul II. The Pope offered a mass before more than 1 million people in the Plaza of the Revolution in January 1998. On that memorable day, the Roman Catholic Pope blessed the fervent multitude at his feet, behind whose backs rose the huge mural of Che Guevara that presides over the Plaza. The Pope thus stood facing Che, and with his back to the famous statue of José Martí and the tall tower which is his monument.

Alberto Korda, who took the classic black-and-white photograph known throughout the world of Che with his beret, star, and mystic gaze, was in the crowd that day and captured the following image in color: the mural of Che in the background, his features very visible, outlined in metal; in the foreground white, black, and mulatto faces. High above their heads is the image of a Catholic Virgin; a Cuban flag, which some arm raises, appears in the midst of the heads, Che, and the Virgin. The sound track of this superproduction achieves a similar impact: The Pope ("the old man," as the Cuban people lovingly called him) dialogues with the human sea, as Fidel has done so many times before, from the same place, breaking protocol and responding to the overly familiar crowd that chants, "John Paul, amigo, the people are with you," "We see, we feel, the Pope is real." The same habitual choruses are directed toward Fidel but with different names. Fidel, in civilian clothes, smiles soberly from a discreet location to the left of the main altar. This story is called, in honor of the image in Lezama's poem, "The Flying Cat."

The study of today's Cuba from the angle of the body and its political connotations intrigues me. I hope to return to these and other themes, which, for the moment, I only wanted to outline, unless my hand may also have to wave good-bye. One would need to think about, for example, the hypothesis that the nineties engendered a "loose" body, not only in the sense of freed or untied but also in the sense of "escaped," thrown out of gear, in some way autonomous or alone. This is how, at a certain level of analysis, formations such as the self-seeking or prostituted body, the body of illegality and "hustling" (*bisneo*), and also of anomie, appear to me. The body of exile. The loose body generates multiple scenarios, from the picaresque to self-exile to madness and suicide. And it occurs to me that a usurping, chameleonlike body also proliferates, which opportunistically installs and deletes identities: a chameleon body that goes to meetings of the Committee for the Defense of the Revolution with a cellular phone—a totally unobtainable object for ordinary Cubans—in order to make its nouveau riche status clear and "to kill with technology" our picaresque pre-modernity, which in return asks this yuppy: What do you "plug" that into? There is, I believe, an aspect of this loose or dislocated, usurping or travestied, body that has renovative and critical force, that is subversive and has allure. Besides, as a friend warns me, perhaps it is not as dislocated as it seems; it forms networks, links, at its level. But that deserves another discussion.

What have I been trying to tell you? That we socialists no longer know how to "make" socialism. That is not news. "And yet it moves." The Cuban body, the bodies of men and women, has passed through a difficult apprenticeship. Now, perhaps, we need confidence in our own strengths or we will misidentify them. Some—many, probably—are tired and prefer not to think, and walk to the beat of the loudspeaker for reasons of prudence or routine. But a community that has given so much democratizing energy in this world (and perhaps other generations I will not live to see) will find a new way to ride the bicycle, and the bicycle will become again a matter of play and technique (that is freedom), and we socialist cyclists will be able to tangle with and crash into each other without feeling guilty, impelled toward ourselves, directly through the eye of the needle, pedaling toward what will be the ecology of freedom rather than the ecology of necessity.

(A baroquely decorated bicycle appears on stage, and I invite the audience, whoever so desires, to get on. I get on, we get on many bicycles, and leave the conference room pedaling.)

Santiago de Chile, Rio de Janeiro, Havana
July 2000

In Medias Res Publicas: On Intellectuals and Social Criticism in the Cuban Public Sphere

Desiderio Navarro

Translated by Alessandro Fornazzari and Desiderio Navarro

In the midst of public things: that is where intellectuals are called upon to carry out their roles in their respective countries. But, as the authors of the Prince Claus Fund document *The Role of the Intellectual* (2000, 3) state, "in a number of respects the role of intellectuals differs from country to country," and the "material, cultural and political constraints" that they experience "differ from situation to situation." These differences must be taken into account if we are to avoid falling into illicit extrapolations, unfounded generalizations, and ethnocentrisms. Hence, as the document adds, "there is a need to understand the role of intellectuals in these contexts and to discuss key dilemmas."

This essay was presented at the international conference "The Role of the Intellectual in the Public Sphere," organized by the Prince Claus Fund, Beirut, 24–25 February 2000. The English translation was first published in *Nepantla: Views from South* 2.2 (2001) 355–71. It is reprinted here with permission from the Prince Claus Fund for Culture and Development.

The following observations and reflections attempt to contribute to the understanding of the role of the artistic intelligentsia in the public sphere in revolutionary Cuba, that is, in the last forty years of my country's history. This text deals with a long and complex period of Cuban culture that is still awaiting monographs of historical synthesis, and which would be impossible to present and analyze meticulously within this article's narrow framework. This is the reason for its sketchy nature and for the minimal exemplification of the following historical background.

In June 1961, in a famous meeting with some of the most important personalities of the Cuban intellectual scene, Comandante Fidel Castro (1961, 11) uttered a phrase that, because of its brevity, construction, and categorical nature, has functioned, from that moment until the present, as a summary of the Revolution's cultural politics: "Within the Revolution, everything; against the Revolution, nothing." Taken out of context and in the hands of circumstantial hermeneutists and exegetes, this versicle, part of a speech known since as "Palabras a los intelectuales" [Words to the intellectuals], proved to be extraordinarily polysemic, which allowed it to become the guiding principle for the successive periods and tendencies in struggle.[1]

The country's cultural and social life would repeatedly bring up many more specific questions that never got a well-developed, clear, and categorical answer: Which events and processes of Cuban social and cultural reality form part of the Revolution and which do not? How can one distinguish which cultural texts or practices act against the Revolution? Which act for it? And which simply do not affect it? Which social criticism is revolutionary and which is counterrevolutionary? Who decides what is the correct answer to these questions? How and according to what criteria is this decision made? Does *not* going against the Revolution imply silence on the social ills of the prerevolutionary past that have survived or on the ills that have arisen due to erroneous political decisions and unresolved problems of the revolutionary period? Doesn't being for the Revolution imply publicly revealing, criticizing, and fighting these social ills and errors? And so on.

---

1. In October 1977, in the closing remarks of the Second Congress of the Unión de Escritores y Artistas de Cuba (UNEAC; sixteen years had passed since the first congress), Armando Hart (1978, 142), then the Minister of Culture, acknowledged that "the deficiencies, difficulties, and gains that marked the period between the first and second congresses of the UNEAC are partly related to the varying levels of understanding that each person has had of the most profound essence of Fidel's statement that, synthesizing everything, proclaimed, 'Within the revolution everything; against the Revolution nothing,' or when he said, 'Art is a weapon of the Revolution.'"

After the 1959 revolutionary victory, and especially after the 1961 proclamation of the socialist nature of the revolution, relations between the political avant-garde and the intellectual or artistic avant-garde—to use designations of the time—experienced strong but localized and passing tensions in matters of cultural politics (for example, in regards to the prohibition of the public showing of the Sabá Cabrera Infante film *P.M.* or the sectarianism of 1961–62). Nonetheless, the intellectual avant-garde widely adhered to the decisions and projections of the political avant-garde in all the other spheres of national public life. On the other hand, in September 1966 Roberto Fernández Retamar (1967, 186), one of the most outstanding thinkers of the intellectual avant-garde, still could present the critique of the politicians' errors as a duty that is consubstantial to the intellectual's adherence to the Revolution, and as a diagnostic and corrective factor that the "actually existing" Cuban politicians of the time took into account:

> A theoretical error committed by someone who can turn his or her opinions into decisions is no longer just a theoretical error: it is a possibly incorrect measure. We have come across incorrect measures, and they pose a problem of conscience. The revolutionary intellectual is not really acting as such when applauding what he or she knows to be an error of *his or her* revolution; rather, he or she acts as a revolutionary in showing that an error has been made. The intellectual's adherence, if he or she really wants to be useful, can only be a critical adherence, since criticism is "the practice of judgement." When we have detected such errors of the Revolution, we have discussed them. This has been done, not only in the aesthetic sphere, but also with erroneous ethical conceptions that have been translated into infelicitous measures. Some of these measures have been rectified and others are in the process of being rectified. And this has occurred, in some measure, because of our participation. . . . In some way, as modest as it may be, we contribute to the modification of this process [the Revolution]. In some way we *are* the Revolution.

Faced with the often utilized hypostatization of the synecdoche that makes an individual political leader or a collective of them "the Revolution" and then makes their ideas and decisions the ideas and decisions of "the Revolution," Fernández Retamar recalled that revolutionary intellectuals are also a part of the replaced whole in that Grand Synecdoche.

For the majority of the revolutionary intellectuals—but not for the majority of the politicians—it was clear that their role in the public sphere should be one of critical participation. Around 1968, intellectual critical intervention in the public sphere made itself felt with considerable strength and from diverse political positions. The relative monologism dominant for years, thanks to spontaneous political consensus and, to some extent, self-censorship motivated by the danger of manipulation of information by the enemy, was broken by isolated intellectual voices that called into question narrow or broad aspects of the revolutionary process, or even the whole of it.

This heteroglosia in political matters appeared even more strident against the backdrop of a prorevolutionary national intelligentsia that, paradoxically, did not publicly intervene in extra-aesthetic discussions. While enumerating "some problems of the revolutionary intellectual," Fernández Retamar (1967, 178–79) first of all had referred precisely to this strange silence: "Recently, in Mexico, Víctor Flores Olea asked me why Cuban intellectuals did not participate, or only rarely, in the discussion of problems such as material stimulation, moral stimulation, the law of value, etc., problems that were usually dealt with by Che, Dorticós, and others. . . . The question . . . touches upon, among other things, the following point: Cuban intellectuals, who have debated so lucidly about aesthetic questions, should consider other matters, otherwise they will remain confined to the limits of their guild." Fernández Retamar then asked for "that expansion of the problematic treated by intellectuals" precisely as a part of the intellectuals' "process of conversion into intellectuals of the Revolution" (179).

On the other hand, in relations with foreign intellectuals an analogous political heteroglosia appeared: a large part of the foreign leftist or progressive intelligentsia (primarily Western European and Latin American) criticized the revolutionary government for its approval of the 1968 invasion of Czechoslovakia by the troops of the Warsaw Pact and for the 1971 detention of the Cuban poet Heberto Padilla. In January 1968, on the occasion of the Cultural Congress of Havana, the intellectual workers of the world, and of Europe in particular, were exalted for intervening in the public sphere with protests and combative mobilizations in favor of causes such as Cuba's position during the October missile crisis, Che's guerrilla movement, the Vietnam struggle, the black people's movement in the United States, and so on, in contrast with the limited or nonexistent public support given to such causes by the world revolutionary avant-gardes, parties, and political organizations. But, soon after the above-mentioned criticisms in 1971, within that intelligentsia a "mafia" of "false intellectuals" was discovered and described as "petit bourgeois pseudo-leftists of the capitalist world who used the Revolution as a springboard to win prestige among the peoples of the underdeveloped countries," and who "attempted to permeate us with their debilitating ideas, to impose their styles and tastes, and even to act as judges of the Revolution" ("Declaración" 1971, 17).

All of a sudden, for most politicians, the intellectual appeared as a real ideological Other who was publicly interpellating them on extracultural matters of national politics. That appearance, along with the knowledge of the role played by Czech intellectuals in the Prague Spring and the growing influence of the Soviet sociopolitical and cultural model in its Brezhnevian stage of "Restoration," were some of the factors that contributed to intellectuals being seen by many politicians as untrustworthy fellow travelers, and even as a potential oppositional political force. Some employed the idea expressed by Che Guevara (1965, 49), in *El socialismo y el hombre en Cuba*, that "the culpability of many of our intellectuals and artists resides in their original sin; they are not authentically revolutionary," while at the same time failing to mention another political dictate that Che formulated in the same paragraph: "We should not create docile wage earners of the official thought or 'scholarship holders' who live sheltered under the budget, practicing a feigned liberty."

From 1968 on, in addition to a series of administrative measures (the most symbolic being the termination of the important journal called, precisely, *Pensamiento crítico* [Critical thought]), a veritable crusade was launched against the intelligentsia's critical intervention in the public sphere. This crusade culminated in the First National Congress of Education and Culture (1971) and was only disarticulated at the beginning of the 1980s with the failure of the last desperate attempt to implement as official doctrine the particular Soviet version of Socialist Realism that was most hostile to social critique. It was precisely at the beginning of the 1980s that new critical voices began to be heard, this time stronger and in greater numbers. They belonged to young intellectuals born and educated in the Revolution—the majority being plastic artists, though there were also fiction writers, dramatists and stage directors, filmmakers, and essayists.

The Cuban art critic Gerardo Mosquera (1988, 26) has described better than anyone the way these young plastic artists conceived of and carried out the role of the intellectual in the public sphere: "One feels [in them] a great urgency to go 'beyond art' in order to bring it directly to bear on society's problems, without making even the smallest artistic concession." He adds that these artists are "advancing a very serious critical questioning of the problems of our reality that, although touched upon in hallways, rarely have moved from an oral discourse to a public discussion in print." Establishing a clear intertextual relationship to Fidel's phrase, Mosquera concludes: "As strong as this expression turns out to be, it is a questioning that emerges within socialism and for socialism" (ibid.).

In mid-1989 Mosquera (1989, 24) noted, "The plastic arts . . . now constitute the most daring platform. Their social criticism analyses very real ills in search of their rectification." And Mosquera mentioned some of these ills: "bureaucracy, opportunism, authoritarianism, rectification but not too much, accommodation, antidemocratic centralism . . ."

Related to this desire for public criticism and discussion, an extraordinary proliferation of cultural spaces of all kinds took place during the 1980s: spaces for exhibits, publication, readings, discussions; institutional and noninstitutional spaces; private and public spaces. One of the unusual characteristics of many of these new spaces was the appearance of spontaneous interventions that were not previously reviewed, authorized, or programmed (i.e., the public reading of texts not submitted days or weeks beforehand to diverse cultural and political institutions for their approval, correction, or rejection).

On the other hand, this critical intellectual activity was characterized by an orientation, never before seen, toward the noninstitutional or antiinstitutional. Faced with the constraints of the institutional spaces and their institutional uses, these intellectuals developed the following strategies:

1. the unexpected irruption into, and the ephemeral, "deconstructive" appropriation of, institutional cultural spaces (sudden uninvited performances in the midst of other people's exhibitions or conferences);
2. the creation of noninstitutional cultural spaces (plastic art exhibits and theatrical representations staged in private homes, a samizdat cultural newspaper), some of which tended to produce noninstitutional institutions (galleries in houses or in a central park); and
3. the more or less ephemeral irruption into and appropriation of public spaces (through graffiti, murals, and performances in the city streets, a baseball game played by artists and critics in a baseball stadium).

But as early as 1988 the intellectual's critical intervention in the public sphere was opposed by a new offensive that—in conjunction with the difficult working and living conditions created by the economic crisis of the early 1990s, and the simultaneous loosening in the granting of exit permits—led the majority of that artistic intelligentsia to join the diaspora in the Americas and in Europe. Nevertheless, in the 1990s, especially in the first half of the decade, cinematographic, narrative, dramatic, and other works continued to appear, although with decreasing frequency, in which the critical spirit of "the 1980s" survived.

In what follows we will examine not the administrative measures that were adopted but instead the discourse legitimizing them and, in general, the ideology and cultural practices that were leveled against the critical attitude of the intellectual, the public character of the intellectual's intervention, and even against the figure of the intellectual in general. That examination will be carried out in a typological and synchronic way, without dealing with the internal history or the variable historical presence of that ideology and those practices in national life; such a historiographical undertaking would require an entire book. Presenting themselves as the guarantors of the ideological and political stability of the Revolution, they have come to be hegemonic in certain periods, but, happily, they have never reigned in an absolute way in all the instances and ramifications of political power and cultural institutions. It was precisely the resistance to them of institutions such as the Casa de las Américas, the Instituto Cubano de Arte e Industria Cinematográficos, or the Unión de Escritores y Artistas de Cuba, and even the very Ministry of Culture—the latter two of which took part in imposing them at other times—that permitted the appearance or survival of certain intellectual spaces of critical thinking.

Within the framework of such anticritical ideology and practices, the role of the revolutionary intellectual as a critic of the Revolution's social reality is seldom openly denied, but it is also seldom forthrightly affirmed or reaffirmed. Most of the time it is passed over in silence or mentioned only in passing as something secondary or optional. Even when the intellectual's critical role is explicitly recognized in a theoretical way, it is immediately neutralized through diverse restrictions and reservations, and carrying it out in concrete social practice becomes the target of all kinds of political and ethical accusations.

The most radical restrictions, of course, are those stated in the name of *raison d'état*: social criticism in the public sphere is not advisable or should not be permitted

1. because the internal and external enemies of the Revolution could capitalize on it for propaganda use, and/or
2. because coming to know certain truths (difficulties and defects of social reality) could disorient, confuse, or dishearten the people, who still do not have the necessary preparation to assimilate them

(N.B.: This is the same people whose political culture, ideological maturity, and lucidity are presented as extraordinary when the goal is to highlight the rational character of its support of the Revolution), and/or

3. because each new critical discrepancy would constitute a heterodoxia, a dissidence that would break the nation's monolithic ideological unity, so necessary for its survival.

Now, if it is accepted that social criticism in the public sphere puts national security at risk, then in practice only a few options are left to the revolutionary intellectual: in the "best" of cases, either silence or the role of apologist, bard of the achievements that actually exist, and, in the worst of cases, the role of idealizer and idyllizer of social reality.

The raison d'état gave rise to the *mystery syndrome*. That is how Cuban popular language dubbed the tabooization of the public investigation and discussion of social phenomena that contain (or could contain) an endogenous negative element (fact, process, effect, etc.). This tabooization, which has existed in different periods with varying degrees of rigor and amplitude, penetrated even the most trivial spheres of everyday life and on occasion reached grotesque extremes.

Often, for the intellectual, it is not even a question of making "the people," or "the public," aware of a particular negative social phenomenon, but simply of discussing collectively that phenomenon, which is in fact an open secret, in the public sphere. For example, the existence of prostitution in Cuba was one of the big taboo subjects: while by the end of the 1980s almost everyone knew of its open and growing presence in the streets, official discourse continued to deny its existence, and it was an intellectual, a young novelist and journalist, who, with a testimonial article, brought the undesirable phenomenon out into public debate. Now, thanks to the intervention of the artistic intelligentsia, something similar is happening with another taboo subject: the persistence of racism in Cuba.

In conjunction or not with the already mentioned restrictions, narrow limits concerning the range of competence are set on the intelligentsia's critical role in the public sphere. It is affirmed that the intelligentsia should not publicly intervene in social problems that are not strictly cultural or politico-cultural because they are not competent to do so, due to their lack of theoretical and empirical knowledge of the concrete social reality, which is the proper domain of professional politicians and "experts" or "specialists" in specific social problems.

This thinking, which reinforces and is reinforced by the aforementioned lack of interest in public social criticism on the part of many intellectuals, determines the thematic profile of local cultural publications. If Cuban cultural magazines are compared with equivalent journals in the former socialist Eastern Europe—for example, *La gaceta de Cuba* with the Soviet *Literatúrnaia gazeta*—one is struck by the strictly artistic-cultural nature of the themes that are dealt with in Cuban periodicals (with recent exceptions), and, in particular, by the absence of social themes like ecology, education, morality, ways of life, and (absent until recently, and still only rarely present) religion, race, and gender.

In addition, it is often affirmed that the intellectual should critically intervene only on specific cultural—literary, artistic—works, not on cultural and social institutions and their influence on the production, diffusion, and reception of those works. More and more non-Marxist critics and theorists from all over the world are recognizing the sterility of an "ergocentric" criticism—that is, a criticism focused on works as if they were suspended in a social communicational vacuum—and the need to investigate texts in the context of their social processes of production, diffusion, and reception. Meanwhile, in the bosom of Cuban socialism, Marxist criticism, among other forms of criticism, is expected not to investigate social aspects of artistic social communication. It is expected to be less sociological, that is, *to be less Marxist or to cease to be Marxist.*

Contrary to expectation, the most frequent way of attacking the intelligentsia's critical interventions in the public sphere is not by signaling the negative consequences that these critical statements might allegedly have, nor by demonstrating the supposedly erroneous nature of these affirmations, but by attributing condemnable hidden intentions to their authors. Intellectuals, or at least some of them, are accused of attempting to make the intelligentsia into *the* Critical Conscience of society, that is, society's only and exclusive critical conscience. This runs contrary to something obvious: the intelligentsia could only aspire to and achieve that status in a public sphere where the rest of society does not or could not intervene critically. Obviously, the intelligentsia has no way to prevent these interventions. Only the absence of critical activity by other social subjects (classes, groups, political organizations, the mass media, etc.) can cause the intelligentsia to be not *a* critical conscience among others, but *the* critical conscience.

Another frequent way of disqualifying the intelligentsia's critical interventions is through the public stigmatization of them with the epithet *hipercrítico* (hypercritical), which is sufficient legitimization to exclude them from the public sphere. In proper Spanish, *hipercrítico* is applied to something that contains an excessively meticulous, scrupulous, or rigorous criticism.

If meticulousness, scrupulousness, and rigorousness in the critical analysis and evaluation of social reality are not in themselves what is reproachable about "hypercriticism," then the problem must be the excessive amount of these qualities: they present themselves "in greater quantities than what is necessary or appropriate." That is, the criterion for correct social criticism would not be the truth but the correspondence of the degree of its meticulousness, scrupulousness, and rigorousness to a certain measure of what is necessary or advisable. Nevertheless, no critical intervention is stigmatized as being "hypocriticism" or "acriticism." Not criticizing at all or criticizing less than what is necessary or appropriate is not considered a reason for reproach or exclusion. This reveals that the "zero," the total absence is, in fact, the ideal degree of social criticism. Once again we must ask: Who decides what is the level of critical rigorousness that is necessary or appropriate for a socialist society? How, and according to what criteria? In other words, how much truth and how much silencing of the truth are necessary or appropriate? And how much silencing of the truth generates a lie by omission?

Another resource used to invalidate criticism, similar to and often associated with the one just described, is the fallacious Socialist Realist requirement that the totality of society be reflected not by the whole body of the works of a culture, but by the individual literary, artistic, or social-scientific work. The work must be a microcosmos in which nothing can be left out. So critical representations of social reality are sharply condemned because they focus on the negative and do not present at all or do not present in their real magnitude (as measured by their statistical proportions or social significance) the positive things that exist in society alongside the negative ones being criticized. Nevertheless, the prevalent uncritical, or even absolutely apologetic, interventions are in no way anathematized for concentrating on the positive and not showing at all or not showing in its real magnitude the negative that survives or arises in society alongside the exalted positive.

Perhaps the most incapacitating of all the attacks is the one that limits itself to signaling in a critical intervention coincidences with prior statements of internal or external counterrevolutionaries. Again, it is not the principle of correspondence to the truth that rules in this case, but rather a "logic" that Engels mockingly called "Gribul politics," which consists in every Marxist thinker's supposed obligation to affirm *automatically* the opposite of what any other non-Marxist author has asserted. But this "logic" is also applied retroactively: if any professed enemy of the Revolution publicly affirms that he or she agrees with an intellectual's earlier critical statement, or gives some direct or indirect indication of his or her approval of it, that statement automatically becomes counterrevolutionary, regardless of how much time has transpired since the intellectual's original intervention. If the politically correct is the opposite of what the Revolution's enemies say, then the intellectual and his or her work are subject to a hazardous and lamentable intellectual dependence with respect to their initiative.

Another way of disqualifying intellectuals' critical interventions is to accuse them of being "undisciplined," of introducing anarchy and disorder into social life. It is a call for us to disregard the truth-content of a critical intervention because it has violated the unwritten (but not for that reason any less rigorous) pragmatic rules that determine where, how, and before whom criticism can be offered on certain subjects (and even who should not offer it). For a critical intervention to be subject to discrediting and any response to it to be declared unnecessary—and improper—it is enough, for example, that the intervention be realized outside the corresponding circle of authorized persons or outside the programmed institutions and meetings, or by a person (a beginner or an amateur) who is not institutionally recognized as an intellectual, or without the envelope of the ritual "constructive" apologetics, or who fails to offer a ready-made solution to the problem the intervention poses.

A particularly effective and frequently used way of disqualifying critical interventions is to present them—in a pathetic and almost always melodramatic and kitsch way—as an "offense to popular sensibility," or a "wound inflicted upon the deepest fibers of the heart of our abnegated people." While in questions of comprehensibility of works what is sought after is—as Che Guevara's famous phrase keenly points out—"what everybody understands, which is what the functionaries understand," in moral and political matters what is sought after is only what everybody approves of, which, in fact, is what the functionaries approve of. In this way, "popular sensibility," which in other social questions is sometimes ignored by the same functionaries, is presented as the supreme and infallible moral and political instance, even though it is often no more than oratory or a mass-media construct embodying what the functionaries consider to be the people's duty to feel regarding this or that matter.

Finally, if the intellectual's critical argumentation is clearly developed with an impeccable Marxist logic and from the perspective of the principles and interests of the Revolution, then an emergency neutralizing mechanism can be employed: instead of publicly discussing the argument or refuting it with Marxist intellectual weapons, the author is accused of simulating a revolutionary or Marxist persona, of disguising him- or herself with a Marxist phraseology. In this way the intellectual part of the matter is considered to be settled and the corresponding moral damage is inflicted on a true revolutionary or Marxist.

The intellectual's critical activity in the public sphere is not only fought directly, but also through indirect routes. One of the indirect means is the administration of memory and forgetting. In each period there is an attempt to erase (minimize or veil) from the collective cultural memory everything related to the intellectual's critical activity of the preceding period, whether it be the memory of the forms that it assumed, the channels that it used, the spaces in which it developed, and the specific personalities who practiced it, or the memory of how it was fought, repressed, or suppressed, and who its antagonists were (which, in the uncertain first half of the 1990s, facilitated the "whitewashing of biographies," "ideological cross-dressing" [*travestismo*] and "recycling" of hard-liners).

Thus, employing conventionally the inexact round-number designations of the periods, we could say that the interventions and critical spaces of "the 1960s" (1959–67) were erased in "the 1970s" (1968–83); that the politico-cultural "errors" committed in "the 1970s" against those interventions and spaces were superficially recognized and immediately erased in "the 1980s" (1984–89); and, finally, that the new 1980s interventions and critical spaces were erased in the 1990s. The modes of operation have ranged from the crude exclusion from dictionaries and historical texts to the subtle immediate acceptance, in the 1980s, of the euphemistic denomination "gray five years" (*quinquenio gris*, 1971–75) for the authoritarian and dogmatic period that, on the one hand, in fact lasted for about fifteen years (approximately from 1968 until 1983), and, on the other, was in fact not gray but black for many intellectual lives and works.

It is not by chance, then, that the 1980s critical interventions struggled to rescue the memory of their 1960s precedents as an interrupted tradition. In a similar way, the rescuing of the memory of the young plastic arts and the other 1980s critical manifestations should form part of the Cuban intelligentsia's historical anamnesis, so necessary in the face of those who take great pains to make our country into what the title of Aldo Baroni's old book proclaimed: *Cuba, país de poca memoria* [Cuba, a country with little memory].

An identical function is to be ascribed to the fact that, from the intellectual production of socialist Eastern Europe that has been made available to the Cuban public, the works embodying a socialist intellectual tradition of critiquing the social reality of actually existing socialism have been excluded or suppressed. These works range from Vladimir Maiakovski's satirical texts to Stanislav Stratíev's, and from Leon Trotsky's political essays to Adam Schaff's or early Rudolf Bahro's.

Another indirect, but highly effective, way of battling the intelligentsia's critical intervention is the stirring up and propagation of anti-intellectualism, which already existed in prerevolutionary Cuban culture and is revived and disseminated for political ends. Already in 1925, in his essay "La crisis de la alta cultura en Cuba," the prominent Cuban thinker Jorge Mañach (1999, 32–33) had noted, while enumerating the factors responsible for that crisis in the young republic, that among the people, in "all the nation's nonintellectual classes," there existed "a silent antipathy, an ironic distrust," an "attitude of indifference toward and even contempt for intellectual concerns." He further observed that: "not only among the lower classes, but even among the bourgeoisie, being or seeming an 'intellectual' is a fault." In this early "tradition" one could discern the diverse but profound influence of the anti-intellectualism of two cultures, those of Spain and the United States, that had participated in the genesis and evolution of Cuban culture.

Thus, in the 1970s the image of the intellectual in mass culture (in songs, soap operas, comic shows) became increasingly ridiculous and unsympathetic. The intellectual was presented not only as unpopular but, in general, as someone lacking "cubanía" (that is, as an aristocratic, pompous, and pedantic person out of touch with social reality, the people, and hard work).

While "the masses" or "the people" had been constructed in the past as the Other of the intellectual elite—the defining term in the opposition—and therefore as primitive, obtuse, irrational, and so on, now it is the intellectual "elite" that was constructed as the Other of the "people" and therefore as extravagant, amoral, and fond of all things foreign.

Taking advantage of the moral ideas reigning in broad popular sectors, homophobia (more precisely, "gayphobia") and the hostility and intolerance toward all lifestyle differences (and toward all the signs of originality—in dress, etc.—frequent among intellectuals), an identification was established between intelligentsia, homosexuality, "extravagance," and political and moral untrustworthiness. Pierre Bourdieu (1984 [1979]) has called attention to this "anti-intellectual machismo" (316) and "the tendency of the ruling fractions [of the ruling class] to conceive the opposition between the 'man of action' and the 'intellectual' as a variant of the opposition between male and female" (315).

The internationally known Cuban film *Strawberry and Chocolate* (1993)—a film that to this day has been deprived of the mass audience of the national television channels—can also be seen as the national intelligentsia's tardy artistic reply to gayphobia and, in general, to the moral and ideological "allophobia," that is actually existing among the people, but that, in the 1970s, was stirred up and directed against the intelligentsia as a whole.[2] (Remember the weight that the intellectual and the cultural have in the portrayal of the homosexual protagonist, as well as the representation of his increasingly friendly communication with the heterosexual member of the Communist Youth.)

The bearers of this anti-intellectualism include not only many of the politicians and much of the popular sector; in Cuba there are also a good number of what Leszek Kolakowski (1986, 112) has called "intellectuals against the intellect." But Kolakowski's explanation for their emergence— a sensation of "rootlessness," of not integrating, and the derived need for a feeling of total commitment or for a consciousness of belonging—do not seem valid in this case. Bourdieu's (1996 [1992], 280) explanation for this "internal anti-intellectualism" seems to be more appropriate here: the resentment and "the violence of disappointed love" that arise in mediocre intellectuals "when relative failure comes along to destroy their initial aspirations to a culture from which they expected everything." This is shown by the fact that the apogee of anti-intellectualism in the cultural milieu coincides with the period already described by many as that of the "mediocracy," of "mediocrity's rise to power," and so on.

These anti-intellectual campaigns were so successful and took such deep root that, still in 1992, the National Board of the Unión de Escritores y Artistas de Cuba had to issue a document (*La cultura cubana de hoy*) in large part devoted to criticizing "anti-cultural prejudices" and those persons who provoke the people's hostility and suspicion toward intellectuals (Consejo Nacional 1992, 5–8).

• • • •

In their respective moments of participation in the public sphere a majority of Cuban critical intellectuals have believed, more so than many

---

2. "The cultural media cannot serve as a setting for the proliferation of false intellectuals who attempt to convert snobbism, extravagance, homosexuality, and other social aberrations into expressions of revolutionary art that are remote from the masses and the spirit of our Revolution" ("Declaración" 1971, 16).

boundary 2

Subscribe to *boundary 2*.

☐ Please enter my subscription (three issues) to *boundary 2* at the annual subscription rate of $32.* Outside-U.S. subscribers: Please add $12 for postage. Canadian subscribers: Please add 7% GST to the subscription rate, in addition to the outside-U.S. postage.

☐ Enclosed is my check, made payable to Duke University Press.

☐ Please bill me (no issues will be sent until payment is received).

Please charge my ☐ VISA ☐ MasterCard ☐ American Express

Account Number   Expiration Date

Signature

Name

Address

City/State/Zip   B23I1

* Individual subscriptions only.

Send your order to Duke University Press, Journals Fulfillment, Box 90660, Durham, NC 27708-0660. To place your journal order using a credit card, call toll-free 1-888-387-5765 (within the U.S. and Canada) or 919-687-3602. www.dukepress.edu

Does your library subscribe to *boundary 2*?
Take this card to your librarian to request an institutional subscription.
Please enter our subscription (three issues) to *boundary 2*. Libraries and institutions: $133 (Canadian libraries add 7% GST to the subscription rate).

Institution

Address

                                                                    B23I1

☐ Purchase order enclosed.
☐ Please bill our agent:

☐ Please send a free examination copy to the address listed above (libraries only).

Volume 30, 2002 (3 issues); ISSN 0190-359

Send your order to Duke University Press, Journals Fulfillment, Box 90660, Durham, NC 27708-0660. To place your journal order using a credit card, call toll-free 1-888-387-5765 (within the U.S. and Canada) or 919-687-3602. www.dukepress.edu

BUSINESS REPLY MAIL

FIRST CLASS MAIL   PERMIT NO. 1000   DURHAM, NC

POSTAGE WILL BE PAID BY ADDRESSEE

Duke University Press
Journals Fulfillment
Box 90660
Durham, NC 27706-9942

BUSINESS REPLY MAIL

FIRST CLASS MAIL   PERMIT NO. 1000   DURHAM, NC

POSTAGE WILL BE PAID BY ADDRESSEE

Duke University Press
Journals Fulfillment
Box 90660
Durham, NC 27706-9942

of the politicians, in socialism's capacity to bear open criticism. They have believed that criticism, far from being a threat to socialism, is its "oxygen," its "motor": a necessity for the survival and well-being of the revolutionary process. The critical intellectuals believe that social criticism can constitute a threat only when it is silenced or even met with reprisals, when it is confined to a closed guild or institutional enclave, when it is placed in a communicational vacuum under a bell jar, or—and this above all else—when it goes unanswered or when, recognized as correct, it is not taken into account in political practice. For these intellectuals, what confirmed the processes that brought about the collapse of the socialist bloc was not—as many politicians, bureaucrats, technocrats, and econocrats believe—that the intellectual's social criticism causes the erosion and fall of actually existing socialism, but that the silencing, confinement, and disdain of social criticism realized by the intelligentsia and the people in general allow social problems and the corresponding unease to grow, multiply, and accumulate beyond what a belated opening of critical public debate could handle.

The fate of socialism after the fall of the socialist bloc will be determined, more than ever, by socialism's capacity to sustain in theory and in practice the initial idea that the intellectual's adherence to the Revolution (like that of any other ordinary citizen), if the intellectual "really wants to be useful, can only be a critical adherence"; by its capacity to tolerate and publicly answer social criticism that is directed toward it from other ideological positions—those of the "nonrevolutionaries within the Revolution" to whom the famous 1961 maxim referred; by its capacity not only to tolerate, but to foster the social criticism of its own management that emerges from those very principles, ideals, and values that socialism proclaims as its own, that is, by socialism's ability to be the Maecenas of a socialist criticism of its own management; and, finally, by its capacity to guarantee that, in order to publish the truth, the intellectual does not have either to resort to samizdat or to "tamizdat,"[3] diasporic public spheres, and other extraterritorial cultural spaces and patrons, or to overcome the "five difficulties in writing the truth" described by Bertolt Brecht (1966 [1935], 265–90) in his famous article. But while this capacity is hampered by the actions of political forces hostile to social criticism, the intellectual, in order to overcome these difficul-

3. "Tamizdat" is a Russian neologism created by analogy with *samizdat*. Combining *tam* (there) and *izdat* (abbreviation of *izdatelstvo* [publishing house]), it refers to the printings, in North America, Western Europe, and elsewhere, of texts of Soviet and other socialist bloc authors that, because of the decisions of political officials, could not be published in the authors' home countries.

ties, will have to display the five corresponding Brechtian virtues: the courage to express the truth, the perspicacity to recognize it, the skill to make it serviceable as a weapon, the discernment to choose the hands in which it will be effective, and the cleverness to disseminate it widely.

References

Bourdieu, Pierre. 1984 [1979]. *Distinction: A Social Critique of the Judgement of Taste*. Translated by Richard Nice. Cambridge: Harvard University Press.

———. 1996 [1992]. *The Rules of Art: Genesis and Structure of the Literary Field*. Translated by Susan Emanuel. Stanford, CA: Stanford University Press.

Brecht, Bertolt. 1966 [1935]. "Fünf Schwierigkeiten beim Schreiben der Wahrheit." In *Schriften zur Literatur und Kunst*. Vol. 1. Berlin and Weimar: Aufbau-Verlag.

Castro, Fidel. 1961. *Palabras a los intelectuales*. Havana: Ediciones del Consejo Nacional de Cultura.

Consejo Nacional de la UNEAC. 1992. *La cultura cubana de hoy: Temas para un debate*. Havana: Consejo Nacional de la UNEAC.

"Declaración del Primer Congreso Nacional de Educación y Cultura." 1971. In *Casa de las Américas*, nos. 65–66: 4–19.

Fernández Retamar, Roberto. 1967. "Hacia una intelectualidad revolucionaria en Cuba." In *Ensayo de otro mundo*. Havana: Instituto del Libro.

Guevara, Ernesto. 1965. *El socialismo y el hombre en Cuba*. Havana: Ediciones R.

Hart, Armando. 1978. "El arte es un arma de la Revolución." In *Del trabajo cultural: Selección de discursos*. Havana: Editorial de Ciencias Sociales.

Kolakowski, Leszek. 1986. *Intelectuales contra el intelecto*. Barcelona: Tusquets.

Mañach, Jorge. 1999. "La crisis de la alta cultura en Cuba." In *Ensayos*. Havana: Letras Cubanas.

Mosquera, Gerardo. 1988. "Crítica y consignas." *La gaceta de Cuba*, November: 26–27.

———. 1989. "Trece criterios sobre el nuevo arte cubano." *La gaceta de Cuba*, 24 June, 24.

Prince Claus Fund. 2000. *The Role of the Intellectual in the Public Sphere: Beirut, Lebanon, 24, 25 February 2000: Reader*. The Hague: Prince Claus Fund.

Postscript for *boundary 2*

I mention in this essay that even criticism from "within the Revolution" can sometimes be met with reprisals. An example of such reprisals is the sorry "response" by certain official sectors to my initial presentation of this text in Cuba at a conference sponsored by the Cuban Artists and Writers

Union (UNEAC) in April 2001. A scant week after the event, I received not a written or verbal reply to what I had said but instead a notice informing me that the small building that had been granted a year earlier to *Criterios*— the journal of international literary and cultural theory I founded and edit— to serve as the home for a new Center for Theory and Culture, and that was in the process of being remodeled for that purpose, had been assigned in error and would have to be returned to the ministry in question.

Mambí (Rap)

Obsesión (Alexey Rodríguez Mola and Magia López Cabrera)

Translated by Sujatha Fernandes and Kenya Dworkin

Dedicated to Mumia Abu Jamal	*Dedicado a Mumia Abu Jamal*
Come in, Column 2, Column 2, Column 2, for the people, here I am	*Atención Columna 2, Columna 2, Columna 2 pa'l pueblo aquí estoy yo*

American hip-hop first became popular in Cuba among black youth in the early eighties in the urban neighborhoods of Havana and in large suburban working-class housing developments such as Alamar. Cuban rap as a musical and poetic genre, distinct from both Cuban popular music and American rap, began to develop in the mid-nineties and currently comprises a broad and diverse movement that extends from the urban areas of Havana to the eastern city of Santiago de Cuba. Some of the themes that recur in Cuban rap are: the increased racism experienced by Afro-Cuban youth in the "Special Period"; the silencing of race issues in Cuban society in the name of revolutionary political correctness; the identification of Afro-Cuban youth with the political movements of African Americans and left activists in other parts of Latin America; and the struggles of rappers to make their voices heard despite problems of censorship and the promotion of more commercial forms of rap by the state cultural apparatus. *Mambí* refers to the black soldiers, most of them former

boundary 2 29:3, 2002. Copyright © 2002 by Duke University Press.

Chorus:	**Coro:**
Here I am saying	Yo estoy aquí diciendo
OBSESIÓN MAMBÍ in battle	OBSESIÓN MAMBÍ pinchando
Don't wait for luck	Que nadie espere ningún tipo de chance
If Quintín Banderas never gave up	¿Si Quintín Banderas nunca dio masaje,
Why me, then?	porq' yo entonces?
Let's fight!	¡A fajarse!
'Cause the jungle is screaming: I'm me,	Q' la manigua está gritando: yo soy yo
and it's for me the bell tolls.	y es por mí por quien doblan las campañas.
Don't lie.	No metan forros.
The *Morro* knows I run to battle	El morro sabe q' al combate corro y corro
and run with *bayameses*,	junto a los bayameses,
Cuba's proud of me!	¡Cuba, orgullosa de mí!
I'm not afraid of a hero's death.	No le temo a una muerte gloriosa.
So chill, to be a rebel and	Estense quietos q' insurrecto y prieto
Black is whack.	es lío.
Rebambarambara!	¡Rebambarambara!
I raise my machete high,	Alzo la wampara y bien pará mantengo la
And I keep my writing hard and crazy,	escritura dura sin cordura alguna,
so the fat cats don't make more money,	pa' q' los panchos no hagan más fortuna,
and so, one, two, or three,	por eso, una, dos o tres.
What a great beat my troops dance to!	¡Que paso más chévere el de mi tropa!
There is no defeat.	No hay derrota.

---

slaves, who fought in the Cuban war of independence against Spain in the 1890s. One of their leaders was Quintín Banderas. The reference later in the rap to a diary is probably to Che Guevara's *Bolivian Diary*. "Hear this, Nicolás" alludes to the Afro-Cuban poet Nicolás Guillén. —Sujatha Fernandes

Chorus	**Coro**
No more messin' around, I was on the war path with something sticking in my craw, and brave words came out of me, free of fear and I say: I have more than the leopard because I have a good reason for pride like him I'm black. My intention is not to be a pretty black girl on posters, and if you see me that way I know it's 'cause there're still those who want to be the boss, to see me working without rest in the sugar mills, I've suffered this, I've seen this, as Christ also saw it, that's why with one slash of my machete I open a path among so many clever poets. In my case I fight because I exist and to find a way to say this. Now the fat cats are working for me,	*Se acabó el relajo,* *crucé la trocha con el buche molesto* *y el dialecto guapo,* *me escapó así curá de espanto* *y digo:* *yo tengo más q' el leopardo porq' tengo* *un buen motivo pa' echarla como éste:* *yo soy niche.* *Mi intención no es salir como negrita linda* *es los afiches,* *y si me ven así es porq' se* *q' todavía hay quien quisiera ser* *mayoral,* *pa' verme trabajando sin descanso en los* *trapiches,* *eso lo he sufrido, lo he visto,* *como también lo ha visto Cristo, por eso* *de un sólo tajo me abro paso entre tantos* *poetas listos.* *En mi caso, me fajo porq' existo y de qué* *manera encajo esto.* *Ya tengo a to' los panchos limpiándome el* *rancho,*

and repeating every two minutes that	y repitiendo cada dos minutos q' soy Magia
I'm Magic on this island.	en esta isla.

Chorus	*Coro*

Without so much fuss	Sin tanto papití ni na'
We're WHO WE ARE	Somo NOSOTROS

What?	¿Qúe?

The rage from my throat sets off	La furia de mi garganta desencadena fuegos
fireworks	artificiales,
since my voice learned it too deserves	desde que sabe q' también merece papeles
a leading role,	protagónicos,
it's logical.	es lógico.
Those who hear me are part of a	Quien me escucha es parte de un
unique, historical movement,	movimiento histórico, único,
'cause I have revolutionary proposals	porq' tengo propósitos revolucionarios
under my arm.	bajo mi brazo.
A diary that accompanies the guerrilla fighter,	Un diario q' no abandona al guerrillero,
its title:	su título.
Yes, I'm a knight-errant	Sí, soy caballero
(so the prologue says),	(y dice el prólogo).
This archipelago gives me more courage	El archipélago me da más valor del
than I need to be who I am and what I	q' necesito para ser quien soy y lo q' soy hoy,
am today, I am myself wherever I am,	lo soy donde quiera q' esté
immersed in this blackness I ask,	sumido en esta negritud pregunto,
Who are you, who calls into question my	¿Quién es usted, q' pone en tela de juicio mi
legitimacy?	procedencia?

Who are you, who questions my decency,	¿Quién es usted, q' cuestiona mi decencia,
integrity and appearance?	integridad y apariencia?
Who are you, who doubts my capabilities	¿Quién es usted, q' duda de mis capacidades
and denies the virtues that are part of	y niega virtudes q' me salen a flor
my flesh and bones?	de piel?
Those winds brought these storms,	Aquellos vientos trajeron estas tempestades,
And so it happened that (suddenly)	resulta q' así (de pronto)
my race had a mountain of	un montón de cualidades cayó
virtues dumped on it	encima de mi raza,
and many went in mass to pass a	y muchos fueron en masa a pasar un
course on how not to be racist,	curso de cómo no ser racistas
they graduated with high honors,	se graduaron con honores y fiestas
and until today they remain hidden	y hasta el sol de hoy permanecen escondidos
behind this phrase:	en la frase esta:
WE ARE ALL EQUAL,	SOMOS IGUALES,
WE ARE ALL HUMAN BEINGS	TODOS LOS SERES HUMANOS
Dear so and so,	Estimado fulano,
if for you black and white hands are not	si para usted no son lo mismo blancas y
the same,	negras manos,
consider yourself invited to my black	considérese invitado a mi concierto
concert,	prieto,
Hear this, Nicolás!	¡Escucha esto, Nicolás!
I am rapping to the beat of my kinky hair,	Estoy rapeando al compás de mis pasas,
my wide nose, my thick lips, my	mi ñata, mi bemba, mi árbol genealógico,
family tree, my history, my customs,	mi historia, mis costumbres, mi religión y
my religion and my way of thinking.	mi forma de pensar.
I know the court is watching me, but	Se q' el tribunal me observa pero yo

I also watch back with fixed gaze,
Grandfather told me:
My son, you cannot hesitate at the
   hour
when you are defusing the bombs,
because of this, in the middle of the
   trial
I dance the conga in front of the
   jury,
since I know my arguments have
prevailed.
I have witnesses who'll swear to
what I say,
Now let's hear the verdict!

también miro fijo.
Abuelo me dijo:
Mi'jo, no se puede titubear

a la hora de desactivar las bombas,
por eso, en pleno juicio bailo conga
   frente a
to' el jurado,

porq' se q' han prevalecido mis
motivos.
Tengo testigos q' donan sangre a
lo q' digo,
¡Ahora q' venga la sentencia!

Four Poems

Omar Pérez

Translated by Kristin Dykstra

Pure Subject, Subject in Pieces

> . . . who wrote hoping to
> corrupt the ages to come.

Who wrote with the intention of doing damage, suborning
future generations
readers of solid reputation, emancipated
in the dull sacra of libraries and conversations
and, again, libraries;
who wrote with the illusion of making enemies.
Who wrote with the intention of extorting from posterity
readers, pale or bronzed, erect (obscenely)
on top of cultural protocols and boredom's protocols
and, again, boredom's protocols;
who wrote with the pretension that they'd slander him.
Who wrote, it's said, with the illusion of making enemies—

boundary 2 29:3, 2002. Copyright © 2002 by Duke University Press.

unexpectedly, they add, he was distracted or hindered;
he came apart, leaving the work half done.

Camilo in the Clinic Hallway

Camilo possesses himself of the clinic hallway
in the photo that's too old for me
and too new for anyone who can bear this kind of place any longer.
Camilo is laughing alone in the hallway
and he who laughs alone
recalls a more clear and simple time
he who laughs alone
deposits a comprehensible heart
in a sink as credit.
Camilo laughs alone
it's clear that I have just one way out,
I mimic him
and as if I were a sort of spoiled saint
and as if I were an unyielding saint
I chew over the smoldering ash from a more difficult time,
he mimics me.

Diogenes Has Shown

Diogenes has shown that the tongue is like a sponge
adding that this is true for all of us; me included.
Diogenes activated all the resources of his grandstanding tongue
in sight of friends, see? (me included) and women
he crushed it brutally between his index fingers and thumbs
to force the last drop of meaning out.
Through his beard, which is already silvery, see?, streamed
brilliant words of saliva or words intrinsically brilliant,
when it was over, though, Diogenes noted sadly
that no one, none of us, me included,
can squeeze everything out of a sponge.

Victory of the Disobedient

In the crowd
a man has slyly nudged a pigeon with his foot
many times before picking it up.
There is just one life and we'll shield it with scales
There is just one life and we'll cover it with the words of others.
We'll pat it slyly several times before deciding that we want it.

The Supervised Party

Antonio José Ponte

1

I would like to tell the story of how money and parties—*fiestas*—reappeared in Havana. To do this, it would be necessary to talk about the blackouts, because money and parties spring out of the dark, since it is in the dark that certain things can best be seen.

There would be, then, a dark city, with power shortages. A dead city or one awaiting more bombardments. Deserted, with no cars driving around, no public transportation. And here and there, by virtue of the foreign tourists who come to visit, spots of light from the hotels, bright fishbowls in the night.

It would be in these hotels where, at first, money and parties were concentrated. And those who were determined not to do without them would go there. They would be known by their style of dress, a uniform: close-fitting clothes, the women's legs and navel and the men's arms exposed. The navel serves to signify in a not very concealed way what is hollow, and the legs promise a firm grip on whoever enters that hollowness. And the bare arms of

boundary 2 29:3, 2002. Copyright © 2002 by Duke University Press.

the men allude, as do the women's legs, to penetration and, on a secondary level, to the penis.

Black clothes preferably: camouflage in the dark zones between one hotel and the next. Sober, priestly, and, ideally, expensive. Shoes that increase height and improve posture. High heels for the women and buck-led boots with shiny metal pieces for the men. The female vampire and the urban cowboy, more or less. *Jineteros* (prostitutes) they would be called or they would call themselves.

With nightfall and no electricity in their homes, they would go out to prostitute themselves in the war zones around the hotels, lit up in spite of the danger in which the city was immersed. They would be content to spend hours over a drink or seated in a brightly lit lobby, not too concerned (at least not visibly so) with the pace of business.

To be inside the hotels meant something as miraculous as the flow of electricity. It meant being free of police vigilance, entering a world bent on putting into motion waiters to please the guests, facilitating their trade in contraband goods and black market deals. A beer, a comfortable sofa, the movement of people, would be enough to justify going out. And, meet-ing the foreign clients, no unnecessary agitation, on the way to their hotel rooms. Instead, sinuosity, a meandering prostitution. Something like high-class prostitution or call girls. (The country's president, who had abolished prostitution decades before, would have to recognize publicly that it had returned. And before the television cameras he would take pride in the fact that the country boasted the most sophisticated prostitution in the world.)

Indeed, the old trade had returned. But some part of it, of its mecha-nisms, seemed to have been lost along the way. Because, applying the con-cept of efficiency to the total effort of getting oneself up, avoiding the police, and paying for a drink in order perhaps to get nothing in return from the night, that prostitution proved as inefficient as the economic enterprises of the country.

Even easygoing pimps would have disqualified the work of such pupils. What were they doing wasting time in lobbies and long preambles, delaying the moment when they would take one of the elevators? In a coun-try devastated by war and the expectation of still more war, they inevitably confused needs with desires. A beer, that cold bitterness: They could pros-titute themselves in their slow, inefficient manner for as little as a beer. They would have discovered some new sentimentality, a form of affection exac-erbated by items found only in hotels, paid for in foreign currency.

And in the same way in which they simulated pleasure in order to give it—the necessary condition of all forms of prostitution—they were capable of feigning affection and a quite secondary interest in money. They surprised their foreign clients with a different way of understanding their charges. They would stay in the room after collecting the amount agreed on, when the taxi meter was no longer running. (There was still blackout at home.) If even basic necessities of life were elevated, given the impossibility of satisfying them, to the level of extravagances, likewise it would also be difficult to draw the line between a love affair and prostitution.

And now, their clients would ask, without being able to get rid of them, What do you want? Somewhat metaphysical male and female prostitutes, the majority of the *jineteros* would place little importance on the physical act. Veterans at prostitution, in spite of being very young, they were above mere sex. They would offer, above all, time to their clients. And they would want to be reciprocated, not with the confusion of money but rather with an invitation to travel. They exchanged history for geography.

What is the difference between a transaction effectuated with money, compared to one in which time is offered in order to obtain space in exchange? Surely little. They would struggle to find a way out to other places where hotel life was not such a big exception. They wanted to put their bodies in another space. They hung out around hotels because they could not do the same around embassies and consulates.

They entered the illuminated fish bowls, evaded the guards and the rules of tourist apartheid that prohibited Cuban nationals from entering. They bribed doormen and police, elevator operators and receptionists. They unwittingly fulfilled, in an almost animalistic fashion, the desires that the rest of the population, isolated in the darkness of their homes, were forced to deal with in both theory and practice.

They bet on beauty, another name for the party. They would see a hotel as the rudiment of possible life. A beer, a song, perfume, anything beautiful passing by that gave some value to time would be, for them, a symbol as powerful as money. And while official discourse declared that the country maintained the armor of its dignity untarnished, the new prostitution took it upon itself to ensure that the armor of beauty was not neglected. They centered their dignity on this. The defense of a necessary dose of joy and beauty constituted their pride as a clan. The *jineteras* and *jineteros* were the aesthetes of the Special Period.

2

In one of the notes for the book on the Paris Arcades he never finished, Walter Benjamin wrote that, during the Commune, the clocks on the faces of buildings were favorite targets for revolutionary sharpshooters.

Practically all the public clocks in Paris ended up stopped by bullets. The gunshots of the Communards sought to stop time forever, to quell their anxiety at the little importance time attributed to the revolutionary triumph. Because time had dedicated only a moment to that triumph, as if it were nothing special, in its haste to move on to something else.

The revolution in power would undertake to punish such insolence, to combat time. It would call attention over and over again to that precious moment of triumph, it would make it history, meaning, density in a moment. It would invent commemorations, the calendar of the Revolution, a new astronomy, a kingdom of self-torture and guilt: How does one call oneself revolutionary when everyone, sympathizers or not of the abrupt change, innocents, accomplices or executioners, now finds him- or herself, forever, outside the moment of the Revolution?

Whoever was not there during the fighting would not be able to say, then, that he or she was in the Revolution, would not be able to narrate it truthfully to his or her grandchildren. Even those who held pistols on the barricades and might have managed to put a bullet in the machinery of a city clock presumed too much in the very process of carrying out their act, since from the instant the shot sounded that act became elegiac. Two epitaphs coincided at the same moment: the epitaph of the old regime and the epitaph of the Revolution.

Enormous efforts would be made to relive this first moment, and they would always fail. In astronomical terms, institutionalized revolutions describe an absurd model: that of an orbit composed of a single point. The worst of alchemies is a revolution when it is put to do battle against time. It empties time until it achieves a crushing appearance of eternity, of a dead season, of summer heat. And by taking on time along with one of time's emblems, money, it is left with only two options: to be accursed or inane.

The Revolution manages to make evident, in the same way as the lucidity and hallucinations of misery, the symbolic character of money. It insistently unmasks one of the certainties that any other society needs to forget in order to continue operating: that money, the representation of everything, can also represent nothing, be nothing.

Creating the spectacle of a currency devalued to zero, organizing lines to humiliate, in front of bank tellers' windows, those who were only yesterday the proud ones, the triumphant revolution changes money in the same way it changes the calendar. It has bonfires at its disposal, *autos-da-fe* for the paper money belonging to the old regime. New bills are circulated to commemorate other dates, and each transaction is a turn of a Tibetan prayer wheel of revolutionary phrases, a new remembrance of the epic moment. Only in this way, exorcized by its capacity to commemorate, does money find a way to enter the Revolution.

With the frontiers of the country closed, and the field of experiments narrowed down, one proceeds, then, to throw out of kilter all forms of behavior related to money. Giving it away sometimes in exchange for no effort, withholding it other times when it has been justly earned, making it available generously, while, at the same time emptying the shelves of any merchandise it could be used to purchase, making it scarce when shops and stores are better stocked—the Revolution's techniques of using money are approximately the same as those found in a manual of torture: dizzying changes, dislocation of the sense of time, rupturing of the sense of filiation and of any link that tries to relate an effect with some cause.

The new society manages thus to explode the base of all previous societies, making impossible any relationship between work and advancement in life. Soon, with the march of the revolutionary economy, it is discovered that something in the alchemical experiment from which so much was expected has stopped working and that from the ashes of the old money no phoenix has succeeded in taking flight. The bills of the Revolution are hardly more than flyers celebrating the disappearance of the currency, confetti to toss out when the carnival of communism arrives. Each substitute invented (moral incentives, they used to be called) is an even more ridiculous expedient than the previous one. And the ghost of the old money begins to rise.

To create a rigidly centralized economy is, in a way, like trying to control the weather. Money escapes from our hands, flows, has the shape of the clouds (as a pickpocket might have thought on some occasion), is too ungovernable. The fifth element, Joseph Brodsky called it. It flows like liquids; what differentiates it from liquids is the property that any receptacle that contains it will adopt the form money lends to it.

In the desire to eliminate money, as in the desire to paralyze time, there is something of Xerxes whipping the sea, something tragic or ridiculous, depending on how it is seen. Just like prostitution, money, after being banished, had to return. And the possession of foreign currency stopped being seen as a crime; they stopped putting people in jail for walking around with four U.S. dollars in their pockets.

In order to be credible again, money had to come from other lands. Foreign currency turned out to be the only kind of money magically endowed. The national currency, however, would use this intrusion to its advantage. To find a level of equivalence with the dollar, whatever that equivalence might be, was in itself a sign of existing. And the Cuban peso would lose a little of its character as sugar mill scrip, worthless outside the company store.

3

A few years ago I was able visit the ruins of Sloppy Joe's bar in downtown Havana. The metallic curtains of the mythical Havana bar, closed for decades, were drawn back by a team that was filming a documentary.

We got permission to visit what had become a cave. Inside, rats scurried around, water leaks formed stalactites, and there was almost nothing left of the mirrors. But the magnificent bar was still standing. One member of the film crew, used to cinematographic expedients, sprayed pressurized water on the floor and managed to clear away the grime. The writing inscribed on the floor appeared like the moon from behind the clouds. Sloppy Joe's was once again, for a moment, open. The party reappeared, the musicians once again unpacked their instruments.

(Sometime later, someone told me that he had at home, using it as a home bar, a piece of the bar from Sloppy Joe's. If that were true, they had sold that bar as a relic, in the same way that splinters of the Santa Cruz or bricks from the Berlin Wall were sold.)

In *Our Man in Havana*, shot in 1959 or 1960, after the triumph of the Revolution, Alec Guinness, playing the role of someone playing the role of a spy, is pursued by a group of musicians who always play the same song, a *guaracha*. He enters the Seville Biltmore hotel, walks along the Prado, patronizes the bars in the old section of Havana, and is even filmed sitting in a somewhat empty Sloppy Joe's. (A few years more and nothing would remain of that life.) Wherever he goes, he is besieged by a *guaracha*, which, because of its persistence, seems to be a secret message, some incomprehensible spy signal.

Currently, the Havana movie theaters go out of their way not to show this film. (It would be shocking to see the city of the fifties on screen and to go out afterwards to the spectacle of its destruction.) Sloppy Joe's continues to await restoration, reopening. The street musicians, whose return coincides with that of the *jineteras*, now corral foreign tourists with new *guarachas*, secret messages that, when deciphered, are unmistakably sexual or laments for the profound transparency of the beloved presence of Comandante Che Guevara. And, curiously, the lyrics of dance tunes have recently been the object of censorship and literary attention.

The repertoire of the bands that make Havana hotel life pleasant during part of the year and that dedicate the other part of the year to fulfilling commitments abroad is now under review. Official censorship discovers in the songs of the best popular musicians vulgarity, filthy language, and misogyny; it poses as a standard the most idyllic tunes and blatantly ignores the central, openly erotic, core of Cuban music. Official censorship does not seem disposed to recognize that vulgarity reigns in the streets where these musicians perform. It forgets that vulgar humor and gossip have also been a revolutionary political weapon.

Immersed in the life of the neighborhood or the ambience of the hotels, trying to catch the moment with their songs, the salsa songwriters are obliged as a matter of course to come to terms with the business of prostitution. (Perhaps the public that offers the best dividends to the bands may be the *jineteras* and *jineteros*.) The theme of the rights and privileges of money and sex mix in songs that become immediately popular. The misogyny of some of the lyrics results from what a man experiences working in an environment of generalized prostitution.

Before dedicating itself to scrutinizing their songbooks for political correctness, politics had tried to find a useful ideological resource in the work of these musicians. Those who set and policed the quotas that dictated how much national music was to be aired on the radio were obliged to rely on the musicians for product. Popular dance music was, first and foremost, nationality, nationalist discourse in the face of foreign music. Salsa lyrics and nationalist political discourse could feel bonded in the mixture of diatribe, exasperation, ostentation, complacency, and exacerbated masculinity they shared.

Diatribes, in some cases against the perjured woman, in others against a world that stubbornly refused to accept as its salvation the Cuban Revolution, could be played together. And it was not by chance that for a while official ceremonies included performances by these same bands. The salsa musicians functioned as the backdrop for the speakers or vice versa.

In the long run it was all a misunderstanding. Beyond the lyrics, what official censorship was not happy with began to be clear. The relative economic independence achieved by those who played music, their trips abroad, their ostentatiousness (in the eyes of revolutionary asceticism, of dictated misery), would find no pardon even after taking into account the participation of these bands in political gatherings. So those in charge of artistically staging the official commemorations had to rely once again on the rather melancholy songwriters of the so-called Nueva Trova, the poets of misery.

Although the return of money was inevitable, it had been hoped that it would come back in a "politically correct," egalitarian way. Demonetized money in the style of decaffeinated coffee, nourishment for old delicate organisms. The resurrection of a taxation system directed at artists and owners of small businesses would not be enough. With artists, there was still ideological coercion, censorship.

The ostentation of the new prostitutes that could never be forgiven (they would pay for it through repeated arrests) was also going to be punished in the musicians. What would be punished in them (and in all self-employed workers) was the economic hybridity that power had been obliged to allow to ensure the continued celebration of the revolutionary calendar.

What had been planned, in essence, was a country of university graduates who worked as waiters, the most cultured waiters in the world, capable of calculating in a microsecond the precise moment to twist the cone when serving ice cream. (The enormous number of university graduates presupposes that professionals will never succeed in living as such within the Revolution.) A country of waiters, whose tips are tightly controlled.

If the spectacle of the new prostitution seemed to incite change, it was mainly due to the lost opportunity to have the state function as pimp. The party, the happiness that was content with commemorating itself, was going to be accepted reluctantly. The party was a cure, but one that needed to be supervised.

4

Small entrepreneurs run restaurants with only four tables, rent rooms in their own homes to foreigners, pedal bicycle-taxis, transport passengers in North American cars of the forties and fifties (or in what seem to be the oldest Soviet cars), fill the market stalls with food, give value once again to any number of gestures, and restore confidence in work.

They have become as necessary as the *jineteros*. In the same way that beauty and joy were defended by the *jineteros* in the darkest moments of the Special Period, the small private enterprises rescue formulas lost for many years. Simple and effective formulas that relate work to monetary gain and return money and time to us.

Many things are changing among us, even when the sluggishness of the pace of change makes us impatient. That which was necessarily exiled has begun to initiate its return, and one day the Revolution will have ended. The country will lose its mission as the beacon for the whole continent, the last sentinel of the socialist watchtowers, the bone sticking in the mouth of the North American empire. And with all these roles exhausted, let us hope that we do not end up becoming with the same fervor the party town for the rest of the world.

I suppose that when that time comes, it will be very dangerous to consider, tangentially, from the single remaining point of connection, its end, the years of the Revolution in power. To deny completely what happened would be as absurd as it has been to move in the imaginary geometry of an orbit composed of a single point. Joseph de Maistre, whom it would be very difficult to accuse of revolutionary inclinations, made his companions of the Bourbon exile recognize that to act as if the French Revolution had not occurred would be like emptying Lake Geneva and bottling its waters in order to store them afterwards in a cellar. Lake Geneva stored in the cellar of nostalgic reaction and the shoulders of the sea whipped into action by the Xerxes of revolutionary voluntarism are two beautiful hydraulic impossibilities.

What from the Revolution will seem useful when it has ended? It is still too soon to know what will be missed.

Every afternoon, between six and seven, whoever walks in Havana along the Avenida del Puerto will encounter along the seawall a large group of fishermen with rods. A school of fish seeks shelter every afternoon in this part of the bay. The fishermen fish quickly, attentive to the slow movement of the fish. When the school begins to shift, they move along the seawall. They hurry like the paparazzi or stock market brokers of old. It is lovely to see the school of fish next to the shoreline, and the activity of the fishermen who try to catch them is also lovely. There is an abundance of exclamations, protests, pushing, and stockbroker-like shouting.

One afternoon, after much rushing back and forth, as he was tossing his hook into the new site of the school of fish, I heard one of these fishermen shout something that, at the time, seemed to explain a lot of things to me. I don't know now what his outburst can tell me, and I don't know with any precision why I remember that group of fishermen enjoying themselves by the bay. Perhaps it was because of the extremely slow, almost stationary and hypnotic advance of the school of fish and the impatience, the anxiety, that consumed the fishermen.

"Shit, what luxury!" was what the fisherman shouted.

Havana, May 2000

Chango's Little White Horse

Raúl Rivero

I believe it was true that he loved Cuba, all of Cuba. In the complex Havana of the nineties, he drove around in a black 1957 Chrysler, almost offensive in its majesty, cruising through a landscape of piles of garbage and urban decay, with a prostitute at his side, or a cultural functionary, or a queer, or a writer.

He liked black women with names of flowers or countries or continents. I know several of his "Black girls, my little Black girls," as he used to say.

Jazmín, Rosa, Miosotis, Argentina, Africa and America, Camelia and Azucena, all mulattas, all tall, all religious, and part-time dancers or "language students studying on their own."

In Havana, he tried to open a center for studies of contemporary European poetry. This kept him in contact with the professionally upbeat cultural functionaries, with journalists alert for a story, and the plague of young poets (*jineteros liricos*) hunting phantasmagoric foreign fellowships in order to take a vacation from the Special Period for awhile.

He made a habit of renting private homes in Vedado, which was cen-

boundary 2 29:3, 2002. Copyright © 2002 by Duke University Press.

trally located, still almost clean, with the best hotels near at hand and also near the cultural centers. But he liked the action in Centro Habana, where he would hang out at night in the bars drinking cheap rationed *peleón* rum, listening to a *guaguancó* beat played on a leather stool and a rumba and some boleros, and where the people didn't use his complicated name full of consonants, but Juanito the *sss*mooth one, Juanito the *sss*weet one, or Chango's little white horse.

He started coming to Cuba in the seventies, met everyone, became a saint, and Chango always protected him on his tragic pilgrimages to Los Hoyos in Santiago, on his wanderings through Bayamo and Ciego de Ávila, on his medical trips to Brazil and Santo Domingo, and even in the snow and cold of his homeland, where our saints have to pass themselves off as domestic animals or doves. Where the god Eleggua needs more rum and more tobacco and there is a shortage of coconut candy, and remedies are more difficult to obtain because the deities of the tropics don't know where evil comes from in winter.

I am sure that María Elena Cruz [a dissident journalist] remembers him. She remembers him as being magnificent and generous in my home in Centro Habana at the party to celebrate her release from jail. She remembers him standing in front of a battery of bottles on my glass table, while she sang of treachery and desire with her sad almond and melon voice.

Many writers in trouble remember him. They remember him apologizing for bringing them a small gift, something for the day or the week, something to ease the severity of the blockade. What blockade? "Are the piglets coming from Europe? Is taro root being sown in Boston? Have the little chickens departed for Miami? Have those cows of yours committed suicide? Take that spaghetti and that cheese and a bottle of Rhine wine."

Here he always presented himself as what he was, a man from another place, an intellectual who joined in affectionately, interested in the life and the culture of a country.

No politics, keeping himself always at that middle distance said to be ideal in boxing. This is how he is known on this now unlucky Island, where he has had free entry to bars and hangouts, homes and institutions, where he has been loved, this Gentleman from Europe good at rum, poetry, friends, and "Black girls," very much the gentleman (*caballero*), Chango's little white gentleman/horse (*caballito*).

For Juanito the Smooth Guy, before the sweet guy, my house is in the same place, not a house he saw collapse from age and neglect in neighborhoods like Oquendo and Neptuno, in Cayo Hueso, but one nearer, where, bitter and gloomy, sad for him and sad for me and Cuba, I am writing down our last conversation in the bar of the Inglaterra Hotel this spring, during which his nervous fingers made a strange little music on the counter.

"The journalist Pedrito de la Hoz has told me that I shouldn't visit your house anymore because it's dangerous for me. They can deny me another entry visa to Cuba. They are filming me every time I enter your building."

I said nothing. Juanito stood up without looking at me, took a large empty glass and started to go from table to table asking for money for the pianist.

Two Prose Poems

Reina María Rodríguez

Translated by Kristin Dykstra and Nancy Gates Madsen

watery light

through the porthole, then passing through the old and flowered cloth of a small white curtain, a watery light entered that made me look—though unwilling—at the cracks in the building, the weight of the uncovered water tanks, the iron beams that have lost their casings and creak when the flocks of doves pass, dive, rise, hide from this March splendor, flee perhaps. the girl sleeps with a fever, and he is on the floor (prow) upon a cushion. the cats are looking for some moisture as well and they scatter across the cement—now gray, then red—and I think, or rather I taste, between the light—I repeat— the watery light and that wool protecting the remaining stuffing of a cushion also crushed under the weight, his slender tongue entering my mouth. the sharpest point of the tongue that provoked a certain rejection from me then, and now I taste again (with some of the moisture of an oppressive summer heat that will descend mercilessly upon us) and the doves spread out equi- distantly again. he has already gone. and there's a craving for a misty rain

boundary 2 29:3, 2002. Copyright © 2002 by Duke University Press.

against the boiling skin, the beating skin (I get up and write to conquer that fear of distances, that trembling over losses) the cloud has become a gray mass (a brain) that approaches and warms in order to obscure any visibility through the anchored ship's window of my room. I'll have to move the pen's fine point over his tongue again. I can't understand how a large body like that can end in its stiletto prolongation. weakness bothers me, now it pleases me. it pleases me and it pains me. gray mass that is almost watery and conquers my throat, burning me (that morning I didn't dare, but how good it feels, straddling my chest, my belly, another's waist, like that: upright). my city is a hot mass with too much texture (overabundance of being), dark mucus, uterus that expands and wastes away and sometimes rains water, sometimes blood. my city's noise is interior and gray, it expands—determined by hormones—that color these suburbs, the rooftops, the mezzanines, sandy or metallic to the touch (the temperature has changed radically and a strong, cold wind shakes the hinges). we've eaten boiled sugar beet. here and there, pieces of zinc rise amorphously, I see them flying, they overtake me. the house, a ship among the entrails (stranded), hyperplasia of the endometrium—he has said. there will be a lot of blood, deep swells. I use the stuffing from some of Elís' animals, or rag dolls, wool too. everything helps here to increase—if the quantifiable distinction is possible—the anguish. my friends were always leaving, first some around age twenty, then others through the forties. years tunneling from my vagina to my heart. the gray cloud draws even closer. so much anxiety over building a friendship and then, they leave (I'll repeat, they will return, surely, they'll return, desecrated, to live together). the closer I get, the more I'm feeling the days as pages (commonplace) and the body of the work hurrying to consume its white time. as I turn the pages, I summon a certain shade, a certain color, to seem somewhat different. a French blue, another ultramarine, some gold. (the eyes I like are steel blue) although I accept variations. the days, I repeat, beyond a shade (a trick), an oblique movement of color, or a cloud's gradual halting, like today, are identical (the feeling of the page that fills itself with signs of weariness to delay death, or to change). and this noise that I know as discomfort, a buzzing in my ear that reveals itself as cheap jewelry (it's not gold yet, just plastic). I write those pages that the days give me with their different twilights contemplated from the hammock (there my luxury, my obsession) of preferring to watch the expanse that makes an end distinct. I was so distracted, so entertained, that I never accepted reality . . . (my luxury) at noon, with the summer's intense heat, to open my legs and let that slim tongue wander there again, delving for a way to get into the city, to meet its noise, to know whether I were true behind a cape of pure scents, or acid ones, mixed (scents that exceed any pH, earth, virility, femininity, scents that a perfume designer decided to combine with shades of red, strawberry, clear, purple) and I'm wondering what he's discovering there below the vertigo, what formula he's really making with me out of his saliva. a page turns in the act of opening and closing my legs and I don't know what I'm doing. how many identical, unique and different tastes you have to reabsorb in order to choose. but the city, which has expanded its cracked walls (morphology of the cell) doesn't allow itself to be penetrated easily. I pull up my jeans. the neighbor lady was shouting because she saw a parachute with its para- chutist fall out of the bluish backdrop, right over her rooftop—a mercenary, she shouted—and it was only a hot air balloon blown off course (when I embrace you there is a warm, very human reconciliation to trouble; its ema- nation—I would say—gives form to a presence that's necessary for being saved through fear). my ship stays at anchor by imagining itself this way: one day follows another and all together they leave to alter their living book, a book that closes for another new one, fresh, without marks, not yet faded, that sparks a desire stronger than the previous one. (I'm like a book with too many marks, underlines, some with a yellow highlighter.) the need to describe the voice of the uterus: a soft, serious voice at dawn that lulls you to sleep when heeded, softly loved within, draining. no one caresses you on the inside. your mama's going to make a delicious treat, something spe- cial. today's sugar beet is already boiling. in the end, we are women. when I issue an invitation, those I invite aren't there. the others are the ones who come. (Clarise with her green dress sewing one fold after another letting her recall every stitch, every step, a little of the past) "the Lamb that was slaugh- tered since the beginning of the world . . ." Plantagenet with his refractory bricks fortifying his obsession; or Stephen Dedalus changed into the name of an alley cat, my characters left too. and Virginia and Dinesen and the rest? all dead, dead or fugitives. stop this infernal game! Richard Reich keeps laughing from the mirror, at the shadow of a gallows where I find Nerval, or the little broken windowpane where, when I was opening my legs—and my eyes—I could see Saint Teresa, watching me. it's sugar beet spread. this city that we've built slowly with divine matter, with the dead and with uter- ine substance (anguish about overcoming a state of anguish (ego) and a tremendous penis, now for me, it's just literature). of course, the neighbor lady who saw the mercenary fall won't think the same way, there's the differ- ence, she expects truths. a penis is pink? it's blood, dragon's resin? sepia? maybe burnt sienna (this coloring book has made me understand that it's hard for me to distinguish shades, their pains). sometimes I entertain myself remembering them, I stroke them, remembering them. you were saying my name again, like a lament, like an ending . . . and then, your face stayed trapped there forever, in the ship's window, next to the curtain—which used to be a white skirt—my white flag. I swallowed that semen afraid of poisoning myself (it wasn't any different) but all the same, it was unique. you were possessing yourself in me. your ear reddening with desert-colored paint. here there's quite a singular mystery, what degradation did I suffer in exchange? the storm has just passed and at the foot of the wet buildings, a light illusion of harmony, ecstasy (intensification or reduction of intensity; the cool and warm colors, juxtaposed, intensify each other mutually). perfection is the body and the blood on the altars.

the artist

. . . the music from the house next door is a remote cry across the night. player piano: I return. the balcony has fallen. crash of rock on mud. astonished, people look at each other and watch it falling still without a sound, almost fantastic. with her flashlight, a woman illuminates the broken supports (the number of the slot through which they give out spices), the choice, she trains the light on me and I get scared. I'm exposed by the light, by the glass in a window that has fallen down from above, I protect myself . . .

(. . . I see another street, no less devastated, inside me. if I were patient enough to narrate all of that, what it was like. I feel sorry for those people, faced with frustrations, who seek illusion in the fissure, the illusion of being able to leap, of being sustained in weightlessness by the current of a river with no tributaries . . . "without the eyes of pragmatism to evaluate the relativity that supports them"—you'd say—"rather than an absolute," so that no one would feel the true current and compensate only for the frustrations, to substitute, they are the disorders of necessity . . .)

. . . together, gas pedal and brake try to create in us an illusion of existing. you spend your life like that, waiting to begin, on the edge. when what is hardly begun completes its ending, unreflective, the figure surprises us . . . that figure is me, out looking for you . . .

(. . . when I was a little girl, I used to scribble in my books, we all did. when someone would say the words that I made up, I would be perplexed, and at the same time, sad. because everything was known; everything was known. growing up, the scribbles—formerly lines of delirium and undeciphered words—took on precise forms, drawings, systems, maturity had been achieved, that's it, representation, its construction. now I want to break up the conscious drawing, its dark line, which led me from one abstraction to the other, and I want to unmake myself in those original scribbles—not the same—because I already learned to control the game of making them and destroying them . . . sketched desires are of a different breed, when we've learned the artificial desires of any power, or possession, it's hard to achieve the others . . .)

. . . a protagonist sick with cancer, a crusted crab. "Sweet November"—that movie where she satisfies a different man every night, until dawn, leaving her cancer, her pain, in other bodies and in each contracted muscle, kiss and death . . . (it's always when laughing at death that you take your own life—said Edmond Jabès) . . .

(the violence of the need)

. . . cancer and woman, there's no contradiction. it's the end of the movie, the month, the year, the century, the project; the era, the end of illusion. the inner street gives back my black silhouette, also overheated between two lights, without pain, without odor, without flavor, without rancor, phantasmagoric. fiction of an inverted (magic?) lamp looking for its contents in the window-pane: some light—bright, momentary, against that other, oblique light . . .

. . . "fragile, like things that are expensive, that don't come back . . ."

(plagiarizing Socrates, Osvaldo, myself, anyone, with the fragility of simply supporting a life)

. . . I don't have a glow anymore, I lost the glow, the possibility of enamel and with these fingernails, holding fast and demanding some truth, I'm gradually losing my appearance while giving it another discourse, which no longer includes birds, or the sorrows of birds, or shadows. perhaps I've been the most ambitious creature, watching you deceive; touching objects to make them marvelous, deceiving them. behind the appearance, which I've lost, there's no longer any other; behind that closed door, only the most prominent cheekbones, the bones of a passion I never lived, its pale lips . . . (thoughts fall to pieces at the foot of the unthought, like birds at the edge of the sky, wrote reb Farji)

. . . when I abandon the simulacrum, the acting, the desire to seem, the fable, the plagiarism of a system of action, do I cease to be "the artist"? . . .

Grilled Shrimp Pasta

José Prats Sariol

> Old injustices were being corrected, new injustices were beginning to be perpetuated.
> —Milan Kundera, *The Book of Laughter and Forgetting*

The entrance to Hops Restaurant-Bar-Brewery flashes its *Welcome* sign like the river of cars moving along Pine Pembroke Avenue. The lights are barely noticed by the patrons arriving at the restaurant this Friday night; they go immediately to pick up the electronic cards that will tell them when their table is ready. The hostess rewards them with a pasted-on smile, framed between her freckled cheeks like a logotype. She turns the smile on the party of three just approaching the door and delivers the prescribed message:

"We're here to please you. We want to attend to your every need, make your pace our pace, your style our style, and any special request an opportunity to please you."

David looks at his Cuban father-in-law, unsure whether his English is good enough to metabolize the message. But he senses immediately that

boundary 2 29:3, 2002. Copyright © 2002 by Duke University Press.

Fernando has gotten the gist of it, although some words probably remain hanging in his ears. Marta smiles, knowing that her father pretends to speak Oxford English, more exact than *Webster's Dictionary*.

The couple is unaware that Fernando is dealing with another problem altogether: How to bring up the topic he knows is unavoidable but that will crash noisily on the tablecloth like a packet of firecrackers going off over the plates and leftovers, the silverware and glasses.

"Shall we go to the bar?" Fernando asks in Spanish.

"Let David go. Can you go to the bar, baby, *please*?"

"Sons-in-law can be . . . He is passing all the tests. I swear."

"Seriously, Daddy? If I didn't know you . . ."

Fernando smiles for the first time since they had gotten out of the Ford Explorer Marta and David bought just days before. He knows that his daughter hangs on his reactions like a spider, suspended between anxious anticipation and approval. He understands that he has absolutely no right to rain on her parade. But he looks at her now as he did when she was three or four years old, after the divorce, and he took her back to the Sevillano in a number 13 bus where they did not give him a seat. He takes her by the arm before responding:

"It seems that David has in his favor his Irish mother and a father who is the son of Germans. Ireland is also a Catholic country."

"But without *Yemayá*."

"Yes, but I'm sure they have their own goddess of the waters. Probably the one they call Molly Bloom, who knows? And what about the Germans with *Odin* and his tribes? There's David on his way back."

"Maybe he was able to get seats at the bar."

"Do you talk with him about Cuba?"

"Of course, but what's important is that his Spanish not sound like a *señorrita's* . . ."

"And that your English not sound like mambo."

"I'll never get rid of my accent. Besides, I'm dark-skinned; besides, I don't feel like it."

"My grandchildren won't have this confusion: Perfect English for them."

"Don't be silly, Daddy, they'll be bilingual: Who better than you to teach them Cuban?"

"Dreams, Marta. They will jabber in Spanish, use it on Christmas Eve and at birthdays. A family relic, which when they grow up they may perhaps find they need for their work."

"Here comes David."

"Please. Seats. Go."

"Okay, let's go."

Fernando thinks the gaudy decoration of the bar, somewhere between a Western saloon and a Pullman car, forms a curious synthesis of Yankee comfort. He notices that the design of the room distributes spaces with efficient rationality. It is simultaneously tight and roomy, informal and ceremonial. No one gets in the way, even in the corridors that lead to the kitchen. There, behind glass walls, the heart of Hops is like a Chaplinesque machine whose moving parts are the cooks, kitchen hands, and waiters. Everything displays the same standard quality as the beer they make—or appear to make—in the rear of the restaurant, behind another glass partition that offers a view of the bronze kettles and coils.

At the bar, there are only two stools free. Marta takes the one in the corner, and David insists on Fernando taking the other. The bartender has a narrow nose and high-pitched voice. He asks them what they want to drink. David suggests they try the Lightning Bold Gold beer, or the strongest one, Hammerhead Red. They decide on the latter, named thus because of its amber color. They also order a plate of Ultimate Nachos to nibble on. The order arrives promptly.

"Cheers!"

"To my Daddy's arrival."

"May you both be happy."

"Fernando, liking it?"

"Delicious, it must be the tradition of the German emigrants. In Cuba, too, they used to make a beer like this, dark, but I think it had more alcohol, and it was thicker. Dangerous! I think they have started making it again now . . ."

"Now that the economy is dollarized, no?" Marta asks ironically.

Fernando, instead of answering Marta, looks up at the ceiling and shrugs his shoulders. To answer would be to complicate things, to introduce in the conversation viruses that will spoil the dinner. He tries a nacho, submerged in a chunky salsa, and takes another long swig of beer:

"They make it very well, with just the right bitterness. It was a great idea, David, this place is welcoming, and the service is incredibly fast for a Cuban from Cuba."

"There being Cubans not from Cuba?"

"Excuse me, I meant that the more than one million who have left won't be surprised that the service is efficient . . ."

"We are all Cubans, right, Daddy?"

"Of course, dear, which doesn't mean that we are in agreement, because, among other things, that would be very boring."

"Yes, but in Cuba some people say that those of us who leave the country aren't really Cuban."

"The troglodytes . . . But there are extremists here in Atlanta, too, and, I don't need to remind you, in Miami. Maybe we Cubans should get used to—really get used to—living together with people who don't think like us, whether we are exiled or, if I may coin a phrase, 'insiled' (*sean insiliados o exiliados*)."

"I to be agree with your Dad. The United States of America to be exile country. To come from all parts."

"David doesn't understand. Why don't we talk instead about you two, your plans?"

"Ay, Daddy, now we're not going to be able to talk about anything! Well, anyway . . . We've been thinking of living closer to the lab. Renting or selling our condo and putting a down payment on a house in Boca Raton."

"Gain an hour daily, *you know? Time. . . .*"

"And health reasons and less risk on the freeway and the possibility of using the extra time to swim, read, whatever . . . Have you made an offer?"

"We spoke with an agent, who promised to get back to us next week. There's a new section in Boca we just love, although the cost of the down payment is very high."

"Give to choose *more than* thirty model residence."

"Just like in Cuba, right, Daddy?"

"Just let them discover more oil, diamonds, whatever . . . though tourism is doing well, and the mixed enterprises . . ."

"Just let the state monopoly end."

"You think so?"

"There'll be less bureaucracy, big investments from the Cuban community here in the States, more money transfers to family."

"Family dwelling, *new*. Much content!"

The electronic buzzer they are holding tells them they can move over to the restaurant section. David goes to check on the table. He is back in a minute. They eat some more of the Ultimate Nachos. Their table is on the left side. Fernando finishes the rest of his beer. He thinks that the Hops machine moves with the precision of a Swiss watch. Even the murmur of the conversations, the soft rock background music, the patron's orders seem to be part of the *performance*.

As soon as they are seated, David hands out the menus. The three-some casts glances at the tables around them, trying to identify the dishes against the names, imagining how they will taste by how they look. Fernando knows that he can't spoil the dinner, nor the pride his daughter feels at invit-ing him, so he again hesitates making the decision he knows he has to, puts it out of mind . . .

It dawns on him that the mulatto waitress is Dominican. She must have at least a few years as an immigrant already, because the level of her English, at least the English she uses to attend to her customers, is not the common Spanglish of Miami, of the Cuban immigrants intermixed with Cen-tral Americans and West Indians. She smiles, but David, Marta, and Fer-nando sense that it is not a spontaneous smile: This is what she is taught, indeed obliged, to do, from the first to the last customer of the night. Marta chooses the Chicken Caesar Salad and David the Jamaican Top Sirloin. Fer-nando reads the ingredients of the Grilled Shrimp Pasta: *Large gulf shrimp, seasoned and grilled, then toasted with fresh linguine in a white wine gar-lic cream sauce. Topped with fresh grated Parmesan cheese. Served with toasted garlic bread.* And, without giving it another thought, he asks for one. All three order the same beer, Lightning Bold Gold this time, which is smoother, just right for their meal, and the Hops Stickers as an appetizer.

They overhear a middle-aged couple at the next table talking loudly — in melodious Guantanamero Spanish — about the huge bills they have run up on their credit cards, which their monthly statement has reminded them of like a sharp slap or the U.S. military base located in the bay of their native town. A little further away, in another corner, a group of young people are laughing and asking for another round of Hammerhead Red. Now it is coun-try music that flows through the restaurant, soothing their hunger pangs until the Dominican waitress returns with the foaming beer mugs and the order of six egg rolls:

"Hop Stickers to be to lick fingers," David says in his garbled Spanish.

"Is there a Yankee cuisine proper?"

"Hamburgers and hot dogs, right? And baked beans (*frijoles colo-rados con salsa medio dulzona*) . . . Pancakes with maple syrup? Bacon, sandwich, grilled chicken, ham and egg?"

"*Yes*, sir. Our to eat. Tasty, tasty. *Sabrioso.*"

"In reality, the Yankees don't have anything of their own. They say that in the planet there are three cuisines, the Chinese, the Mexican, and the French. The others are variations, and the one here especially, although it has the rare capacity to corrupt recipes by adding ketchup and mustard,

melted synthetic cheese, and a side of French fries, even with stuffed pota-
toes."

"Ay, Daddy, you're too much!"

"Please don't get me wrong. There are delicious dishes. The combination of Coca-Cola and hamburger is perfect, for example."

"Excellent! Favorite *lunch*. I like eat *everyday* McDonald's. But Marta
lunch yogurt and vegetables."

"This bobo doesn't respect my diet, Daddy. I've already told him that
McDonald's is for weekends, Sundays. Just imagine, I would become like a
milk cow. Grease everywhere, lard with lard. No, darling, none of that! It's
not good for anyone, it raises your cholesterol and puts on fat. And afterwards, it's difficult to lose the weight. Here they spend their lives inventing
diet plans, but it's because they don't watch what they eat. Have you noticed
the number of fat people around?"

"Yes. But most of them seem to be Latinos or blacks; I suppose they
are the ones who have experienced the most hunger."

"Hunger. Come soon, Grilled Shrimp Pasta, okay?"

"Daddy, no one goes hungry over here. That's down there."

"Yes, but the immigrants eat less fruit and also have less money.
There's also a psychological hunger brought in the suitcase, and habits . . .
Like the Galicians who emigrated to Cuba, eating bean stew (*garbanzada*) in
the middle of August, with pork sausages, black pudding, pork shoulder . . ."

"And can they get all that through the ration book now, Daddy?"

"Now our order has finally arrived. Here comes the Dominicana with
our tray!"

"Good Lord! Look *sabriosa*, delicious."

"*Sabroso*, David, *sa-bro-so*, de-li-cious. Daddy, don't feel bad cor-
recting him. That way he'll learn better."

"It's just that . . . Well, we're not in a classroom. The conversation
would turn to lead."

The waitress puts the plates down without removing the smile on her
face, asks if everything is all right, and leaves with the same agility. Marta
looks at and sniffs her Chicken Caesar Salad; David, his Jamaican Top Sirloin; Fernando, his Grilled Shrimp Pasta. The three share this complicity,
reexamine the surgical instruments before them, and throw themselves into
the battle with the vigor of a Mongolian horde.

The praises of the chicken, the steak, and the spaghetti with shrimp
are not long in coming. Fernando exalts the texture of the white sauce but
is careful not to ask how to make something similar at home. His thoughts

move instead to the topic that has obsessed him since embarking on this trip to the United States: "How to avoid being on one side or the other, exile and insile, fatalism, painful immobility?" He savors the Parmesan cheese and the white wine in the fabulous sauce and reflects: "Polarization favors railway tracks."

Marta and David smile at him with the unspoken satisfaction of seeing the spaghetti disappear from his plate, but Fernando, without showing on his face the whirlwind of thoughts passing through his mind, continues his monologue: "Each railway track rolls against time. Dialogue is foreign to railway tracks. They have parallel thoughts. Parallel, *para-lelos*, for fools . . ." And now his smile does not have to be false, and he elaborates as he slowly savors one of the larger shrimp: "The two lines of track have a train that joins them: a locomotive that needs crisis, that goes from fanatic station to fanatic station, never arriving at the terminal, at the present." As he takes a long swig of the Lightning Bold Gold, he finds himself asking: "Can you rule a country as if it were a primary school in the sixteenth century?"

He takes a piece of garlic bread from the basket and thinks to himself: "The beliefs of one or other railway track are like affective bacteria, resentments. They love specters, specters as sinister as the apparent end of discriminations. The majorities, already conservative and fearful, confused by two voluntaristic elites, allow the misfortunes the country has undergone, from the Spanish viceroys to the North American soldiers and ambassadors, from the dictators of our mutilated republic to the tragic end game of today, to reach a point of culmination. The failure is as spectacular as this sauce."

He chews, savors, clears his throat as if he were giving a talk: "The two enemies do not go beyond willful thought, the subjective intentionality of Madame Bovary. Both sides offer a teleology full of ahistorical aphorisms, ineffable judgments, sentimental bromides, and populist slogans." He wipes his mouth with the napkin, because the shrimp, which he has just speared with his fork, was so large that it came out at the sides of his mouth when he raised it to his lips.

"These shrimp are size XL!" he notes aloud with satisfaction to David and Marta, who beam back as if they had caught them themselves.

"Ah, well!" exclaims Marta, "aren't you going to give me one?"

"Of course, so that the two biochemists can analyze it in their laboratory in Boca Raton."

But Fernando is already retreating into his head again, pontificating to himself now, as if Hops Restaurant-Bar-Brewery were a symposium: "At times, even the least passionate, by a curious psychological mechanism of

self-justification that comes upon them inadvertently, tend to distort historical facts or such obvious phenomena as the transnationalization of capital,
electronic globalization, postmodernist eclecticism in thought . . . The mistake is plausible: the goal mortgages their intelligence, blinds them. They
are stupefied, they swim in stupidity, and so cannot think."

He is vaguely aware, between mouthfuls, that the more Grilled
Shrimp Pasta he eats, the more academic his analysis becomes. But he
cannot avoid another paragraph: "Two abstractions mold my position. The
most important one is ethical in nature. I presuppose an integrity that is very
far from existing in fact, above all in some of the small groups that drive the
locomotives down these rails. The masks, be they of cowardice or opportunism, succeed each other as in Greek tragedy. The excessive pride of
believing oneself to be the master of truth, and the consequent repression
of wizards and witches is as shameful as if we were to leave the restaurant without paying the bill or to embarrass the Dominican waitress. I also
commit an insolence: You cannot compare a railway track that has power
with one that has lost it. The threat of a bloodbath, the neocolonial danger, the extreme bad luck of being the recipient, at the same time, of the
good graces of Soviet-style communism and those of a peripheral capitalism, these things are not shrimp. Neither are the vicissitudes of the home-
less or those who live in houses that are falling down the magical inventions
that pass for food in Cuba, the nightmares of our dilapidated transport system, the feeling of not having a say in the decisions that are truly important
for the country . . ."

After a moment, he adds: "A third track is foreseeable when the fanat-
ics of today disappear, God willing, peacefully. It will be a technocracy supine
in the face of electronics and globalization, in the face of a new myth of
progress that will paper over the growing triviality of culture and education,
ecological depredation, mindless functionalism. It is going to be less visible
than the former two tracks, and because of that it will be more dangerous.
It will insist on converting individuals en masse, emptying life of choices,
creating false needs, impeding critical thought that opposes computerized
resignation. That prospect is also reason to hasten the liquidation of the two
sclerotic tracks. The longer we delay, the more defenseless we will be in the
face of the third track."

Fernando rests his gaze on the breadbasket and thinks: "Underneath
these three aberrations is Cuba. But the first railway track lacks a vocation
for self-liquidation; the second, courage; and the third, maturity. The mouse-
trap is not perfect; many start to move in new directions: youth, Christians,

and especially blacks, women, homosexuals, people from the provinces."
He takes another sip of beer and thinks: "No one wants to be turned into a
statue of salt or to have to listen to the tired refrain that a revolution can be
permanent. In Cuba, even the jailors are in prison . . ."

He decides to shift to some questions, but they get tangled up in his
fork along with the spaghetti: "Will we be capable of taking our foot off the
brakes? Will we be able to think without railway tracks? What stops us from
buying sponges? How to overcome reluctance? We have had since the end
of the eighteenth century an abundance of those who have known how to
scratch the philosopher's stone, how to dream of the union between eman-
cipation and well-being. But isn't it true that the planet is different now, that
the problems of 2000 are new ones, that the utopias ended in the sea?"

David interrupts his father-in-law's thoughts. The strain of composing
the sentence, partly in English, partly in his rudimentary Spanish, shows:

"*I'm sorry, you* seem other side."

"He's like that, David, he goes off every now and then, *se va de onda
a cada rato* . . . Right, Daddy?"

"I'm enjoying this sauce with the spaghetti, the shrimp, so much that
I seem to you to have gone off on a tangent, but none of that, I'm right here.
You two give the same impression with your chicken and steak. Enjoy it!
Delicious! *Sabroso.*"

"*Sabrooooso!*"

"Now you said it right. *Okay.*"

Each one returns to his and her plate, and Fernando, almost unwillingly, goes back to the line of thought David had interrupted. Now he is writing an essay. The vanities of the academic lecturer vanish, he punctures
another shrimp and continues: "Is the Cuban emigration in fact annexationist, unpatriotic? Do all of those here regard with pity those who stayed, do
they look down on them, do they help them fight poverty in order to feed
their own self-esteem? Grudges, arrogance, revenge? How do we close the
cracks? Is it David and Goliath, the backyard of the Empire? How do we deal
with the paradox that never before did Cuba depend so much on the United
States?"

Fernando dips a piece of garlic bread in the sauce that remains in
a corner of the plate, summons up more evidence, stumbles against mon-
sters: "We are afraid of neoliberal models of development, the projects of
drastic changes that lead to brutal inequalities, the proliferation of corruption
and runaway capital, Russian-style politicos and Polish-style entrepreneurs.
And the consequences a transition will bring? The process of reforms? And

the immobilism of the military officials and government functionaries, of the rats and the parrots?"

Fernando scratches his thigh, scratches the fact that the majority of the Cuban population of today hardly knew, or was born after, the famous dispute with the United States. He says to himself: "They know it by hearing or reading about it, nothing more. They respond to other values, they aspire to a different society. Against the vitality of three new generations there is little petulant old men can do. There are no museum pieces in politics, much less in economics. Forgetfulness has always been their overwhelming characteristic."

He is happy to think that the majority of Cubans were born after 1959. "They don't have any reason to suffer the mistakes of their parents, much less their grandparents," he notes. "The more they wait, the worse it'll be. Being apolitical is a sign of ideological supersaturation, also of conformism. The illusion of emigration as a paradise and the desire for an empty consumerism void of spirituality concerns us all, regardless of where we are or our points of view. It's simple. So alarming. Yes or no?"

He tries to answer his own question: "To favor debate is to demand integrity. I dream of avoiding the 'it's not worth it' group, the 'tomorrow is another day' group, the devitalizing effects of 'it's the other side's fault' or the registers of self-pity that egotism archives. Exile and insile, our greatest aberration, deserves a happy ending, Brazilian soap-opera style . . . Ah! A happy ending?"

He shakes his head as if he had both hands full and a fly was fluttering around his nose. He thinks that all of what he has just told himself is due to the effects of the Grilled Shrimp Pasta, that if his ideas were accompanied by salted corn fritters they surely would not be the same. When he lifts his gaze toward his daughter, he sees her giving David a bit of chicken to taste. The idea of the essay he had crudely sketched while eating the Grilled Shrimp Pasta begins to fade. Marta realizes that he is looking at her and invites him to taste a piece of her Chicken Caesar Salad. Fernando accepts, squinting his eyes to erase his train of thought. He sips his beer to clear his palate. When he opens his mouth, there no longer remains a trace of the railway tracks.

"Nice!"

"You really liked it?"

"Very nice. It makes you want to come to Hops every day, to try all of the dishes."

"And now we're going to order desserts to top things off. There's one . . ."

"Desserts. I want the Brownie. Is *a rich gooey chocolate brownie loaded with mixed nuts and lots of Hops tasty treats. Topped with real chocolate syrup and homemade whipped cream.*"

"I want the same as David, but there's also the Apple Walnut Crunch, the Homemade Key Lime Pie, or a Milk Shake . . ."

"The Key Lime Pie should be rich, but good, but this won't be the only time we come here, right? So ask for three Brownies. Here comes the Dominicana!"

"Three Brownies, please."

While the waitress goes off in search of the desserts, Fernando, again without meaning to, returns to the caricature he has just drawn. He clicks his tongue as a sign of annoyance because he understands that his analysis is filled with holes and precipices, and arguments still to be made. But two certainties make him happy: that the youth are the only ones capable of solving the dilemmas and that his reflections have ended up confirming the decision, which, in a few minutes, after the Brownie, he will communicate to his daughter.

"Gone off again, Daddy?"

"Not at all. Just waiting for that chocolate!"

"You'll see how good it is."

"I will try it."

"Not try, swaaaaallow. *Nuts*?

"*Nueces.*"

"Come waiter."

"Waitress, David. It's a woman, female, feminine."

"Thanks, Marta, soon better my Spanish. Your English."

A rock ballad sung by Tina Turner accompanies the ceremony of dessert. The three savor their brownies enthusiastically, sticking their tongues on the roof of their mouth to enjoy the taste with the greatest intensity. And now Fernando is ready to let drop onto the table of Hops Restaurant-Bar-Brewery his decision. He finishes eating, looks first at David, then at his daughter, and says:

"Marta, forgive me, perhaps this is not the right place to talk about this, but it is best if I tell you now. I'm going to go back. It's not a duty, it's also about pleasure, desires . . . I hate the aberration that has transformed us into exiles and insiles, here and there, this absurd thing with no head and no feet, that nothing can really explain or justify. I don't know if returning is the easiest or the most difficult thing. I'm not interested in judging anything. But I know that my place is there, in what was once your home. I'm sorry, I'm going back to Cuba."

When they leave, it is drizzling. In the distance, Pembroke Pine Avenue has less traffic on it than when they arrived. The Hops Restaurant-Bar-Brewery falls away behind them as they walk toward the dark green Ford Explorer in the parking lot. Marta thinks about how to rescue her father from his error; David, about improving his Spanish; Fernando, about nothing. He walks without thinking anything. The rain begins to worsen, they run a little, laughing, full. The bright *Welcome* sign continues to flash its invitation to enter. It silhouettes them against the car.

Havana, 2000

Resistance and Freedom

Cintio Vitier

Nations have to criticize themselves, because criticism is health; but with a single heart and a single mind.
—José Martí, "Nuestra América

1

During the heyday of Sartre and Camus, Europe, and above all France, tried once again to enlighten us, this time with the thesis of the committed intellectual, just when we were beginning to discover that Spanish American culture, given its anticolonialist origins, was structurally revolutionary. This does not mean that there have not been reactionary or regressive tendencies in that culture. On the contrary, these currents have been powerful and are always lying in ambush, but they have had to function within a contextual dilemma—either we are independent or we are not—and so they have never been able to be, neither will they be, masters of the direction of our destiny, because the search for freedom and justice is inseparable from our creative expression, and our creative expression is inseparable

boundary 2 29:3, 2002. Copyright © 2002 by Duke University Press.

from its innate tendency to convert itself, in one way or another, into historical acts. Because of this, we can say that our culture has known only intellectuals committed to or against the project that is bound up with their being,
and in the most diverse ways, including those that are ironic, indirect, and
invisible. The Cuban Revolution, without lacking the usual fools and syco-
phants, made this invisibility visible. For example, in an unexpected inversion, it revealed how Julián del Casal and José Lezama Lima had evaded,
in their hyperaestheticism, a detestable reality only to create an imaginary
reality desirable for the future of the nation. Years later, the Sandinista Revolution would perform the same service to the living memory of Rubén Darío,
with fewer objections and more explicit declarations of praise. In this way,
we discovered what we already suspected, that our escapists were also
founders, and, moreover, that the theory of the intellectual as the "critical
conscience" of the culture in the face of power, in all time and space, was
as old-fashioned for us as a London top hat. What was lacking for us was
not what Octavio Paz called "the myth of criticism," the idea of European
modernity according to which the only truth is criticism itself, but rather José
Martí's "To love: that is criticism," because what is at stake is engendering
justice. What we lacked was not the permanent supervision, impugnation,
and rebelliousness deriving from the supposed purity of a spiritually privi-
leged caste but rather participation in collective work that would lend to the
community dimensions that correspond to it. Among these dimensions, of
course, is the critical function in an organic and, one might say, biological
sense, as the regulating sign of experiences in which one participates: a
criticism whose main form is not professional or so-called "art" criticism,
although this type of criticism can also be necessary and useful, but rather
a criticism that takes place in the sphere of intellectual and artistic creation
itself.

2

As we delve deeper into the challenge of the nineties, each step we
take, however small it may be, has to be against an enemy and in favor of
our resistance. Above the seemingly unstoppable waterfall of the Empire, as
above Niagara Falls, the mirage of a rainbow of supposed options appears,
none of whose colors suit us, because they are the false colors of foam and
vapor. We have the immense power of the waterfall and its false rainbow
against us. But, paradoxically, we also have against us the habit of resisting
the Empire, which tends to keep us firm in our conviction but also immo-

bile, as if hypnotized by resistance. To convert resistance into the mother of a new freedom is the challenge that imposes itself on us. To meet this challenge, there is no better inspiration than the libertarian spirit of Martí, which comes from Heredia, the first poet of the Cuban nation, and from José de la Luz, who said: "Freedom, the *fiat* of the moral world." The *fiat*, the injunction *do it*, is what makes the word an act, like the word in every Genesis. If we don't free the generative forces implicit in resistance, we risk converting it into a paralyzing idol. Nothing could be more contrary to the inspiration of our people, which is who we need to listen to every day. If liberation is already a historical and political fact among us, freedom never is, neither here nor any other place, a consummated fact. It is, rather, something that has to be conquered or extended daily. It is not enough to remain content with the *no* of resistance. It is not enough to seek a mimetic "freedom" as imported as that idea of the intellectual as "critical conscience," a freedom that is the real breach the enemy opens up. Rather, we must discover a freedom extracted from the resistance to the Empire, the daughter of resistance, the prize of resistance, our mother. Our popular resistance is desirous of its own originary freedom, which is specific to this time, which has to grow from popular and revolutionary power with no other condition than the level of social justice attained. We may help to propitiate its plenitude as if it were—because it should be—the birth of a collective poem, since history for us is not reason or the absurd but rather is poetry. To the Hegelian formula "all that is real is rational"—and to its surrealist inversion "only the irrational is real"—we oppose the causality of hidden gestation and birth as eruption, the causality of poetry, not the logical causality of reason but rather the nuptial and maternal causality of poetry, in which it is possible for resistance to be pregnant with freedom. It is what I believe Martí, a Martí now present among us beyond the obligatory quotations from his work, the essential Martí who vibrates in our blood and our soul, is asking us in the face of the challenge at the end of this century.

3

The collapse of East European socialism, including the USSR, has not provoked in Cuba, in spite of the enormous economic trauma we are suffering, the ideological vacuum expected by the United States and the Cuban reactionaries who want to take control of the island again. The reason is simple: However important our alliance with the socialist countries may have been, it was no more than that: an alliance. Where they expected to find an ideological vacuum, they found Carlos Manuel de Céspedes, Antonio Maceo, and Martí—that is, something more than an ideology, a concrete vocation of justice and liberty. The Cuban national-popular interpretation of Marxist-Leninist socialism was to put it to the service of that vocation. From the first generation of Cuban Marxists, those of the twenties, it was clear that the national tradition, culminating in Martí, would not be subsidiary to Marxism; rather, the reverse. Curiously, it is this hierarchization that explains, in the sphere of our popular culture, why the ideological values of socialism have not been destroyed among us by the collapse of the above-mentioned alliance. It is not that Cubans are more Marxist than anyone else but rather that our way of assuming "what is" Marxist in the intuitive popular interpretation has those ancillary characteristics that the collapse brings out into the open and leaves intact, since they have made possible a work of justice that is visible to all and that our concrete historical vocation clamored for. The defense of socialism has thus been expressed as the defense of the country itself, a slogan that would be untenable at this point in history if it didn't have a real foundation in a national project in which all previous failed efforts are accumulated. However, precisely because what is involved is survival as an independent nation, it is no longer enough simply to defend what has already been achieved. To limit oneself in this way would be to lose initiative and, in a deeper sense, to retreat. The tense resistance of the Cuban people is sounding another note which, until now, perhaps had not rung with so much depth and urgency. By merging desire for justice with total resistance to the Empire, what that resistance seems to ask for is not only the firmness of the fortress, which is not in doubt, but also the free and at the same time attached motion of the flag above it.

4

The close of this century again raises, in a particularly aggravated and singular fashion, the problem of 1898: The nascent imperialism of that time is hegemonic today, the fervor for national independence crushed back then cannot be so easily defeated today, the same current of reformism asserts its privileges (*fueros*) and the same current of annexationism its crimes (*desafueros*). The Spanish republican project, which also emerged after 1898, and which we Cubans passionately supported, was crushed as totally as our drive for independence and has not been able to reassert itself fully, as our nationalism has, except on the basis of an accommodation that has put Spain more on the side of a Europe allied with the United

States than on the side of Spanish America, in spite of the fact that Spanish America is its greatest historical responsibility. It is true that, in an attempt to compensate for this unfortunate situation, a broad movement of regional solidarity toward Cuba has manifested itself in Spain. The strengthening of that initiative seems to us of vital importance, not only for the material aid it can provide, but also because of our need to reestablish our link with the Hispanic—and the African—at the "family" level. When Martí said in the *Manifesto of Montecristi*: "We Cubans began the war and we Cubans and Spanish will end it," beyond the exalted project of a war for common justice, "with all and for the good of all," he was pointing, or so it seems to us today, toward a root community of Hispanic cultures, which, given its popular ethical essences, could contribute more than any other to what he called the "balance of the world." God grant that for her and our own good, the Spain of Martí and Unamuno, the Spain of Darío and his Hispanic disciples, prevails. Meanwhile, solitude and solidarity, coming into relation with each other, invade the space of our political and cultural context. And it is here that the qualitative force of our resistance can offer, is already offering, a capacity for dialogue, understanding, and sympathy that is para-ideological. It is certainly not a question of receiving "assistance" passively, like a needy man on his sickbed, or like someone grateful but deaf to the diversity of the world. It is a question of receiving the world in order to understand it and embrace it beyond the dominant arrangements, receiving as brothers what as brothers, from our poverty, we have ourselves given so many times. What we can offer now is, above all, an example. Not necessarily the example of Numancia, the Iberian city that committed collective suicide rather than submit to Roman domination, but a quotidian one of dignity, laughter, and rhythm in the midst of danger and scarcity, of an inventive and industrious spirit, of unforeseeable imagination. These are all forms of freedom, as well as personal character, initiative, opinion, which now more than ever we, in the manner of Martí, should encourage.

5

The great political, ethical principles of Martí are anti-imperialism, solidarity with the poor and the oppressed, the "Republic of the workers," "the integral exercise of self, and the respect, as a kind of family honor, for the integral well-being of others." These five principles suffice to give a foundation to our socialism and our democracy. The latter two are the most difficult to put into practice in the embattled trench into which our Revolution has been increasingly forced. A trench is not a parliament. Martí himself, by saying "trenches of ideas are worth more than trenches of stone," accepted that, in the face of the enemy, ideas have to become entrenched, united for a resistance without fissures; and he diagnosed the degrees of freedom possible according to the circumstances when, referring to two models for a free press, he wrote:

> One thing is freedom of the press, and the *greater its freedom*, when, *in the republic* that is at peace, it strives, with no other armor than this republic, to defend the freedoms from those who invoke them to violate them, from those who make them merchandise, and from those who attack them as contrary to their privileges and authority. But the press is different *when it is faced with the enemy*. Then, softly, the signal is given. What the enemy will hear is none other than the call to attack.

What we hear in this special historical conjuncture is that popular resistance in the face of the enemy, without intending that the trench become a parliament, asks for the tense freedom of the flag—we repeat: that at once waves freely and remains attached to the pole. Waves in the wind that agitates it; remains subject to the flagstaff planted in necessity. The greater our difficulties, the greater has to be our freedom in order to endure and resolve them. All the pressure has to come from the difficulties themselves, from the fatality they suppose. Beyond this pressure, which generates our resistance, we should be as free as the words of a poem. But the words of the poem *are owed* to the poem, they are committed to it and are at its service, as our freedom and our criticism should be at the service of our resistance. Resistance and poetry. Resistance and freedom: possible freedom, always greater, always more deserved. To be born out of ourselves. To slowly climb upward with the people. When I write these words, I seem to recall something. I don't come from some lines in Martí's poem, I go toward them. Martí magnetizes us: All we feel and think goes toward him or comes from him. Indeed, he said, "The people, the afflicted masses, are the true leader of the revolutions," and "What is best is to be in the innermost recess of the people and to climb upward with the people!" To climb upward with Martí, with the people: This is the only path for our conscience, our culture, our national *poiesis*.

June 1992

Books Received

Abbott, H. Porter. *The Cambridge Introduction to Narrative*. New York: Cambridge University Press, 2002.

Archer, John Michael. *Old Worlds: Egypt, Southwest Asia, India, and Russia in Early Modern English Writing*. Stanford, Calif.: Stanford University Press, 2002.

Atwood, Margaret. *Negotiating with the Dead: A Writer on Writing*. New York: Cambridge University Press, 2002.

Back, Rachael Tzvia. *Led by Language: The Poetry and Poetics of Susan Howe*. Tuscaloosa: University of Alabama Press, 2002.

Bauer, Dale M., and Philip Gould, eds. *The Cambridge Companion to Nineteenth-Century American Women's Writing*. New York: Cambridge University Press, 2002.

Berg, Allison. *Mothering the Race: Women's Narratives of Reproduction, 1890–1930*. Champaign: University of Illinois Press, 2002.

Burt, Richard, ed. *Shakespeare After Mass Media*. New York: Palgrave, 2002.

Crane, Gregg D. *Race, Citizenship, and Law in American Literature*. New York: Cambridge University Press, 2002.

Culler, Jonathan. *The Pursuit of Signs: Semiotics, Literature, Deconstruction*. Ithaca, N.Y.: Cornell University Press, 2002.

Des Forêts, Louis-René. *Ostinato*. Translated and with a preface by Mary Ann Caws. Lincoln: University of Nebraska Press, 2002.

Desmet, Christy, and Robert Sawyer, eds. *Harold Bloom's Shakespeare*. New York: Palgrave, 2002.

Diprose, Rosalyn. *Corporeal Generosity: On Giving with Nietzsche, Merleau-Ponty, and Levinas*. Albany: State University of New York Press, 2002.

Dobie, Madeleine. *Foreign Bodies: Gender, Language, and Culture in French Orientalism*. Stanford, Calif.: Stanford University Press, 2002.

Easthope, Antony. *Privileging Difference*. Ed. Catherine Belsey. New York: Palgrave, 2002.

Echols, Alice. *Shaky Ground: The Sixties and Its Aftershocks*. New York: Columbia University Press, 2002.

Elliott, Dorice Williams. *The Angel out of the House: Philanthropy and Gender in Nineteenth-Century England*. Charlottesville: University Press of Virginia, 2002.

Emery, Kim. *The Lesbian Index: Pragmatism and Lesbian Subjectivity in the Twentieth-Century United States*. Albany: State University of New York Press, 2002.

Farquhar, Judith. *Appetites: Food and Sex in Post-Socialist China*. Durham, N.C.: Duke University Press, 2002.

Fiol-Matta, Licia. *A Queer Mother for the Nation: The State and Gabriela Mistral*. Minneapolis: University of Minnesota Press, 2002.

Frank, Joseph. *Dostoevsky: The Mantle of the Prophet, 1871–1881*. Princeton, N.J.: Princeton University Press, 2002.

Gardiner, Judith Kegan, ed. *Masculinity Studies and Feminist Theory*. New Directions. New York: Columbia University Press, 2002.

Glazier, Loss Pequeño. *Digital Poetics: The Making of E-Poetries*. Tuscaloosa: University of Alabama Press, 2002.

Glowacka, Dorota, and Stephen Boos, eds. *Between Ethics and Aesthetics*. Crossing the Boundaries. Albany: State University of New York Press, 2002.

Graham, Colin. *Deconstructing Ireland: Identity, Theory, Culture*. New York: Columbia University Press, 2002.

Head, Dominic. *The Cambridge Introduction to Modern British Fiction, 1950–2000*. New York: Cambridge University Press, 2002.

Hopenhayn, Martín. *No Apocalypse, No Integration: Modernism and Postmodernism in Latin America*. Trans. Cynthia Margarita Tompkins and Elizabeth Rosa Horan. Durham, N.C.: Duke University Press, 2002.

Horowitz, Gregg M. *Sustaining Loss: Art and Mournful Life*. Stanford, Calif.: Stanford University Press, 2001.

Huang, Yunte. *Ethnography, Translation, and Transpacific Displacement: Intertextual Travel in Twentieth-Century American Literature*. Berkeley: University of California Press, 2002.

Izzo, Donatella. *Portraying the Lady: Technologies of Gender in the Short Stories of Henry James*. Lincoln: University of Nebraska Press, 2002.

Joshi, Priya. *In Another Country: Colonialism, Culture, and the English Novel in India*. New York: Columbia University Press, 2002.

Keller, Catherine, and Anne Daniell, eds. *Process and Difference: Between Cosmological and Poststructuralist Postmodernisms*. Albany: State University of New York Press, 2002.

Latham, Rob. *Consuming Youth: Vampires, Cyborgs, and the Culture of Consumption*. Chicago: University of Chicago Press, 2002.

Law, John. *Aircraft Stories: Decentering the Object in Technoscience*. Durham, N.C.: Duke University Press, 2002.

Llatham, W. T. Jr. *Deliberate Speed: The Origins of a Cultural Style in the American 1950's*. Cambridge: Harvard University Press, 2002.

McReynolds, Louise, and Joan Neuberger, eds. *Imitations of Life: Two Centuries of Melodrama in Russia*. Durham, N.C.: Duke University Press, 2002.

Mann, Thomas. *The Cambridge Companion to Thomas Mann*. Ed. Ritchie Robertson. New York: Cambridge University Press, 2002.

Marrouchi, Mustapha. *Signifying with a Vengeance: Theories, Literatures, Storytellers*. Albany: State University of New York Press, 2002.

Massumi, Brian. *Parables for the Virtual: Movement, Affect, Sensation*. Durham, N.C.: Duke University Press, 2002.

Matthews, Steven. *Les Murray: Contemporary World Writers*. Manchester and New York: Manchester University Press, 2002.

Monroe, Jonathan, ed. *Writing and Revising the Disciplines*. Ithaca, N.Y.: Cornell Paperbacks, 2002.

Moore-Gilbert, Bart. *Hanif Kureishi*. Manchester and New York: Manchester University Press, 2002. Distributed in U.S. by Palgrave.

Munck, Ronaldo. *Marx@2000: Late Marxist Perspectives*. New York: Zed Books, 2002.

Nelson, Deborah. *Pursuing Privacy in Cold War America*. New York: Columbia University Press, 2002.

Preece, Julian. *The Cambridge Companion to Kafka*. New York: Cambridge University Press, 2002.

Ravetto, Kriss. *The Unmaking of Fascist Aesthetics*. Minneapolis: University of Minnesota Press, 2002.

Reiss, Timothy J. *Against Autonomy: Global Dialectics of Cultural Exchange*. Stanford, Calif.: Stanford University Press, 2001.

Roberson, Susan L., ed. *Defining Travel: Diverse Visions*. Jackson: University Press of Mississippi, 2001.

Rosello, Mireille. *Postcolonial Hospitality: The Immigrant as Guest*. Stanford, Calif.: Stanford University Press, 2002.

San Juan, E. Jr. *Racism and Cultural Studies: Critiques of Multiculturalist Ideology and the Politics of Difference*. Durham, N.C.: Duke University Press, 2002.

Santiago, Silviano. *The Space In-Between: Essays on Latin American Culture*. Ed. Ana Lúcia Gazzola. Durham, N.C.: Duke University Press, 2002.

Segalen, Victor. *Essay on Exoticism: An Aesthetics of Diversity*. Trans. and ed. Yaël Rachel Schlick. Durham, N.C.: Duke University Press, 2002.

Shostak, Stanley. *Becoming Immortal: Combining Cloning and Stem-Cell Therapy*. Albany: State University of New York Press, 2002.

Simpson, David. *Situatedness, or, Why We Keep Saying Where We're Coming From*. Durham, N.C.: Duke University Press, 2002.

Smyth, John Vignaux. *The Habit of Lying: Sacrificial Studies in Literature, Philosophy, and Fashion Theory*. Durham, N.C.: Duke University Press, 2002.

Steinberg, Philip E. *The Social Construction of the Ocean*. New York: Cambridge University Press, 2002.

Wallace, Mark, and Steven Marks, eds. *Telling It Slant: Avant-Garde Poetics of the 1990's*. Tuscaloosa: University of Alabama Press, 2002.

Williams, Jeffrey J., ed. *The Institution of Literature*. Albany: State University of New York Press, 2002.

Winston, Jane Bradley. *Postcolonial Duras: Cultural Memory in Postwar France*. New York: Palgrave, 2002.

Contributors

Carlos A. Aguilera is a poet and critic. He coedits the journal *Diáspora(s)*. His own work includes a collection of poems, *Retrato de A Hooper y su esposa* and essays on Severo Sarduy and Virgilio Piñera.

Miguel Barnet is a well-known Cuban poet and literary figure of the generation of the sixties. He is perhaps best known as the author/compiler of *Biography of a Runaway Slave / Biografía de un cimarrón* (1966), the book that founds the genre of testimonio (testimonial narrative).

John Beverley is professor of Spanish and Latin American literature and cultural studies at the University of Pittsburgh. His most recent books are *Subalternity and Representation: Arguments in Cultural Theory* and *Una modernidad obsoleta: Estudios sobre el barroco*.

Tania Bruguera is a performance and installation artist who exhibits both in Cuba and abroad.

Michael Chanan is the author of the definitive study of Cuban film of the Revolution, *The Cuban Image*. He teaches film studies in England. Tomás Gutiérrez Alea died several years ago. He is generally considered the most important modern Cuban film director (his work includes the classic *Memories of Underdevelopment* from the sixties and the recent *Strawberry and Chocolate*).

Haroldo Dilla Alfonso is a sociologist. He was associated with the influential independent think tank for social research founded by the Cuban Communist Party, the Center for Studies of the Americas (CEA), which was shut down in 1996 for supposedly exceeding its mandate. He now is research coordinator for the Latin American Social Sciences Faculty program in the Dominican Republic.

Antonio Eligio Fernández (Tonel) is a painter and installation artist, art critic, and curator. He is on the editorial board of the Cuban journal *Artecubano* and has been the recipient of Rockefeller and Guggenheim fellowships.

Ambrosio Fornet is one of the foremost literary critics of the Revolution. His work spans both contemporary and nineteenth-century Cuban literature. He is credited with coining the term *quinquenio gris* (grey five-year period) to describe the repressive phase of Cuban cultural policy in the seventies.

Víctor Fowler belongs to a generation of poet-critics born after the Revolution. He works at the José Martí National Library in Havana and has written a great deal on Afro-Cuban themes in Cuban literature. His most recent books are *Desnacional* and *Malecón Tao*.

Fina García Marruz is one of Cuba's oldest and most distinguished poets. Along with her husband, Cintio Vitier, also represented here, she is associated with the influential literary group that precedes the Revolution, *Orígenes*.

Rafael Hernández is a political scientist and also a poet and dramatist. He is the editor of the important journal of social theory and research *Temas*. A translation of his own very influential book *Mirar a Cuba: Ensayos sobre cultura y sociedad civil* (1999), from which his essay here is drawn, is forthcoming from the University Press of Florida.

Fernando Martínez Heredia is another social scientist closely associated with the initiatives toward greater independence and realism in the Cuban social sciences and some sectors of the Communist Party in the eighties and early nineties. The essay translated here is from his book, *En el horno de los noventa*.

Margarita Mateo Palmer is a literary critic and professor at the University of Havana. Along with the late Salvador Redonet, she has studied the production of a group of young writers—something like a Cuban Generation X—that emerges after 1989 in *Ella escribió postcrítica* (1996) and the work of José Lezama Lima, the topic of her recent book, *Paradiso: la lucha de Eros y Thanatos*.

Nancy Morejón is director of the Center for Caribbean Studies affiliated with the Cuban cultural center Casa de las Américas. One of the best-known poets of the generation of the Revolution, she focuses on both Afro-Cuban and women's themes. Her most recent collection is *Quinta de los molinos*.

Gerardo Mosquera is an art critic and curator closely associated with the so-called New Cuban Art movement of the eighties. He is visiting curator at the New Museum of Contemporary Art in New York. He lives in Centro-Habana.

Magaly Muguercia is a journalist and theater and performance artist working in Havana.

Desiderio Navarro is Cuba's best-known expert on literary and cultural theory. He is the founder and editor of the Cuban journal of cultural theory *Criterios*.

Obsesión is a contemporary rap group whose songs focus on the black experience in Cuba.

Omar Pérez is a poet, essayist, and translator who lives and works in Havana. The four poems included here are from his 1996 collection *Algo de lo sagrado*. His most recent book is *Como les guste*, a translation of *As You Like It*.

Antonio José Ponte is a poet, essayist, and novelist. His books include *Cuentos de todas partes del imperio* and the novel *Contrabando de sombras*, recently published by Mondadori in Barcelona. He serves on the editorial board of the émigré journal *Encuentro*.

Raúl Rivero is a poet and journalist. He is the director in Havana of the independent press agency CubaPress. He was one of the signatories in 1991 of the Letter of the Ten, one of the first public statements of opposition to the regime. His books include *Firmado en La Habana* and the forthcoming *Puente de guitarra*.

Reina María Rodríguez is a poet. The weekly gatherings in her rooftop apartment in Centro-Habana, dubbed *La Azotea*, were one of the focal points for Cuban writers of various generations, but especially younger ones, in the nineties. She edits with Antón Arrufat the journal *Azoteas*. Her most recent books of poetry are *Traveling* and *La foto del invernadero*. Two collections of her work, edited and translated by Kristin Dykstra, *La detención del tiempo/Time's Arrest* (www.factoryschool.com), and, with Nancy Gates Madsen, *Violet Island and Other Poems*, are available in English.

José Prats Sariol is a novelist and essayist. He has written on (and identifies with) the tradition of Cuban liberal thought. His books include a novel, *Mariel*, and a recent collection of stories, *Cuentos de sediciones y fricciones*.

Cintio Vitier is one of the figures most closely associated with the *Orígenes* group, which included the major novelist José Lezama Lima. Vitier's edition of Lezama's Lima's *Paradiso* is considered definitive, and his own *Lo cubano en la poesía* is a classic of Cuban criticism that has recently been reissued in Cuba. His essay here is from a 1995 collection, *Resistencia y Libertad*.

Translators

Dawn Duke, who is from Guyana, is working on a dissertation on Cuban and Brazilian women's poetry at the University of Pittsburgh.

Kenya Dworkin is an associate professor of Spanish at Carnegie Mellon University in Pittsburgh. She is working on a book about theater and society in the Tampa Cuban community.

Kristin Dykstra was associated with Charles Bernstein's poetry group at SUNY Buffalo and is now assistant professor of English at Illinois State University.

Sujatha Fernandes is finishing a dissertation on Cuban film and rap at the University of Chicago.

Marta Hernández is working on a dissertation about the concept of civil society in Cuba at Duke University.

Nancy Gates Madsen is finishing a Ph.D. in Spanish at the University of Wisconsin–Madison.

Achy Obejas is a well-known Cuban American writer whose novels include *Memory Mambo.*

American Literature

Call for Papers

Special Issue:

"Aesthetics and the End(s) of American Cultural Studies"

Reclaiming the aesthetic, emphasizing the "literary" in literary studies, conceptualizing a new formalism: such appeals represent the latest turn in ongoing debates about art and aesthetic ideology. Too often this debate has been characterized by predictable oppositions that set art against social action, structure against cultural practice, and the so-called imaginaries of affect against the putative reality of politics.

Will an aesthetic turn only augur a weakening of social and cultural thinking? Can a study form, for instance, produce an understanding of how legitimacy, normalcy, and convention are secured and perpetuated? What's new about the "new aesthetics"? Submissions might examine what methodological purchase aesthetics provides beyond the oppositions between formal structure and specific historical content that have long concerned American writers and critics. Essays might also consider the historical insights provided by a genealogy of aesthetic concerns of American cultural studies thus far. What new light can the study of aesthetics shed on the performative identities of race, class, sex, gender, and citizenship, or on the specularized history of democracy? In an effort to probe these and other questions, the editors of this special issue, Christopher Castiglia (Loyola University, Chicago) and Russ Castronovo (University of Wisconsin-Madison), invite essays on the uses and history of aesthetic formalism to initiate a series of dialogues on literary studies in, against, and after American cultural studies. Four double-spaced copies of each submission (between 10,000 and 12,000 words, including endnotes) should be sent by 1 April 2003 to *American Literature*; Box 90020; 327 Allen Building; Duke University; Durham, North Carolina 27708; the envelope should be clearly labeled "Special Issue Submission." For more information, contact Christopher Castiglia, Department of English, Loyola University Chicago, 6525 N. Sheridan Road, Chicago, Illinois 60626; or Russ Castronovo, Department of English, University of Wisconsin-Madison, Madison, Wisconsin 53706.

Dissent from the Homeland: Essays after September 11

Stanley Hauerwas and Frank Lentricchia,
special issue editors

James Nachtwey/VII

In this special issue, well-known writers and scholars from across the humanities and social sciences take a critical look at U.S. domestic and foreign policies—past and present—as well as the recent surge of patriotism. These dissenting voices provide a thought-provoking alternative to the public approval, both at home and abroad, of the U.S. military response, to the September 11 attacks.

Contributors

Jean Baudrillard	Catherine Lutz
Mike Baxter	Jody McAuliffe
Robert N. Bellah	John Milbank
Daniel Berrigan	James Nachtwey
Wendell Berry	Peter Ochs
Vincent J. Cornell	Anne R. Slifkin
Stanley Hauerwas	Rowan Williams
Fredric Jameson	Susan Willis
Frank Lentricchia	Slavoj Žižek

Order Information
Single issues, U.S. $12
Pages: 216, 11 color photographs
Available September 2002

Subscription to *SAQ* (quarterly),
$35 U.S. individuals
$120 U.S. institutions

Contact Information
Duke University Press
1-888-387-5765 (toll-free within the U.S. and Canada) or 919-687-3602.

E-mail: subscriptions@dukeupress.edu
Web site: www.dukeupress.edu/SAQ

a special issue of
South Atlantic Quarterly
volume 101, number 2

JOURNAL OF MODERN LITERATURE

The *Journal of Modern Literature,* edited by Morton P. Levitt
and published four times a year by Indiana University Press, is widely
recognized as the journal of record for modern literature and addresses
all literature written in the twentieth century.

Global Freud: Psychoanalytic Cultures and Classic Modernism
Daniel T. O'Hara, Editor

Volume 25, Numbers 3 + 4 • $18.95

Visit our web site at **iupjournals.org**

SUBSCRIPTIONS:
Individuals, $37.50
Institutions, $97.50
Foreign surface postage, $12.50
Foreign airmail postage, $28.00

SINGLE ISSUES:
Shipping and handling: $5.00 for one,
$1.00 for each additional

SEND ORDERS
with payment or credit card information to:
Journals Division, Indiana University Press,
601 N. Morton St., Bloomington, IN 47404.

FAX credit card information to 1-812-855-8507

CALL 1-800-842-6796 or 1-812-855-9449

EMAIL to journals@indiana.edu

Visit our website and enter discount code KPRF to receive a 20% discount
off the single issue price.

Pedagogy
Critical Approaches to Teaching
Literature, Language, Composition, and Culture

"Add my name to the list of supporters.
It's high time someone in the U.S.
began examining pedagogy in higher ed."
—Linda Brodkey, University of California, San Diego

Pedagogy is devoted to teaching in the broad field of English, including the teaching of literature, literary criticism, and writing. The journal seeks to create a new discourse surrounding teaching, fusing theoretical approaches with practical realities. As a journal devoted exclusively to pedagogical issues, *Pedagogy* offers a forum for critical reflection as well as a site for spirited and informed debate from a multiplicity of positions and perspectives. The journal strives to reverse the long-standing marginalization of teaching and its scholarship and instead to assert its centrality to the work of scholars and professionals. *Pedagogy* will energize the conversations surrounding teaching excellence in higher education; in particular, it will radically affect the shape of undergraduate and graduate instruction in the humanities, particularly English studies.